Palgrave Studies in European Political Sociology

Series Editors
Carlo Ruzza
Department of Sociology and Social Research
University of Trento
Trento, Italy

Hans-Jörg Trenz
Department of Media, Cognition and Communication
University of Copenhagen
Copenhagen, Denmark

"Based on unique international survey data, this book shows us a much needed, and exceptionally detailed, picture of the solidaristic acts and ideas of Europeans in the context of pressing economic, cultural, and political challenges. A timely, insightful, and thought-provoking contribution to our understanding of the viability of solidarity as a cornerstone of social organization in Europe."
— Professor Wim van Oorschot, *KU Leuven, Belgium*

"Solidarity in Europe is a timely book. Austerity measures, the inflow of refugees, and the rise of populism have placed considerable strain on European solidarity. This insightful book provides a rich and variegated picture of solidarity in Europe, and redresses false conceptions about solidarity and further addresses a key issue: our capacity to live together and to create social cohesion".
— Professor Florence Passy, *University of Lausanne, Switzerland*

"A most timely empirical analysis of attitudes of solidarity in Europe! With a range of different indicators, it demonstrates national variations and common patterns of attitudes in eight countries and stimulates the reader to reflect on present challenges for solidarity in general and particularly for the European Union."
— Professor Emeritus Steinar Stjernø, *Oslo and Akershus University College of Applied Sciences, Norway*

Palgrave Studies in European Political Sociology addresses contemporary themes in the field of Political Sociology. Over recent years, attention has turned increasingly to processes of Europeanization and globalization and the social and political spaces that are opened by them. These processes comprise both institutional-constitutional change and new dynamics of social transnationalism. Europeanization and globalization are also about changing power relations as they affect people's lives, social networks and forms of mobility. The Palgrave Studies in European Political Sociology series addresses linkages between regulation, institution building and the full range of societal repercussions at local, regional, national, European and global level, and will sharpen understanding of changing patterns of attitudes and behaviours of individuals and groups, the political use of new rights and opportunities by citizens, new conflict lines and coalitions, societal interactions and networking, and shifting loyalties and solidarity within and across the European space. We welcome proposals from across the spectrum of Political Sociology and Political Science, on dimensions of citizenship; political attitudes and values; political communication and public spheres; states, communities, governance structure and political institutions; forms of political participation; populism and the radical right; and democracy and democratization.

More information about this series at
http://www.palgrave.com/gp/series/14630

Christian Lahusen • Maria T. Grasso
Editors

Solidarity in Europe

Citizens' Responses in Times of Crisis

Editors
Christian Lahusen
Department of Social Sciences
University of Siegen
Siegen, Germany

Maria T. Grasso
Department of Politics
University of Sheffield
Sheffield, UK

Palgrave Studies in European Political Sociology
ISBN 978-3-030-10356-9   ISBN 978-3-319-73335-7   (eBook)
https://doi.org/10.1007/978-3-319-73335-7

© The Editor(s) (if applicable) and The Author(s) 2018 This book is an open access publication.
Softcover re-print of the Hardcover 1st edition 2018
Open Access This book is licensed under the terms of the Creative Commons Attribution 4.0 International License (http://creativecommons.org/licenses/by/4.0/), which permits use, sharing, adaptation, distribution and reproduction in any medium or format, as long as you give appropriate credit to the original author(s) and the source, provide a link to the Creative Commons license and indicate if changes were made.
The images or other third party material in this book are included in the book's Creative Commons license, unless indicated otherwise in a credit line to the material. If material is not included in the book's Creative Commons license and your intended use is not permitted by statutory regulation or exceeds the permitted use, you will need to obtain permission directly from the copyright holder.
The use of general descriptive names, registered names, trademarks, service marks, etc. in this publication does not imply, even in the absence of a specific statement, that such names are exempt from the relevant protective laws and regulations and therefore free for general use.
The publisher, the authors and the editors are safe to assume that the advice and information in this book are believed to be true and accurate at the date of publication. Neither the publisher nor the authors or the editors give a warranty, express or implied, with respect to the material contained herein or for any errors or omissions that may have been made. The publisher remains neutral with regard to jurisdictional claims in published maps and institutional affiliations.

Cover illustration: Cyndi Hoelzle / EyeEm

Printed on acid-free paper

This Palgrave Macmillan imprint is published by the registered company Springer International Publishing AG part of Springer Nature.
The registered company address is: Gewerbestrasse 11, 6330 Cham, Switzerland

Acknowledgements

Results presented in this book have been obtained within the project European paths to transnational solidarity at times of crisis: Conditions, forms, role-models and policy responses (TransSOL). This project was funded by the European Commission under the Horizon 2020 research and innovation programme (grant agreement No. 649435). The TransSOL consortium was coordinated by the University of Siegen (Germany), and was formed, additionally, by the Université de Genève (Switzerland), the Fondation Nationale des Sciences Politiques (France), the Glasgow Caledonian University (United Kindgom), the University Panepistimio Kritis (Greece), the University of Florence (Italy), the University of Warsaw (Poland), the University of Copenhagen (Denmark), the University of Sheffield (United Kingdom), and European Alternatives Ltd (Germany and United Kingdom). We thank all the members of the TransSOL research consortium for their contributions to the project.

Contents

1 **Solidarity in Europe–European Solidarity: An Introduction** 1
Christian Lahusen and Maria Grasso

2 **Toward a New Conditionality of Welfare? Reconsidering Solidarity in the Danish Welfare State** 19
Hans-Jörg Trenz and Maria Grasso

3 **Solidarity Activism in Germany: What Explains Different Types and Levels of Engagement?** 43
Johannes Kiess, Christian Lahusen, and Ulrike Zschache

4 **Pulling Together or Pulling Apart? Solidarity in the Post-Crisis UK** 73
Tom Montgomery, Simone Baglioni, Olga Biosca, and Maria Grasso

5 **Solidarity Practices in Poland and Their Social Capital Foundations** 103
Anna Kurowska and Maria Theiss

6 The Social and Political Dimensions of Solidarity in Italy 127
   Nicola Maggini

7 Volunteering for Refugees and Asylum Seekers in Greece 169
   Stefania Kalogeraki

8 Civic and Political Solidarity Practices in Switzerland 195
   Eva Fernández G. G.

9 Trajectories of Solidarities in France Across Fields
   of Vulnerability 227
   Manlio Cinalli and Maria Jimena Sanhueza

10 Solidarity in Europe: A Comparative Assessment
   and Discussion 253
   Christian Lahusen and Maria Grasso

Index 283

Notes on Editors and Contributors

Editors

Maria T. Grasso holds a Chair in Politics and Quantitative Methods at the Department of Politics, University of Sheffield, UK. Her research focuses on political sociology and political engagement. She is the author of *Generations, Political Participation and Social Change in Western Europe* (2016). Her research has been published in *British Journal of Political Science, European Journal of Political Research, Electoral Studies, Acta Politica, Work, Employment & Society, Mobilization*, and other journals. She has been awarded over £800,000 in research funding to date and is the principal investigator/work-package leader on two collaborative EU projects funded by the European Commission in the Horizon 2020 scheme: TransSOL on transnational solidarity in times of crisis and EURYKA on youth participation and inequalities.

Christian Lahusen holds a Chair of Sociology at the Department of Social Sciences, University of Siegen, Germany. He studied sociology in Düsseldorf and Madrid, received his PhD from the European University Institute (Florence), and obtained his habilitation from the University of Bamberg. His research interests include social theories, political sociology, and the sociology of European societies and European integration. He has directed and participated in a number of national and international research projects on topics relating to contentious politics, civil society, and social exclusion, most of them with a European and comparative perspective. He was the coordinator of the TransSOL project (Horizon 2020).

Contributors

Simone Baglioni is Professor of Politics in the Yunus Centre for Social Business and Health at Glasgow Caledonian University (GCU), UK. Before joining GCU he worked at academic institutions in Italy and Switzerland. His research interests focus on youth unemployment, civil society, social innovation, and social movements.

Olga Biosca is Senior Lecturer at the Yunus Centre for Social Business and Health at Glasgow Caledonian University in the UK. She holds a PhD in Economics from the University of Sheffield and an MSc degree in Development Economics from the Autonomous University of Madrid, Spain. Biosca is co-investigator in the FinWell project funded by the Scottish government, examining the potential link between fair finance and health and well-being. Biosca is also a co-investigator on the TransSOL project and the Marie Sklodowska-Curie RISE project FAB-MOVE (For a Better Tomorrow: Social Enterprises on the Move).

Manlio Cinalli is a research professor at CEVIPOF (CNRS—UMR 7048), Sciences Po Paris, France. He has delivered teaching and research in various leading universities and institutes across Europe and the US. He has published widely on citizenship and integration in international journals, and he is also the author of *Citizenship and the Political Integration of Muslims in France* (Palgrave). His research draws on quantitative and qualitative methods. It is noticeable for having developed a multidisciplinary approach combining contentious politics, network analysis, claim making, and public policy studies. He has many large grant awards that have contributed more than £2.5M of research funding to host institutions.

Eva Fernández G. G. works as a research assistant at the Institute of Citizenship Studies of the University of Geneva, Switzerland. Previously, she worked for several years in the public health sector, primarily at the World Health Organization, and then at The Global Fund to Fight AIDS, Tuberculosis and Malaria. Eva holds a degree in Political Science and Public Administration from the Universidad Complutense de Madrid (2008) and an MSc in Environmental Sciences from the University of Geneva (2011). She is a Candoc at Department of Political Science and International Relations of the University of Geneva.

Stefania Kalogeraki is Assistant Professor of Quantitative Methods in Sociology and Social Demography at the Department of Sociology, University of Crete, Greece. She holds a BSc in Statistics (1998), an MA in Sociology with Research Training with Distinction (2002), and a PhD in Sociology (2007, University of Reading, UK). She has participated in European projects (such as GGCRISI, LIVEWHAT, TransSOL, EURYKA) and been the principal investigator in Greek research projects. Her main research interests focus on questionnaire design, comparative social research, social demographic analysis, and mixed method designs.

Johannes Kiess is a researcher at Siegen University, Germany, and employed in the EU Project EURYKA, focusing on political participation of youth and inequality. He received his MA from University of Leipzig; he has also studied at Ben-Gurion University of the Negev, Beersheba and recently was a visiting researcher at the Max Planck Institute for the Study of Societies, Cologne, and at Georgetown University, Washington DC. His PhD investigates the framing of the crisis by German social partners. He has published various articles, chapters, and books on right-wing extremism, particularly focusing on attitudes, European sociology, and trade unions.

Anna Kurowska is Assistant Professor at the Institute of Social Policy at the University of Warsaw, Poland. She holds a PhD in Social Policy (2010) and an MSc in Political Sciences with Distinction (2004, University of Warsaw) and in Economics (2007, Warsaw School of Economics). Her main research interests are in capability approach in social policy, work-family reconciliation, maternal employment, and comparative analysis of welfare states. She is involved in several international projects, including TransSOL, and leading two of them. Kurowska has had her work accepted in highly ranked journals, including *Social Policy & Administration*. For more information, visit orcid.org/0000-0002-3578-4517.

Nicola Maggini is Research Fellow at the Legal Sciences Department of the University of Florence, Italy and a member of CISE (Italian Centre for Electoral Studies). He has published on Italian and international journals, including *RISP-Italian Political Science Review*, *Journal of Contemporary European Research*, *Studia Politica-Romanian Political Science Review*, *Italian Politics and Society*, and *Czech Journal of Political Science*. He is the author of *Young People's Voting Behaviour in Europe: A Comparative Perspective* (Palgrave Macmillan, 2016), co-author of several book chapters, and co-editor of volumes for the 'Dossier CISE' series. He is working on transnational solidarity issues for 'TransSOL' Horizon 2020 project.

Tom Montgomery is a researcher on the TransSOL project based at Glasgow Caledonian University, UK. He holds an MA (Hons) in Politics from the University of Glasgow and an MSc in Political Research from the University of Strathclyde, and he is completing his PhD at the Yunus Centre for Social Business and Health at GCU, where he is examining the role of social innovation in addressing youth employment issues in Glasgow and the west of Scotland focusing on the impact of the political context on socially innovative organisations and the fragile labour markets navigated by young people.

Maria Jimena Sanhueza is Research Fellow at Sciences Po Paris working in the research project "European Paths to Transnational Solidarity at Times of Crisis: Conditions, Forms, Role-models and Policy Responses (TransSOL)" funded by the European Commission. Previously, she worked on the project "Pathways to Power: The Political Representation of Citizens of Immigrant Origin in Seven European Democracies" funded by the French National Research Agency, the 2017 French Presidential Electoral Compass, and the Naval Postgraduate School (USA). Prior to joining Sciences Po, she worked as a project manager for Academics Stand Against Poverty, and as a consultant for Lawyers Without Borders. Maria Jimena's research interests include comparative politics, institutions, political representation, and public opinion.

Maria Theiss is Assistant Professor at the Institute of Social Policy, Warsaw University, Poland. Her research focuses on the issues of social citizenship, social capital, civic society, and the local level of social policy. She was the PI of the Polish team of the project LIVEWHAT and conducted a number of research studies in Poland, including 'Local social citizenship—the example of childcare services'. She is an author and co-editor of four books on issues of poverty, social exclusion, and governance processes at the local level in Poland as well as articles and book chapters.

Hans-Jörg Trenz is Professor at the Centre for Modern European Studies at the University of Copenhagen, Denmark and Research Professor at ARENA, Centre for European Studies, University of Oslo, Norway. His main fields of interests are the emergence of a European public sphere and of European civil society, European civilisation and identity, migration and ethnic minorities, cultural and political sociology, and social and political theory. His recent publications include *Narrating European Society: Toward a Sociology of European Integration*, 'Understanding the Mechanisms of EU Politicization: Lessons from the Euro-zone crisis' (co-authored with Paul Statham) in *Comparative European Politics* (2015), and *Europe's Prolonged Crisis: The Making or the Unmaking of a Political Union* (edited together with Virginie Guiraudon and Carlo Ruzza) (Palgrave Macmillan).

Ulrike Zschache is a postdoctoral research fellow at Siegen University, Germany, and co-applicant of the TransSOL project. She holds a dual PhD in European and Global Studies from Lancaster and Siegen University and studied sociology, cultural and political sciences, and journalism at the Universities of Leipzig and Rome (La Sapienza). Her research interests lie in the area of European integration, European public spheres, transnational solidarity, and the sociology of European societies. Ulrike is particularly interested in public discourses on European policy issues and the diffusion and appropriation of European ideas. She has published various books, book chapters, and articles.

LIST OF FIGURES

Fig. 4.1	The hierarchy of solidarity in the UK	85
Fig. 8.1	Marginal effects on civic solidarity practices by target group	213
Fig. 8.2	Marginal effects on political solidarity practices by target group	214

List of Tables

Table 2.1	Engagement in solidarity action at national, European and global level	28
Table 2.2	Type of solidarity action at national level	28
Table 2.3	Engagement in solidarity action at national, European and global level by age group	29
Table 2.4	Engagement in solidarity action at national, European and global level by gender	30
Table 2.5	Engagement in solidarity action at national, European and global level by place of residence	30
Table 2.6	Engagement in solidarity action at national, European and global level by education	31
Table 2.7	Engagement in solidarity action at national, European and global level by occupational class	31
Table 2.8	Engagement in solidarity action at national, European and global level by social capital (frequency of meeting friends)	32
Table 2.9	Engagement in solidarity action at national, European and global level by attachment to country and fellow citizens	33
Table 2.10	Engagement in solidarity action at national, European and global level by political interest	34
Table 2.11	Engagement in solidarity action at national, European and global level by party attachment	34
Table 2.12	Engagement in solidarity action at national, European and global level by closeness to political party	35
Table 2.13	Engagement in solidarity action at national, European and global level by opinion on EU membership	36

Table 2.14	Engagement in solidarity action at national, European and global level by opinion on whether country benefits from EU membership	36
Table 2.15	Engagement in solidarity action at national, European and global level by support for EU debt relief	36
Table 2.16	Engagement in solidarity action at national, European and global level by what the respondent feels they receive relative to others in their country	37
Table 3.1	Frequencies of engagement over levels and fields of solidarity	48
Table 3.2	Multiple forms of actions over levels and fields of solidarity	50
Table 3.3	Multinominal regression models 1a–1f (socio-economic variables)	51
Table 3.4	Multinominal regression models 2a–2f—socio-structural determinants	53
Table 3.5	Multinominal regression models 3a–3f—cultural-ideational determinants	54
Table 3.6	Multinominal regression models for European level solidarity	57
Table 3.7	Multinominal regression models for solidarity with refugees	59
Table 3.8	Multinominal regression models for solidarity with unemployed people	60
Table 3.9	Multinominal regression models for solidarity with people with disabilities	62
Table 4.1	Descriptive statistics	79
Table 4.2	Solidarity practices in different geographical areas by constituent country in the UK	80
Table 4.3	Solidarity practices with vulnerable groups (refugees, unemployed, disabled) by constituent country in the UK	82
Table 4.4	Solidarity practices to support the rights in different areas and groups	86
Table 5.1	Socio-demographic characteristics of Polish respondents in TransSOL survey	110
Table 5.2	Explanatory variables—frequencies, means and standard deviations	112
Table 5.3	Participation in march, protest or demonstration in order to support the rights of people: in respondent's country, in other countries in the EU and in countries outside the EU	114
Table 5.4	Donating time in order to support the rights of people in respondent's country, in other countries in the EU and in countries outside the EU	115
Table 5.5	Donating money in order to support the rights of people in respondent's country, in other countries in the EU and in countries outside the EU	117

Table 5.6	Solidarity practices in Poland with different scopes of beneficiaries	118
Table 5.7	Logistic regression results (expβ) for the model of *general solidarity* and model of *transnational solidarity*	120
Table 6.1	Type of reported solidarity activities in favour of three target groups	134
Table 6.2	Reported solidarity activities in order to support the rights of people/groups in different contexts	134
Table 6.3	Importance of development aid from the EU to assist certain countries outside the EU in their fight against poverty and in support of their development	135
Table 6.4	Evaluations of solidarity-based public policies	135
Table 6.5	Solidarity actions towards target groups by basic socio-demographic characteristics	137
Table 6.6	Solidarity actions towards target groups by income level and subjective social class	138
Table 6.7	Solidarity actions towards target groups by social capital	139
Table 6.8	Solidarity actions towards target groups by political involvement	140
Table 6.9	Solidarity actions towards target groups by left-right self-placement and libertarian-authoritarian index	141
Table 6.10	Solidarity actions towards target groups by voting intentions	143
Table 6.11	Solidarity actions towards target groups by social beliefs: reciprocity, conditionality, and deservingness	145
Table 6.12	Solidarity actions towards target groups by religiosity	146
Table 6.13	Estimated effects on solidarity actions towards different target groups for some predictors, separated models by blocks of variables	147
Table 6.14	Estimated effects on solidarity actions towards different target groups for some predictors, full model	150
Table 6.15	Variables used for the analysis: original wording, recoding, and distributions within the sample	160
Table 7.1	Volunteering for refugees/asylum seekers, unemployed and disabled in countries participating to TransSOL project	171
Table 7.2	Volunteers'/non-volunteers' associations with specific demographic attributes, human capital indicators, informal social interactions and conventional political behaviour	180
Table 7.3	Volunteers'/non-volunteers' differences in social trust, religiosity and unconventional political behaviour	181
Table 7.4	Binary logistic regression analysis of volunteering for refugees/asylum seekers in Greece	182

Table 8.1	Proportions of solidarity practices towards vulnerable groups in Switzerland	204
Table 8.2	Logistic regression models on civic solidarity engagement strength (odds ratios)	208
Table 8.3	Logistic regression models on political solidarity engagement strength (odds ratios)	211
Table 9.1	Overall support and specific forms of solidarity actions per field	234
Table 9.2	Individual versus collective *repertoire*	236
Table 9.3	Solidarity towards the disabled individual factors	239
Table 9.4	Solidarity towards the unemployed individual factors	239
Table 9.5	Solidarity towards refugees individual factors	239
Table 9.6	Solidarity towards the disabled individual and political factors	240
Table 9.7	Solidarity towards the unemployed: individual and political factors	240
Table 9.8	Solidarity towards refugees individual and political factors	240
Table 9.9	Solidarity towards the disabled individual and political factors (controlled)	242
Table 9.10	Solidarity towards the unemployed individual and political factors (controlled)	243
Table 9.11	Solidarity towards refugees individual and political factors (controlled)	244
Table 10.1	Personal support of other people	255
Table 10.2	Eliminating inequalities	257
Table 10.3	Development aid	258
Table 10.4	Fiscal solidarity: pay public debts	259
Table 10.5	Fiscal solidarity: help refugees	260
Table 10.6	Fiscal solidarity: reasons	261
Table 10.7	Immigration policies for EU citizens	263
Table 10.8	Immigration policies for non-EU citizens	264
Table 10.9	Immigration policies for Syrian refugees	265
Table 10.10	Migrants and social rights	266
Table 10.11	EU membership good/bad	267
Table 10.12	Benefited from EU membership	268
Table 10.13	Effect on jobs and employment if country was *outside* the EU	269
Table 10.14	Referendum on EU membership	270
Table 10.15	Should the UK remain a member or leave the EU?	270
Table 10.16	Solidarity and support for EU membership	271
Table 10.17	Attachments	271
Table 10.18	Solidarity and attachment to the EU	272

CHAPTER 1

Solidarity in Europe–European Solidarity: An Introduction

Christian Lahusen and Maria Grasso

Introduction

Solidarity has received heightened attention in public debates during the last decade, because the various crises affecting the European Union have put the idea of European solidarity under stress. This is true in regard to the economic and financial crisis that has severely hit many European countries since 2008. Even though the European Union has developed a number of policy measures (e.g., the 'European Financial Stability Facility', the 'European Stability Mechanism', and the 'Stability and Growth Pact') which have opened the door to financial assistance, the European Union remained committed to a bail-out policy package that discarded a communitarization of debts and put the main burden on countries threatened with bankruptcy by imposing strict austerity measures. As a reaction, most commentators converged upon the conviction that international solidarity was dead (see Habermas 2017; Balibar 2010). A similar conclusion was drawn in regard to the issues emerging in reaction to the

C. Lahusen (✉)
Department of Social Sciences, University of Siegen, Siegen, Germany

M. Grasso
Department of Politics, University of Sheffield, London, UK

© The Author(s) 2018
C. Lahusen, M. Grasso (eds.), *Solidarity in Europe*,
Palgrave Studies in European Political Sociology,
https://doi.org/10.1007/978-3-319-73335-7_1

increased inflow of refugees from Syria and other regions affected by wars in 2015 and the inability of the EU institutions and its member states to agree on a coordinated asylum policy and mechanisms of admission and integration. Consensus could only be reached in regard to the external dimension (e.g., frontier controls, fight against human trafficking), leaving the issue of fair burden sharing through national quotas and relocation programs unsolved.

The success of populist parties in many European countries (e.g., France, the United Kingdom, Denmark, Italy, Spain), the Brexit vote, and the mobilization of Eurosceptic and xenophobic protests across Europe has raised further concerns that European solidarity might be at risk in a more fundamental and all-encompassing manner. In times of crisis, we might not only be witnessing the erosion of cooperation between member state governments but also the corrosion of social cohesion at the level of the European citizenry, thus threatening the social foundations on which EU institutions and policies are built. Does the crisis of European integration translate into a crisis of European solidarity, and, if so, what are the manifestations at the level of individual citizens? Is European solidarity really on the retreat within the European citizenry? How strongly is solidarity rooted at the individual level, both in terms of attitudes and practices? And which driving factors and mechanisms tend to contribute to the reproduction and/or corrosion of solidarity in times of crisis?

We are urgently in need of sound empirical evidence in order to answer these questions. Public debates and contentions continue to return to this issue, but we so far have very little empirical evidence on which to draw in order to inform this debate. Listening to these public debates, it seems as though pessimists are on the forefront. According to these views, the various crises affecting the European Union are putting European solidarity under strain. In times of economic growth and optimistic economic outlook, it should be easier to profess cooperation and help, while solidarity seems to be much more difficult to sustain in times of recession and scarcity. This is particularly true given that populist and xenophobic political entrepreneurs can draw on the exacerbation of citizens' fear and grievances and that the crisis overlaps with a long history of ineffective policies in key domains, such as poverty and unemployment, immigration, and asylum. Under these circumstances, political debates seem to be marked increasingly by antagonism, conflict, and mistrust between governments and citizens, to the detriment of social cohesion and solidarity. In spite of this pessimistic outlook, there is, however, some room for optimism left.

It remains to be said that 60 years of European integration have gradually established feelings of belongingness to the European community, enabled shared identification with European institutions, as well as European and cosmopolitan identities (Delanty and Rumford 2005; Beck and Grande 2007). Moreover, European integration has furthered cross-national experiences and contacts among citizens, as well as transnational trust between European peoples (Delhey 2007). Finally, public opinion polls show that, in the midst of the European crisis, a majority of respondents still agree that it is desirable to give financial help to other countries in the name of European solidarity between member states (see Eurobarometer 2011; Lengfeld et al. 2012). The same is true for the readiness of European citizens to support a fair burden sharing in regard to refugees, if this is necessary to uphold the achievements of the European Union, such as Schengen (de Vries and Hoffmann 2016).

This book tries to systematically shed light into this debate by presenting findings of a population survey among citizens of eight European countries, namely, Denmark, France, Germany, Greece, Italy, Poland, Switzerland, and the United Kingdom. The survey was conducted in the context of an EU-funded research project devoted to the study of European solidarity ('European Paths to Transnational Solidarity in Times of Crisis'—TransSOL). TransSOL aimed to increase knowledge about solidarity within the general population, organized civil society, and the media. The consortium consisted of members from the following institutions: the University of Siegen (Germany), the Université de Genève (Switzerland), the Fondation Nationale des Sciences Politiques (France), the Glasgow Caledonian University (United Kingdom), the University Panepistimio Kritis (Greece), the University of Florence (Italy), the University of Warsaw (Poland), the University of Copenhagen (Denmark), the University of Sheffield (United Kingdom), and European Alternatives Ltd. (Germany and United Kingdom). The project received funding under the Horizon 2020 program (Grant Agreement No: 649435). The survey was subcontracted to a specialized polling company (Info GmbH).

The aim of the survey was to build a comparative dataset that would allow us to measure levels of solidarity among the member states' citizenry and to help identify those social and political factors that might promote or inhibit solidarity both within the member states and across their borders. This study was demanding, given the fact that solidarity is a complex phenomenon that requires careful reflection, definition, and operationalization and that a nuanced conceptualization is particularly necessary when addressing the notion of European solidarity. Hence, before we move to the presentation of findings for each of the eight countries, it is thus necessary to engage in a conceptual discussion of European solidarity. For this purpose, we will present available evidence on the topic and systematize this knowledge within a conceptual framework apt to guide our empirical analyses.

Contributing Knowledge to an Established Field of Research: Concepts, Measurements, and Assumptions

Solidarity is one of the key phenomena studied in the social sciences. Research in sociology, economics, political sciences, and psychology, among others, has been inquiring for many decades into the forms and conditions of social integration and cohesion in order to better understand the social foundations of societies (Durkheim 1893/1997; Marshall 1950; Parsons 1966). However, the focus has been on national societies, which means that our knowledge about the transnational dimension of solidarity, and in particular about European solidarity, is rather limited. The limitations are even more serious once we move to the individual level and inquire into the attitudes and practices of the European citizenry with reference to European solidarity. How strongly is the idea of European solidarity shared by citizens throughout Europe, and to what extent are they engaged in solidarity-related activities? Is solidarity limited to specific communities or target groups, or do we detect also a universalist or cosmopolitan philanthropy dimension? What can we say about the social traits, beliefs, and convictions of people engaged in solidarity activities? And which are the factors inhibiting solidarity dispositions and practices?

In order to answer these questions, we need to develop a clearer understanding of what we mean by (European) solidarity. In this regard, we propose to follow a much quoted definition by Stjerno who defines solidarity as the preparedness to share one's own resources with others, be that directly by donating money or time in support of others or indirectly by supporting the state to reallocate and redistribute some of the funds gathered through taxes or contributions (e.g., Stjerno 2012: 2). Under this wide conceptual umbrella, research has tended to focus on a series of different expressions of solidarity. Studies have been interested in interpersonal 'social' solidarity in informal groups or networks (e.g., Hechter 1987; Markovsky and Lawler 1994; Komter 2005). They have addressed volunteering, membership and support of voluntary associations, civil society organizations, and social movements (Curtis et al. 2001; Putnam et al. 2003; Giugni and Passy 2001). And they have focused on citizens' support of the welfare state and its redistributive policies (e.g., Svallfors 1997; Fong 2001; Amat and Wibbels 2009; Rehm 2009; Rehm et al. 2012).

As useful as this initial definition might be, it does not yet grasp what we consider to be the specific nature of solidarity. In fact, we see the need to distinguish solidarity more clearly from charitable help, care, or humanitarian aid by stressing the group-boundedness and reciprocity of solidarity. According to this conceptualization, solidarity is tied to an (imagined) community or group, whose members are expected to support each other in order to fulfill the mutual rights and obligations associated with group membership (Hunt and Benford 2004). While this conceptualization is admittedly close to the notion of political solidarity (Scholz 2008), as it leans toward a rights-based definition, we argue that it is applicable to social and civic solidarity between individuals, as well. In fact, 'solidarity groups' might be informal cliques, formal organizations, or full-fledged nation-states, but all of them will be based on the idea that membership is tied to the expectations of mutual support, even if these expectations might range from informal to formalized, from voluntary to binding rights and obligations.

This definition has many advantages for the analysis of European solidarity. On the one hand, we need to remember that European solidarity is only one of the many potential group-bound solidarities, besides the region, the nation, or humanity, among many others. On the other hand, we must acknowledge that solidarities are in themselves contentious, because groups maintain both complementary but also competitive relations to each another (Bandy and Smith 2005; Scholz 2008). As an individual, one might feel in solidarity with one's own family, neighborhood, region, and nation, and this feeling might not stand in competition to a sense of solidarity with Europe or humankind in general. In this case, national and European solidarities would be part of a more encompassing, universalist or cosmopolitan notion of solidarity. However, particularly in times of crisis, where citizens are exposed to feelings of scarcity, relative deprivation, and distributional conflicts, (Grasso and Giugni 2016) group solidarities might be either prioritized or sorted out. And this could mean that citizens center their solidarity more strongly on their own country and/or specific groups therein, even if they do not discard—in principle—the need to help other Europeans. In this sense, group solidarity acquires a particularistic orientation, because one's own support of others is conditional on the ego-alter's membership in the same group, or at least dependent on its social proximity to it.

These conceptual clarifications highlight that we are dealing with a complex and multifaceted phenomenon that requires prudent operationalization. For this reason, we developed a questionnaire that aimed at measuring individual solidarity along its major components. First, our survey insisted on the need to measure solidarity in its different manifestations. In this regard, we opted to look at attitudes and reported activities at the same time. This differentiation is necessary because it is to be expected that the preparedness to help others does not translate inevitably into factual activities. The latter might disclose prioritized group solidarities much more neatly than the mere readiness to help. We thus opted to include a number of questions in our survey that gather information about the respondents' reported activities of solidarity. These questions presented a wider range of potential activities, ranging from more conventional to more unconventional activities, for example, donating money or time, buying or boycotting products, and active participation in voluntary associations and protest actions (Grasso 2011, 2016).

Second, our conceptual framework insists on the need to measure solidarity in its charitable and political dimensions. Scholarly writing has tended to focus on the (financial) help to the needy, thus privileging the charitable dimension of solidarity. While this aspect is important, it downplays the political and rights-based dimension of solidarity. In fact, people demonstrate solidarity with other persons in struggle or in need when participating in collective actions (e.g., public claims-making, political protests, communication campaigns) that strive to improve the situation of these groups by mobilizing on behalf of their rights and entitlements (Giugni and Passy 2001; Scholz 2008). This political dimension seems of particular importance when dealing with the European Union. In fact, European solidarity is present when people help other European citizens to raise their voice and make it heard, particularly if we are speaking of social groups at the fringes of society that are severely hit by the European crisis (Balme and Chabanet 2008; Lahusen 2013; Baglioni and Giugni 2014; Giugni and Grasso 2018). The survey aimed at measuring both dimensions of solidarity, the charitable and the political. In particular, the questions about reported solidarity activities were based on a rights-based concept of solidarity, because it asked respondents whether they actively supported the rights of various groups by means of the activities listed in the questionnaire. Additionally, we assembled information on political activities and orientations related to solidarity, ranging from protest participation to policy-related issues (e.g., European solidarity measures).

Third, solidarity can be organized at different levels of organization and aggregation, as indicated by previous research. Studies have focused on social solidarity at the micro level, that is, on the interpersonal relations of mutual support between individuals (Hechter 1987; Markovsky and Lawler 1994; Komter 2005). Research has also shown that solidarity is a collective endeavor promoted—at the meso level—by civil society organizations and social movements (Hunt and Benford 2004; Giugni and Passy 2001; Curtis et al. 2001). And, finally, scholars have focused—at the macro level—on welfare state institutions and social policies as an instrument of redistribution committed to the idea of solidarity (Fong 2001; Rehm 2009; Alesina and Giuliano 2011; Rehm et al. 2012). This differentiation provides tools for survey-based research, because it allows measuring individual solidarity as a multiscalar phenomenon. In our survey, for instance, we included questions that asked individuals to report interpersonal practices of support within and beyond their country, to indicate whether they supported civil society organizations or social movement activities and whether they are against or in favor of redistributive policies within their country and between European member states. Even though the focus of this book is primarily on the micro- and meso level, we will see that these various levels of organization and aggregation make a difference. Reported activities of individual solidarity seem to be less diffused, when compared to forms of delegated solidarity, that is, the support of civil society and the welfare state.

Finally, the analysis of solidarity has to take the group-boundedness of solidarity seriously. This means in particular that solidarity might be, more often than not, a particularist commitment. Previous research has consistently shown that solidarity is of little analytic and practical use when conceived of as a generalized disposition or practice. Studies recurrently highlight that solidarity is tied to specific groups (Hechter 1987; Hunt and Benford 2004; Scholz 2008) and thus conditional on the assumed social proximity, neediness, or deservingness of the targeted recipients (van Oorschot 2006). For this reason, it is not enough to measure a general disposition to help others. More than that, it is essential to list various potential target groups. In spatial terms, it is necessary to differentiate between solidarity with people within the respondents' countries, with other people within the European Union, and beyond Europe. Moreover, it is important to assess whether citizens make a difference when dissimilar target groups are addressed, such as refugees/asylum seekers, the unemployed, and the disabled.

The conceptual clarifications presented so far guided the design of our survey and allowed us to assemble a comprehensive comparative dataset. Our data enables us to describe levels of solidarity dispositions and activities within the eight countries under study and give a nuanced and differentiated picture of various forms of (target-specific) solidarity. Among other things, we are able to contextualize European solidarity and compare it with other (group-bound) forms of solidarity. This descriptive aim, however, was not the only objective of this survey. More than that, TransSOL was geared to shed light on those factors that are beneficial or detrimental for solidarity at large, and European solidarity in particular. Building on previous research, as indicated below, we know that solidarity among citizens is highly patterned by a battery of factors, namely, sociodemographic traits, social class, political allegiances, social capital, religious beliefs, and values among others; we included these variables in our study. In order to systematize this evidence, we propose to distinguish between three strands of inquiry.

A first source of inspiration comes from empirical research about redistributive preferences. These studies are interested in identifying those factors that guarantee the support of citizens for the welfare state at large, and various social policies in particular, and thus spur the backing of institutionalized forms of wealth redistribution and help (Alesina and Giuliano 2011; Amat and Wibbels 2009; Fong 2001; Rehm 2009; Rehm et al. 2012; Svallfors 1997). Studies have addressed a variety of social policy fields, among them pensions (Jaime-Castillo 2013), poverty (Alesina and Glaeser 2004; Scheepers and Grotenhuis 2005), and immigration (Banting and Kymlicka 2006; Mau and Burkhardt 2009). Evidence suggests that the support for redistributive preferences is influenced by the respondents' position in society, for example, the 'rational calculations' tied to their state of vulnerability (Iversen and Soskice 2001; Rehm 2009). Additionally, cognitive and ideational factor also play a role. Research has pointed to the role of religion and religiosity (Stegmueller et al. 2012; Lichterman 2015) and political socialization (Grasso et al. 2017a), but also general beliefs about the causes of income inequality (Fong 2001) and perceptions of deservingness (van Oorschot 2006) are important factors, too. In regard to the latter, research has identified several criteria that influence the judgment of deservingness: (1) the level of perceived responsibility and neediness, (2) social and spatial proximity and identity, including loyalties to ethnic groups, and (3) the recipients' attitudes and the degree of reciprocation (receiving and giving) (van Oorschot 2000, 2006; Alesina and Glaeser 2004; Luttmer 2001).

Second, the extensive field of studies on social capital and social cohesion is relevant for our discussion here, as well. In part, this research strand measures a similar phenomenon, as it is interested in forms of voluntary engagement within civic groups and organizations (Putnam et al. 2003; van Oorschot et al. 2006). However, social capital is not identical with solidarity, because social capital refers to those resources or ingredients that need to be mobilized into acts of solidarity. In this sense, this research strand provides helpful indications for our explanatory purposes, as it is interested in the conditions of interpersonal help and support. Here, in particular, it highlights the importance of interpersonal and institutional trust, of norms of reciprocity, and of informal networks as necessary ingredients of social cohesion (Chan et al. 2006; Jeannotte 2000; Delhey 2007) and thus as determining factors that help in explaining interpersonal solidarity. Moreover, studies of social cohesion have corroborated the importance of social class, age, and gender. They have shown that post-materialist values and religious beliefs play a beneficial role, whereas societies with social cleavages, political conflicts, and less developed welfare state institutions provide a less conducive environment (Kumlin and Rothstein 2005; van Oorschot and Arts 2005; Gelissen et al. 2012).

Finally, there are also lessons to be drawn from research on political behavior, in general, and social movement and protest participation, more specifically. These strands of research focus on the political dimensions of solidarity, and thus help to answer the question of whether political solidarity is determined by similar factors as the ones discussed above. Scholarly writing seems to support some of the research assumptions presented before, by showing how political behavior is patterned by social inequalities and forms of social exclusion (Brady et al. 1995; Kronauer 1998; Grasso 2013; Dunn et al. 2014; Giugni and Grasso 2015a; Grasso et al. 2017b). Moreover, studies agree on the fact that solidarity is also highly patterned by political preferences and orientation, for example, along the left-right scale (Likki and Staerklé 2014). Social movement analysis adds relevant knowledge by pointing to the importance of mobilization processes lead by existing organizations and groups, with the latter considered as collective means of mobilizing, organizing, and perpetuating (transnational) solidarity in terms of binding norms, commitments, and behaviors (Smith 1997; Balme and Chabanet 2008; della Porta and Caiani 2011; Baglioni and Giugni 2014; Giugni and Grasso 2015b). That is, being a member or follower of a certain initiative, association, organization, or movement implies a commitment not only to specific norms of solidarity but also to palpable acts as well (e.g., membership fees and charitable donations, joint political protests, events of claims-making).

Based on these insights, the survey included a series of questions that geared to gather data on all these explanatory factors. This information should allow us to identify those variables that tend to boost or inhibit solidarity dispositions and practices along the various dimensions identified before. In particular, it will enable us to ascertain whether European solidarity is inhibited or promoted by the same factors as solidarity with other reference groups. First, we are interested to see whether sociodemographic characteristics like age, gender, and race make a difference in regard to solidarity activities and dispositions. The study of civil societies, for instance, has shown that voluntary engagement tends to replicate the public/private divide by centering more strictly on male-dominated and 'public' activities, to the detriment of female networks of care and help (Neill and Gidengil 2006; Valentova 2016). It has been shown that younger and older citizens are more active in social movements, following different grades of 'biographical availability' in the life course (Beyerlein and Bergstrand 2013). And we know that migrants are often involved in cross-national networks of support and help (Glick Schiller et al. 1995; Morokvasic 1999; Recchi and Favell 2009). Second, we wish to test whether solidarity is patterned by the differential access of citizens to valued resources and skills, such as income and education, by the respondents' social status and affiliation to social class (Verba et al. 1978; Cainzos and Voces 2010) and by different levels of social exclusion and deprivation (Kronauer 1998). Third, we wish to analyze to what extent solidarity is conditioned by social capital, following the propositions of research devoted to civil society and social movements (Putnam et al. 2003; van Oorschot et al. 2006; Jenkins 1983). In particular, we wish to highlight the role of institutional and interpersonal trust, of informal networks and social relations, and of associational involvement in a wide range of social, cultural, and political organizations and groups. Fourth, we aim to identify the interrelation between political orientations and behaviors on the one side, and solidarity dispositions and practices on the other. In particular, we try to assess whether relevant factors investigated at the national level, for example, levels of political participation, political preferences, and ideological orientations (e.g., Blekesaune and Quadagno 2003; Amat and Wibbels 2009; Likki and Staerklé 2014; Giugni and Grasso 2017), also differentiate citizens with regard to solidarity. Finally, we wanted to identify the role of ideational and cognitive factors, too, assuming that the collective identities and the attachment to groups and communities might condition levels of solidarity (Luttmer 2001; Komter 2005) as much as religion and religiosity (Stegmueller et al. 2012; Lichterman 2015), moral norms, and visions of a desirable social order (Stets and McCaffree 2014).

Structure and Objectives of the Book

This book is based on data gathered by a comparative research project and aims to answer a number of questions related to solidarity. How developed are solidarity attitudes and practices among citizens of European member states? How diffused are these orientations when comparing various target groups, among them refugees/migrants, unemployed people, and the disabled? And how strongly are citizens engaged in helping people outside their country, both within and outside Europe? Which groups in the European citizenry are strongest supporters of European solidarity, and which segments exhibit distance from European or global solidarity? Available studies have shown that the idea of solidarity across borders is supported by a considerable proportion of the European citizenry, suggesting that the long history of European integration has had an impact on the ideas and preferences of the population (Lengfeld et al. 2015; de Vries and Hoffmann 2016). However, this evidence is far from painting a comprehensive picture. Moreover, most studies have focused on the support of public policies of redistribution and burden sharing, to the detriment of studies about civic and interpersonal forms of solidarity.

The survey data presented in this book provides fresh insights into this topic. It is based on an online individual survey conducted in the winter months of 2016/2017 in Denmark, France, Germany, Greece, Italy, Poland, Switzerland, and the United Kingdom. The same questionnaire was administered in the relevant languages to approximately 2000 respondents in each of the countries of the project, thus assembling data on more than 16,000 European citizens. Respondent samples were matched to national statistics with quotas for education, age, gender, and region, and population weights are applied in the analyses presented in this volume. The questionnaire was drafted to measure solidarity in its various dimensions and manifestations, as indicated before, and to assemble data on a number of potential factors that might help to explain this practiced solidarity.

The chapters included in this volume aim to answer the above stated questions in regard to each of the eight countries under study. They are committed to three overall objectives. First, national chapters engage in a descriptive account of levels and forms of solidarity practices in each of the eight countries. The dependent variables consist of reported solidarity practices, such as donating time or money, buying or boycotting products, protest participation, or passive and active associational membership. Depending on the national contextual relevance, the chapters also compare levels of solidarity in regard to various reference groups: for example, solidarity with people from the own country, from other European country, or countries outside Europe; solidarity with disabled people, the unemployed, and refugees/migrants. These findings enable the portrayal of country-specific levels of reported solidarity practices. Second, national chapters analyze the forces that affect practiced solidarity and in portraying the social profile of the most and least solidarity-prone groups of the population. For this purpose, the national chapters engaged with analyzing the explanatory relevance of the different factors introduced in this chapter. On the one hand, chapters focus on the social traits of the respondents, arguing that their position in the social structure impinges on the means and opportunities they have to commit themselves to solidarity. On the other hand, we assume that reported solidarity is conditioned also by attitudinal dispositions and preferences, such as political attitudes, social beliefs, or cultural values. Finally, each chapter explores specific aspects that seem particularly important either for the country under analysis and/or in view of research debates and questions awaiting empirical validation.

The book ends with a concluding chapter that wishes to paint a comparative picture of civic solidarity within and across European member states. For these purposes, we describe the main findings from our survey in comparative terms by presenting and highlighting the various levels of solidarity-driven practices and attitudes, and by identifying the importance of European solidarity, when compared to national or global solidarities in Europe. Moreover, knowledge assembled by the various national chapters will help us to assess whether solidarity—and European solidarity in particular—is driven by similar or different forces in the various countries under analysis. In this way, this volume provides a unique resource for understanding solidarity in contemporary Europe.

REFERENCES

Alesina, A., & Giuliano, P. (2011). Preferences for Redistribution. In J. Benhabibi, A. Bisin, & M. Jackson (Eds.), *Handbook of Social Economics*. San Diego: North-Holland.

Alesina, A., & Glaeser, E. (2004). *Fighting Poverty in the US and Europe: A World of Difference*. Oxford: Oxford University Press.

Amat, F., & Wibbels, E. (2009). *Electoral Incentives, Group Identity and Preferences for Redistribution*. Instituto Juan March de Estudios e Investigaciones Working Paper 246.

Baglioni, S., & Giugni, M. (Eds.). (2014). *Civil Society Organizations, Unemployment, and Precarity in Europe. Between Service and Policy*. Houndmills, Basingstoke: Palgrave Macmillan.

Balibar, E. (2010). Europe: Final Crisis? Some Theses. *Theory & Event, 13*(2). Project MUSE. https://doi.org/10.1353/tae.0.0127.

Balme, R., & Chabanet, D. (2008). *European Governance and Democracy. Power and Protest in the EU*. Lanham, MD: Rowman and Littlefield.

Bandy, J., & Smith, J. (2005). Factors Affecting Conflict and Cooperation in Transnational Movement Networks. In J. Bandy & J. Smith (Eds.), *Coalitions Across Borders. Transnational Protest and the Neoliberal Order* (pp. 231–252). Lanham: Rowman & Littlefield.

Banting, K. G., & Kymlicka, W. (Eds.). (2006). *Multiculturalism and the Welfare State: Recognition and Redistribution in Contemporary Democracies*. Oxford: Oxford University Press.

Beck, U., & Grande, E. (2007). *Cosmopolitan Europe* (C. Cronin, Trans.). Cambridge: Polity Press.

Beyerlein, K., & Bergstrand, K. (2013). Biographical Availability. In D. A. Snow, D. della Porta, B. Klandermans, & D. McAdam (Eds.), *The Wiley-Blackwell Encyclopedia of Social and Political Movements* (pp. 137–138). New York: Wiley-Blackwell.

Blekesaune, M., & Quadagno, J. (2003). Public Attitudes Toward Welfare State Policies: A Comparative Analysis of 24 Countries. *European Sociological Review, 19*(5), 415–427.

Brady, H. E., Verba, S., & Schlozman, K. L. (1995). Beyond SES: A Resource Model of Political Participation. *The America Political Science Review, 89*(2), 271–294.

Cainzos, M., & Voces, C. (2010). Class Inequalities in Political Participation and the 'Death of Class' Debate. *International Sociology, 25*(3), 383–418.

Chan, J., To, H., & Chan, E. (2006). Reconsidering Social Cohesion: Developing a Definition and Analytical Framework for Empirical Research. *Social Indicators Research, 75*, 273–302.

Curtis, J. E., Baer, D. E., & Grabb, E. G. (2001). Nations of Joiners: Explaining Voluntary Association Membership in Democratic Societies. *American Sociological Review, 66*(6), 783–805.

Delanty, G., & Rumford, C. (2005). *Rethinking Europe: Social Theory and the Implications of Europeanization*. Abingdon and New York: Routledge.

Delhey, J. (2007). Do Enlargements Make the European Union Less Cohesive? An Analysis of Trust Between EU Nationalities. *Journal of Common Market Studies, 45*(2), 253–279.

della Porta, D., & Caiani, M. (2011). *Social Movements and Europeanization*. Oxford: Oxford University Press.

Dunn, A., Grasso, M. T., & Saunders, C. (2014). Unemployment and Attitudes to Work: Asking the 'Right' Question. *Work, Employment, and Society, 28*(6), 904–925.

Durkheim, E. (1893/1997). *The Division of Labor in Society*. New York: Free Press.

Eurobarometer. (2011, September). *Eurobarometer 76.1: Financial and Economic Crisis, Financial Services, Corruption, Development Aid, and Gender Equality*. Brussels: EU-Commission (ICPSR 34552).

Fong, C. (2001). Social Preferences, Self-Interest, and the Demand for Redistribution. *Journal of Public Economics, 82*(2), 225–246.

Gelissen, J., Wim, J. H., van Oorschot, W., & Finsveen, E. (2012). How Does the Welfare State Influence Individuals' Social Capital? Eurobarometer Evidence on Individuals' Access to Informal Help. *European Societies, 2012*, 1–25.

Giugni, M., & Grasso, M. (Eds.). (2015a). *Austerity and Protest: Popular Contention in Times of Economic Crisis*. London: Routledge.

Giugni, M., & Grasso, M. T. (2015b). Environmental Movements in Advanced Industrial Democracies: Heterogeneity, Transformation, and Institutionalization. *Annual Review of Environment and Resources, 40*, 337–361.

Giugni, M., & Grasso, M. T. (2017). Blame and Contention: How Perceptions of the Government's Role in the Economic Crisis Shape Patterns of Political Action. *Acta Politica* (Open Access). Retrieved from https://link.springer.com/article/10.1057%2Fs41269-017-0073-x.

Giugni, M., & Grasso, M. (Eds.). (2018). *Citizens and the Crisis: Perceptions, Experiences, and Responses to the Great Recession in Europe, Palgrave Studies in European Political Sociology*. London: Palgrave Macmillan.

Giugni, M., & Passy, F. (Eds.). (2001). *Political Altruism? Solidarity Movements in International Perspective*. Lanham, MD: Rowman & Littlefield.

Glick Schiller, N., Basch, L., & Szanton-Blanc, C. (1995). From Immigrant to Transmigrant: Theorizing Transnational Migration. *Anthropological Quarterly, 68*(1), 48–63.

Grasso, M. T. (2011). *Political Participation in Western Europe*. D.Phil. Thesis, Nuffield College, University of Oxford.
Grasso, M. T. (2013). The Differential Impact of Education on Young People's Political Activism: Comparing Italy and the United Kingdom. *Comparative Sociology, 12*(1), 1–30.
Grasso, M. T. (2016). *Generations, Political Participation and Social Change in Western Europe*. London: Routledge.
Grasso, M. T., & Giugni, M. (2016). Protest Participation and Economic Crisis: The Conditioning Role of Political Opportunities. *European Journal of Political Research, 55*(4), 663–680.
Grasso, M. T., Farrall, S., Gray, E., Hay, C., & Jennings, W. (2017a). Thatcher's Children, Blair's Babies, Political Socialisation and Trickle-Down Value-Change: An Age, Period and Cohort Analysis. *British Journal of Political Science*. https://doi.org/10.1017/S0007123416000375.
Grasso, M. T., Yoxon, B., Karampampas, S., & Temple, L. (2017b). Relative Deprivation and Inequalities in Social and Political Activism. *Acta Politica* (Open Access). Retrieved from https://link.springer.com/article/10.1057%2Fs41269-017-0072-y.
Habermas, J. (2017, March 16). *Why the Necessary Cooperation Does Not Happen: Introduction to a Conversation Between Emmanuel Macron and Sigmar Gabriel on Europe's Future*. Paper presented at the Hertie School of Governance in Berlin. Retrieved May 9, 2017, from https://www.socialeurope.eu/2017/03/pulling-cart-mire-renewed-case-european-solidarity/.
Hechter, M. (1987). *Principles of Group Solidarity*. Berkeley: University of California Press.
Hunt, S. A., & Benford, R. D. (2004). Collective Identity, Solidarity, and Commitment. In D. A. Snow, S. A. Soule, & H. Kriesi (Eds.), *The Blackwell Companion to Social Movements* (pp. 433–457). Oxford: Blackwell.
Iversen, T., & Soskice, D. (2001). An Asset Theory of Social Policy Preferences. *American Political Science Review, 95*(4), 875–893.
Jaime-Castillo, A. M. (2013). Public Opinion and the Reform of the Pension Systems in Europe: The Influence of Solidarity Principles. *Journal of European Social Policy, 23*(4), 390–405.
Jeannotte, M. S. (2000). *Social Cohesion Around the World: An International Comparison of Definitions and Issues*. Paper SRA-390.
Jenkins, J. C. (1983). Resource Mobilization Theory and the Study of Social Movements. *Annual Review of Sociology, 9*, 527–553.
Komter, A. E. (2005). *Social Solidarity and the Gift*. Cambridge: Cambridge University Press.
Kronauer, M. (1998). 'Social Exclusion' and 'Underclass': New Concepts for the Analysis of Poverty. In A. Hans-Jürgen (Ed.), *Empirical Poverty Research in a Comparative Perspective* (pp. 51–75). Aldershot: Ashgate.

Kumlin, S., & Rothstein, B. (2005). Making and Breaking Social Capital: The Impact of Welfare-State Institutions. *Comparative Political Studies, 38*(4), 339–365.

Lahusen, C. (2013). European Integration, Social Cohesion and Political Contentiousness. In B. Andreosso-O'Callaghan & F. Royall (Eds.), *Economic and Political Change in Asia and Europe. Social Movement Analyzes* (pp. 31–52). Dordrecht: Springer.

Lengfeld, H., Schmidt, S., & Häuberer, J. (2012). *Solidarität in der europäischen Fiskalkrise: Sind die EU-Bürger zu finanzieller Unterstützung von hoch verschuldeten EU-Ländern bereit? Erste Ergebnisse aus einer Umfrage in Deutschland und Portugal.* Hamburg Reports on Contemporary Societies No.5/2012, University of Hamburg.

Lengfeld, H., Schmidt, S., & Häuberer, J. (2015). *Is There a European Solidarity? Attitudes Towards Fiscal Assistance for Debt-Ridden European Union Member States.* Report of the Department of Sociology No. 67, Leipzig.

Lichterman, P. (2015). Religion and Social Solidarity. A Pragmatist Approach. In L. Hustinx, J. von Essen, J. Haers, & S. Mels (Eds.), *Religion and Volunteering. Complex, Contested and Ambiguous Relationships* (pp. 241–261). Cham: Springer.

Likki, T., & Staerklé, C. (2014). A Typology of Ideological Attitudes Towards Social Solidarity and Social Control. *Journal of Community and Applied Social Psychology, 24,* 406–421.

Luttmer, B. (2001). Group Loyalty and the Taste for Redistribution. *Journal of Political Economy, 109*(3), 500–528.

Markovsky, B., & Lawler, E. J. (1994). A New Theory of Group Solidarity. In B. Markovsky, K. Heimer, & J. O'Brien (Eds.), *Advances in Group Processes* (pp. 113–137). Greenwich, CT: JAI Press.

Marshall, T. H. (1950). *Citizenship and Social Class: And Other Essays.* Cambridge: Cambridge University Press.

Mau, S., & Burkhardt, C. (2009). Migration and Welfare State Solidarity in Western Europe. *Journal of European Social Policy, 19*(3), 213–229.

Morokvasic, M. (1999). La mobilité transnationale comme ressource: le cas des migrants de l'Europe de l'Est. *Cultures et Conflits, 32,* 105–122.

Neill, B., & Gidengil, E. (Eds.). (2006). *Gender and Social Capital.* New York: Routledge.

van Oorschot, W. (2000). Who Should Get What, and Why? On Deservingness Criteria and the Conditionality of Solidarity Among the Public. *Policy & Politics, 28*(1), 33–48.

van Oorschot, W. (2006). Making the Difference in Social Europe: Deservingness Perceptions Among Citizens of European Welfare States. *Journal of European Social Policy, 16*(1), 23–42.

van Oorschot, W., & Arts, W. (2005). The Social Capital of European Welfare States: The Crowding Out Hypothesis Revisited. *Journal of European Social Policy, 15*(1), 5–26.

van Oorschot, W., Arts, W., & Gelissen, J. (2006). Social Capital in Europe. Measurement and Social and Regional Distribution of a Multifaceted Phenomenon. *Acta Sociologica, XLIX*, 149–167.

Parsons, T. (1966). *Societies: Evolutionary and Comparative Perspectives.* Englewood Cliffs, NJ: Prentice-Hall.

Putnam, R., Feldstein, L. M., & Cohen, D. (2003). *Better Together: Restoring the American Community.* New York: Simon & Schuster.

Recchi, E., & Favell, A. (2009). *Pioneers of European Integration. Citizenship and Mobility in the EU.* Cheltenham: Edward Elgar.

Rehm, P. (2009). Risks and Redistribution. An Individual-Level Analysis. *Comparative Political Studies, 42*(7), 885–881.

Rehm, P., Hacker, J. S., & Schlesinger, M. (2012). Insecure Alliances: Risk, Inequality and Support for the Welfare State. *American Political Science Review, 106*(2), 386–406.

Scheepers, P., & Grotenhuis, M. T. (2005). Who Cares for the Poor in Europe? Micro and Macro Determinants for Alleviating Poverty in 15 European Countries. *European Sociological Review, 21*(5), 453–465.

Scholz, S. J. (2008). *Political Solidarity.* Penn State University Press.

Smith, J. (1997). *Transnational Social Movements and Global Politics: Solidarity Beyond the State.* Syracuse University Press.

Stegmueller, D., Scheepers, P., Roßteuscher, S., & de Jong, E. (2012). Support for Redistribution in Western Europe. Assessing the Role of Religion. *European Sociological Review, 28*(4), 482–497.

Stets, J. E., & McCaffree, K. (2014). Linking Morality, Altruism, and Social Solidarity Using Identity Theory. In V. Jeffries (Ed.), *The Palgrave Handbook of Altruism, Morality, and Social Solidarity* (pp. 333–351). New York: Palgrave Macmillan.

Stjerno, S. (2012). *Solidarity in Europe. The History of an Idea.* Cambridge: Cambridge University Press.

Svallfors, S. (1997). Worlds of Welfare and Attitudes to Redistribution: A Comparison of Eight Western Nations. *European Journal of Sociology, 13*(3), 283–304.

Valentova, M. (2016). How Do Traditional Gender Roles Relate to Social Cohesion? Focus on Differences Between Women and Men. *Social Indicators Research, 127*(1), 153–178.

Verba, S., Nie, N., & Kim, J. (1978). *Participation and Political Equality: A Seven Nation Comparison.* London: Cambridge University Press.

de Vries, C., & Hoffmann, I. (2016). *Border Protection and Freedom of Movement. What People Expect of European Asylum and Migration Policies.* Gütersloh: Bertelsmann Stiftung euopinion 2016/1. Retrieved October 16, 2017, from https://www.bertelsmann-stiftung.de/en/publications/publication/did/border-protection-and-freedom-of-movement/.

Open Access   This chapter is licensed under the terms of the Creative Commons Attribution 4.0 International License (http://creativecommons.org/licenses/by/4.0/), which permits use, sharing, adaptation, distribution and reproduction in any medium or format, as long as you give appropriate credit to the original author(s) and the source, provide a link to the Creative Commons license and indicate if changes were made.

The images or other third party material in this chapter are included in the chapter's Creative Commons license, unless indicated otherwise in a credit line to the material. If material is not included in the chapter's Creative Commons license and your intended use is not permitted by statutory regulation or exceeds the permitted use, you will need to obtain permission directly from the copyright holder.

CHAPTER 2

Toward a New Conditionality of Welfare? Reconsidering Solidarity in the Danish Welfare State

Hans-Jörg Trenz and Maria Grasso

INTRODUCTION

The Danish (Scandinavian) welfare model is based on the principle of universalism: providing equal services in the form of tax-financed benefits to all citizens independently of their individual contributions. Solidarity traditionally has a high value in the small and egalitarian Scandinavian societies and can rely on the homogenous composition of the populations in terms of ethnic, religious and linguistic unity. This is generally seen as generating high levels of support for the welfare state. At the same time, a strong and omnipresent welfare regime can be said to release citizens from the need to invest in substantive support action. The basic needs of vulnerable groups like the unemployed, people with disabilities or refugees are served by the universal welfare state as a centralized care-taker for the well-being of society.

At the same time, the traditional inclusive welfare regime in Denmark has over the last decade undergone an important, and often unnoticed, transformation. In a series of reforms by the liberal-conservative coalition which governed the country from 2001 to 2011 and, again, since 2015, welfare services have, in general, become more conditional and distinctions between various layers of need have been introduced. The new conditionality of welfare services applies, for instance, in the labor market with an emphasis on 'flexicurity' and the measurement of individual contributions on which unemployment and welfare benefits are made dependent (Strøby-Jensen 2011). The inclusiveness of welfare state services has also been questioned with regard to the Europe of free movements, where the same rights apply indiscriminately to all EU citizens moving to and residing in Denmark.

In this chapter, we analyze engagement in solidarity actions in support of marginalized groups within the Danish population. We first provide an overall picture of the level of involvement of Danes in solidarity actions toward different kinds of vulnerable groups at the local, national, European and global level. Second, we look at how Danes contest solidarity toward these groups at different levels. The overall question to be examined is the inclusiveness of solidarity engagement within Danish society and the way in which solidarity in a traditionally welfare-generous country is currently performed in the backdrop of a European context that faces the challenges of migration, economic recession and increasing competiveness. It is argued that universal welfare states are put under pressure by such developments, first by external challenges and the necessity to respond to demands of new and increasingly diverse groups in need of assistance; and second, by the internal contestations of citizens who withdraw their support, oppose a further extension of welfare services and redefine solidarity.

CONTEXTUALIZING SOLIDARITY: THE DANISH CASE

High-tax welfare states, like Denmark, arguably rely on strong ties of solidarity (Jöhncke 2011). The kind of solidarity ties that support redistributive welfare regimes must go beyond schemes of charity and include a notion of reciprocity in terms of sympathy felt toward co-citizens and a notion of shared responsibility in terms of acting together as a political community (Habermas 2013). Solidarity that supports redistribution therefore typically goes hand in hand with a strong civil society and with civic associations that promote trust and mutual support among the members of the political community (Banting and Kymlicka 2017; Hall 2017; Calhoun 2002). To make a strong welfare state sustainable, citizens should not only support the principle of reciprocal solidarity in abstract terms but also put it into practice in their daily interactions of mutual support and ties of sympathy among the citizens.

The advance of neoliberal market economies based on private initiative, including the cutting of public expenditures and deregulation, have posed a threat to this idea of civic solidarity (English et al. 2016; Grasso et al. 2017; Temple et al. 2016). Liberal market policies have been backed by all Danish governments over the last two decades and, in particular, by the liberal-conservative coalitions which have governed the country since 2001. As a consequence of such policies, Denmark has experienced a general retreat of universal welfare services with a new emphasis on individual responsibility (Jensen and Torpe 2016; Larsen et al. 2015). The weakening of social provisions of redistribution and a cutting down of welfare services can be expected to correlate with a decline of solidarity. Taxation as a core indicator to reciprocal solidarity (Stjernø 2004: 2) is challenged as fewer people are prepared to share resources with others, or simply because the capacities of the welfare state to redistribute income are limited. Strong and universal welfare states are in this sense particularly vulnerable, when their solidarity is tested by global developments or pressures of European market competition (Martinsen 2005). This holds in particular for a high-tax country like Denmark, which has adapted the universality of welfare services to the new flexibility of Europeanized and globalized labor markets. On the one hand, such transformations of the welfare state bear the risk of damaging traditional forms of centralized, universalistic solidarity, but, on the other hand, they also open the possibility that at the same time, and parallel or in direct response to Europeanization and market liberalization, new forms and practices of decentralized solidarity toward different groups of society may develop. European integration is in this sense perceived by some groups within Danish society both from the right and from the left as a major threat to national solidarity, but it could also lead to a general reorientation of solidarity practices. As such, solidarity becomes increasingly contested by new organizations and new forms of civic mobilization addressing European and global issues and increasingly operating at a European and global scale. In Denmark, such new solidarity contestations are proposed, on the one hand, by the Danish People's Party (*Dansk Folkeparti*) which is Denmark's second largest party, gaining 21.1%

of the vote in the 2015 general elections and supporting the current right-liberal minority government in Parliament. The Danish People's Party defends an exclusive notion of national solidarity as a community of belonging based on strong ethnic ties. It is opposed to strong and centralized welfare regimes emphasizing instead individual responsibility, subsidiarity and the need to cut down the high-tax burden in Denmark. In the European Parliament, the Party joined the Eurosceptic European Conservatives and Reformists group opposing EU sovereignty transfers, EU redistributive policies and European and global solidarity engagement. On the other hand, solidarity contestations are pushed by the political left, in particular by the Red-Green Alliance (*Enhedslisten*) gaining 7.8% of the vote in the 2015 elections. The left opposition emphasizes the fight against social inequality and poverty as one of their main priorities and is in favor of strengthening and expanding the welfare state. This includes solidarity toward marginalized groups, including foreigners and refugees. As such, *Enhedslisten* combines a perspective of national and global solidarity but is explicitly anti-EU and campaigns for a withdrawal of Denmark from its European commitments.[1]

Civil society associations have reacted to the new conditionality of the welfare state by shifting orientations and providing new services for the increasing number of those who are falling through the security net. As we are able to show in our survey of Danish civil society activism, solidarity actions by civil society organizations is shifting from being supplementary of state-based services to becoming more substantial and also more confrontational. Instead of assisting the state in implementing welfare, civil society is found to increasingly replace the state and to fight in opposition to state imposed restrictions and financial cuts (Duru et al. forthcoming; Spejlborg Sejersen and Trenz 2017).

The economic and financial crisis that was triggered in 2008 marks some further modest changes but not a radical rethinking of the Danish welfare regime. In general terms, Denmark has turned more restrictive toward vulnerable groups in society cutting welfare state expenditures and putting stronger emphasis on the obligation to work. As a result of the most recent policy changes, social benefits for the unemployed, refugees and people with disabilities persons have been cut or have become more conditional with preference given to measures that seek to reintegrate welfare recipients into the labor market.[2] This is however in line with the tradition of the Danish welfare state, which has always combined a generous social safety net and free education with the obligations to pay high taxes and to contribute actively to the wealth of society through work, volunteering and social responsibility (Christoffersen et al. 2013).

The robustness of the welfare system in times of crisis can be explained by Denmark's efficient crisis management and quick economic recovery after having suffered from recession in the initial crisis years. Macroeconomic data shows, in fact, that the country and its population did not suffer from a substantial loss in wealth, and, while recession or economic stagnation were endured in many parts of Europe, Denmark soon profited again from economic growth.[3] Denmark does not only continue to be the country with the most equal income distribution in Europe, its average annual wage is also one of the highest in Europe, while inflation is at an historical low.[4] Unemployment is steadily declining since 2011 with a current unemployment rate (December 2016) of 6.5%, which is below the EU28 average of 8.3% and far below the rate of countries most hit by crisis like Italy (11.9%), Spain (19.1%) and Greece (23.1%). Youth unemployment is with 10% in 2016 far below the average in other European countries were the youth unemployment rate is generally double or more than double the unemployment rates for all ages.[5] This downward trend indicates the recovery of the labor market which offers job opportunities for young adults not only from Denmark itself but also increasingly young mobile EU citizens. More recent periods (2011–2014) saw a strong increase in intra-EU mobility flows toward Denmark (+44%), made up mainly by young adults in the East, South-East and South of Europe who escape economic hardship by moving to Denmark (European Commission 2014: 20–21).

In the field of immigration and asylum, we observe over the last five years a shift in the number of incoming migrants from non-EU to intra-EU mobility, the former group discriminated by new restrictive legislation and the latter group profiting from the principle of nondiscrimination of EU citizenship and attracted by labor and education opportunities.[6] These circumstances have become a concern for the Danish government and society, which—according to Jørgensen and Thomsen (2013)—is reflected in an increasing negative tone in the media toward both groups: EU and non-EU migrants. A more recent stage was marked by the arrival of refugees which has led to a political controversy regarding the humanitarian obligations of Denmark as well as with respect to solidarity within the EU. The Danish government's restrictive policies in the autumn of 2016 were criticized by neighboring Sweden and Germany and ultimately led to the suspension of *Schengen* rules of free movement and border control which still persists to this day.

Despite these general challenges and tendencies in the transformation of the welfare state, Denmark remains exceptional in the European context in terms of the modest economic impact of crisis and de facto economic growth over the last few years. This might explain why the economic crisis also left only a low imprint on the attitudes of Danes, which remain strongly supportive of the high-tax and welfare regime, express high trust in the state, political parties and parliamentary representation[7] and according to the World Happiness Report published annually by the United Nations Sustainable Development Solutions Network continue to be among the world's 'happiest nations'. Happiness, trust and life satisfaction have become a matter of national pride, and the good comparative rankings of Denmark are widely publicized and commented upon in the media and by political representatives. Our survey confirms these patterns, in terms of high life satisfaction, which is also backed by material gains: 72.5% of all Danes are satisfied or highly satisfied (6–10 on Likert scale) with their life (compared to 36% in Greece), and the great majority of Danes (86.7%) declare that their financial situation has improved over the last five years (6–10 on Likert scale where 0 means much worse and 10 means much better), compared to only 11.4% in Greece.

In line with this image of Denmark as the worlds' happiest nation, a strong emphasis is placed on solidarity, which has two components: (1) support of redistribution measured, for example, in the willingness to share income through taxes and (2) trust and civic virtue, measured, for example, in the willingness to engage in solidarity action and contribute actively to the well-being of the community of citizens. This is often paired with an attitude of moralizing solidarity, that is, to emphasize the duties of active contributions to communal life and to blame deviants. Solidarity is a civic virtue but it is also a moral obligation. An attitude of moralizing solidarity can, in fact, be used as a justification of exclusive practices toward 'non-deserving' groups of society, an argumentation often used by populist-right parties. This raises the question whether there is a widening gap between perceptions of Denmark as the happiest country in the world and practices of exclusion toward growing numbers of poor or persons deprived of rights. The Danish pride in welfare and solidarity might thus nourish an illusion, if Danes continue to believe in the uniqueness of their welfare system and continue to trust in the state's capacities of care-taking while at the same time failing to recognize important systemic changes that put pressures on people in need, push more and more Danes into private insurance schemes or exclude them from the net of social security. As has been noted in a recent report published by a NGO active in the field:

> Although Danish society claims to uphold the basic principles of a welfare state—solidarity among citizens and provisions for the needy—in practice, public discourse and government policies have been creating a more libertarian, individualistic model that strays from its founding principles. Until the Danish people stop moralizing about solidarity and acknowledge the changing nature of their welfare system, Denmark's poor and excluded will grow in number to fill this dangerously widening gap between perception and practice.[8]

We have identified and described the changing state-civil society relations and new solidarity practices elsewhere (Duru et al. forthcoming; Spejlborg Sejersen and Trenz 2017). Based on these insights, it is now our task to analyze more closely public attitudes and public attention in relation to these new solidarity challenges and contestations.

We organize our analysis around a set of questions relating to the attitudinal and behavioral dimensions of solidarity. The question is whether public opinion is leaning more toward a universalistic or an individualistic welfare arrangement. Do Danes continue to support universalistic welfare or do they back the new state policies that make welfare conditional of contributions? Are Danes also aware of the European and global dimensions of solidarity and of the challenges and opportunities offered by European market integration? The question is further whether restrictions in welfare state services and policies that affect particularly vulnerable groups within society, such as refugees, migrants or unemployed, are also noticeable in a reorientation of civic practices (so-called solidarity actions). Does solidarity action turn toward these new people, such as for instance refugees or the long-term unemployed, in need of assistance? Is there a general awareness of the transition of the Danish welfare model from universalism providing services indistinguishably to all persons in need to more conditionality?

The overall question thus is whether this new conditionality of the welfare state is also supported by general attitudes and new practices of solidarity. From a European comparative perspective, this is relevant in order to establish whether Danes still support universal welfare regimes and recognize the needs of new groups of recipients for solidarity recognized by the Danish population. We further wish to understand whether such traditional notions of an inclusive, service-oriented welfare state can be combined with an awareness of global solidarity challenges and possible solutions. This includes an analysis of the extent to which citizens themselves are involved in such transnational and local networks or individual forms of solidarity action.

We organize our analysis of reported solidarity practices around an alternative set of hypotheses: the first concerns support of the traditional belief systems and the notion of universal welfare, and the second concerns the conditionality of solidarity based on the notion of deservingness. In the first case, reported solidarity practices and attitudes would uphold the founding principles and distinctive traits of the Danish (Scandinavian) welfare regime. In line with the existing literature (Christoffersen et al. 2013; Jöhncke 2011), we would expect high levels of support for the welfare state and involvement in solidarity practices to be distributed equally among the population encompassing all age groups, gender, regions and ideological and political affiliations. Such a uniform pattern of solidarity would reflect the homogeneity of Danish society represented by centralized state structures. We would further expect that a centralized, strong and omnipresent welfare regime releases citizens from the need to invest in substantive support action. Danes would trust that the universal welfare state takes care of the basic needs of vulnerable groups like the unemployed, people with disabilities or refugees. Mutual support would be voluntary and not required for the subsistence of these persons in need. We would therefore expect Danish civil society to assume a subsidiary function vis-à-vis state-centered welfare: solidarity action would often supplement existing services and not be substitutive for the well-being or survival of vulnerable groups (in contrast to countries where state solidarity is lacking or inefficient). Citizens would rather opt for indirect instead of direct support actions and their solidarity would encompass several levels: trust and mutual assistance at the local and national level and a European and global problem awareness. We would ultimately expect that the universal welfare state releases forces for the mobilization of transnational solidarity, which becomes especially a target of private, individual support action and charity.

In the second case, we would be able to identify patterns of conditionality in the reported solidarity practices. We would be able to describe how Danes distinguish between different recipients of solidarity along criteria of deservingness that justify an unequal distribution of services and differentiated access to welfare. We would further expect that solidarity varies along the lines of the expected contributions of solidarity recipients to Danish society. An instrumental view on solidarity would thus prevail over the inclusive norms of universal welfare. In particular, we would be able to describe whether solidarity is redefined in a way that either claims of welfare chauvinism or claims of nativism become more legitimate. In the first case, we would assume that Danes support the claims that welfare benefits should become conditional on individual contributions measured in terms of 'having served' for the national community (deservingness based on merit). In the second case, Danes would support the claims that welfare benefits should be reserved only for those considered 'natives' by being born into the national community (deservingness based on ethnic and cultural bonds).

As a result of this shift from universalism to deservingness, we would further expect that solidarity would become more confrontational with citizens either supporting restrictions of welfare through the application of criteria of deservingness or opposing them. This confrontation would follow an ideological left-right cleavage, leading to the polarization of the Danish population shifting from the support of center-right or center-left parties to the political extremes. Conditionality in the reported solidarity practices would also encompass several levels, with strong preference given to the local and national enactment of solidarity and more exclusive attitudes toward European and global solidarity action. As regards patterns of transnational solidarity, we would, on the one hand, expect many Danes to be reluctant to extend welfare services to groups of European migrants or refugees and to make access of these groups conditional. On the other hand, following the new confrontational style through which solidarity is negotiated, we would expect Danes to engage in more political forms of solidarity action in direct opposition of state policies or in response to deficits of state welfare.

Findings

Reported Solidarity Practices

First of all, we wish to investigate whether reported solidarity practices in Denmark reflect a new conditionality in the way Danish population distinguishes solidarity receivers as deserving or undeserving. As shown in Table 2.1, approximately half of the population (46.6%) declares to be engaged in some sort of solidarity action in Denmark, but only about one-fourth in the EU (23.9%) and little more than one-third (36%) outside the EU. In line with previous findings on the inclusiveness of Danish welfare, a relatively widespread solidarity culture in Denmark thus persists and is measurable not only at the level of attitudes but also translates into various forms of solidarity practices accounting for the needs of vulnerable groups primarily inside Denmark but also with a strong focus outside of Denmark, both in Europe and globally.

Table 2.2 shows the type of solidarity actions that people become involved in at the national level. Among the solidarity actions listed at national level, low engagement activities such as donating money is by the far the most widespread activity (28.4% of all Danes), followed by buying or refusing to buy products in support of solidarity goals (17.5%). High engagement activities such as donating time (12.8%), engaging as a passive (10.8%) or active (9.6%) member of a solidarity organization rank lower and participating in a protest march lowest (9.2%) among the reported solidarity activities.

Low engagement activities like donating money or consumer awareness are expectedly more widespread than more engaging activities like donating time, protesting in the streets or aligning with an organization. This is in line with our hypothesis that the availability of state help for persons in need correlates with more indirect forms of solidarity action. Solidarity

Table 2.1 Engagement in solidarity action at national, European and global level (% participated in some form of action)

National	EU	Outside EU
46.6	23.3	34.5

Table 2.2 Type of solidarity action at national level (in %)

	Participated
Attended a march protest or demonstration	9.2
Donated money	28.4
Donate time	12.8
Bought or refused to buy products	17.5
Engaged as passive member of an organization	10.8
Engaged as an active member of an organization	9.6

action is however not apolitical, as some political awareness is needed, for instance, when consumers decide as citizens to boycott particular products. Explicit political activism in support of solidarity like participation in street protests or active membership in political groups is however not widespread (Grasso 2011, 2016), that is, only one out of ten Danes engages in such activities.

Looking more closely at conditional factors of solidarity behavior, we first test a number of social structure variables. When it comes to age, we find that solidarity action at national level is equally spread over all generations, but there are greater differences between younger and older people with respect to solidarity action in the EU and outside of EU, that is, the younger generations below 35 is generally more engaged in European and global solidarity action (Table 2.3).

In other words, young people do not withdraw from national solidarity action and replace it with European and global engagement but engage more equally at all levels. There is thus no trade-off between national and European/global solidarity. The higher engagement of young people in transnational solidarity action is even more striking if one considers the necessity to invest higher resources for transnational actions, like time and money that are more easily available for elder generations. Moreover, age differences are more pronounced when it comes to solidarity within the EU. Comparing the young age group of 18–24 with the middle age group of 45–54, their engagement in national solidarity action is identical (both 47.6%), their engagement in global solidarity action is wider (41.1% vs. 32.8%), but the widest gap is to be found in European solidarity engagement (32.2% vs. 20.0%).

Table 2.3 Engagement in solidarity action at national, European and global level (% participated in some form of action) by age group

	National	*EU*	*Outside EU*
18–24	47.6	32.2	41.1
25–34	50.0	30.3	37.7
35–44	44.4	21.1	29.8
45–54	47.6	20.0	32.8
55–64	48.5	22.7	33.6
65 years and older	42.9	18.6	34.2
Total	46.6	23.3	34.5

These differences are even more pronounced when comparing the young generation with the elder generation (above 65), which shows lowest engagement in EU solidarity (18.6%) but a slight increase in global solidarity action (34.2%). Possible explanations for this EU bias are differences in support of the EU between the age groups that translate into different patterns of national, European and global solidarity. Based on political socialization theory, we could hypothesize that perhaps generations coming of age during the time of EU consolidation and making use of EU opportunities for education, work and travel feel more solidarity at this level (Grasso 2014). Other possible explanations refer to differences in support action (like donating money, which typically involves elder age groups and is more typical for expressing global solidarity and less common as an expression of European solidarity).

There are instead no gender differences when it comes to explaining support action at all levels (Table 2.4) and only slight differences when it comes to residence (city or rural areas) (Table 2.5). On the other hand, education explains higher engagement in solidarity action at all levels (Grasso 2013), with differences more marked for European/global solidarity action (Table 2.6). Moreover, there are also important inequalities

Table 2.4 Engagement in solidarity action at national, European and global level (% participated in some form of action) by gender

	National	EU	Outside EU
Male	46.1	22.9	35.3
Female	47.0	23.6	33.7
Total	46.6	23.3	34.5

Table 2.5 Engagement in solidarity action at national, European and global level (% participated in some form of action) by place of residence

	National	EU	Outside EU
A big city	48.7	27.0	36.6
Suburbs or outskirts	49.4	22.8	36.2
Town or small city	43.8	20.7	32.1
Country village	43.8	19.8	32.7
Farm or home in the country-side	50.1	29.6	37.5
Total	46.6	23.3	34.5

by occupational class of chief of household with professionals participating in national actions of solidarity at 15 points higher than those in unskilled manual jobs (Table 2.7). Overall, we can thus conclude that solidarity action is spread relatively equally between genders and places of residence but spread unevenly in terms of social class with individuals holding more resources more likely to get involved (Grasso 2017). Accounting for these class differences is however not only income but also education, occupational opportunities and social capital (as shown in Tables 2.6, 2.7, and 2.8).

Social capital as measured through sociability (i.e. meeting friends) is associated with national level solidarity, that is, with those who meet friends regularly also most engaged in solidarity action at the national level (Table 2.8). Higher social capital does not show a higher likelihood to engage in European and global solidarity, however. Differences in European and global solidarity engagement may be explained therefore rather by the nature of the network of friends (homogeneity/heterogeneity) than by frequency of meetings.

Table 2.6 Engagement in solidarity action at national, European and global level (% participated in some form of action) by education

	National	EU	Outside EU
University or higher degree	54.6	30.0	45.9
Secondary school	48.1	23.9	35.4
Less than secondary school education	38.6	17.6	24.9
Total	46.6	23.3	34.5

Table 2.7 Engagement in solidarity action at national, European and global level (% participated in some form of action) by occupational class

	National	EU	Outside EU
Professional or higher	56.3	30.4	49.0
Manager or senior administrator	52.4	26.6	38.2
Clerical	42.2	17.0	30.4
Sales or services	47.9	22.5	33.3
Foreman or supervisor	46.8	30.1	41.2
Skilled manual work	46.4	25.5	31.0
Semi-skilled or unskilled manual	41.0	18.3	27.3
Other (e.g. farming)	38.2	21.1	26.7
Total	46.6	23.3	34.5

Table 2.8 Engagement in solidarity action at national, European and global level (% participated in some form of action) by social capital (frequency of meeting friends)

	National	EU	Outside EU
Less than once this month	34.0	30.4	49.0
Once or twice this month	45.9	26.6	38.2
Every week	52.9	17.0	30.4
Almost everyday	47.9	22.5	33.3
Total	46.6	23.3	34.5

Summing up the social structure variables, we find that solidarity behavior of the Danish population is overall rather uniform and follows expected patterns. The preferred action forms for Danes are passive activities like donating money, but still a substantial portion of the population also invests in more engaging and political forms of solidarity. Gender and residence do not impact on solidarity engagement, while there are interesting differences between age groups, educational levels and occupational classes.

Among the attitudinal patterns, it is interesting to note that strength of national identity measured in terms of attachment to one's country matters less to explain engagement in national solidarity action but more to explain European and global solidarity. People who feel least attached to Denmark as a country would still engage in national solidarity and are those most likely to engage in European and global solidarity. Whereas people who feel strongly attached to Denmark as a country are engaged in national solidarity action (even though interestingly to a lower extent that those who feel no attachment), these groups of people are the least likely to engage in European and global solidarity.

This is different when the strength of national identity is measured in terms of ethnic belonging: respondents who feel highly attached to other Danes show a very similar pattern of solidarity engagement at all levels with a clear focus on national solidarity compared to the group of respondents who feel a strong attachment to Denmark as a country. People who feel no attachment to other Danes are instead expectedly least engaged in national solidarity but do also show lower solidarity engagement at all levels compared to the group of Danes that feels attachment to Denmark as a country (Table 2.9). Strong ties of ethnic belonging thus translate into strong patterns of national solidarity as much as strong ties of territo-

Table 2.9 Engagement in solidarity action at national, European and global level (% participated in some form of action) by attachment to country and fellow citizens

	Attached to Denmark			Attached to people in Denmark		
	National	EU	Outside EU	National	EU	Outside EU
Not at all attached	51.0	36.9	42.8	38.5	29.8	31.2
Not very attached	49.5	34.5	45.8	51.4	34.0	46.4
Fairly attached	50.8	25.9	37.5	44.3	21.5	31.6
Very attached	45.9	21.5	33.1	49.2	23.3	37.4
Don't know	15.8	13.6	15.7	46.5	22.3	29.5
Total	46.6	23.3	34.5	46.6	23.3	34.5

rial belonging generate national solidarity. Weak ties of ethnic belonging instead translate into weak solidarity engagement at all levels, whereas weak ties of territorial belonging go hand in hand with strong solidarity engagement at all levels.

Danes who feel no or little attachment to other Danes born in the country also engage less in national solidarity action compared to Danes who feel a strong attachment to fellow Danish citizens. Yet the ratio of engagement in European and global solidarity between these two groups is the same, that is, those who feel no attachment to fellow nationals do not compensate their lack of attachment by higher engagement in European and global solidarity, while those who feel a strong attachment to their co-nationals also translate this into solidarity action toward them and engage to minor degrees in global and European solidarity. Again, we find that there is no trade-off between engagement in national and European/global solidarity, which are not exclusive but complementary. A strong feeling of solidarity with co-nationals is thus also a good predictor for engagement in global and European solidarity, while respondents who feel not attached to co-nationals show low solidarity engagement at all levels.

We further find a strong correlation with political interest (Grasso and Giugni 2016), which matters at all levels, but most when it comes to global solidarity and least when it comes to solidarity within the EU (Table 2.10). Political awareness makes it more likely that Danes engage in global solidarity and to a minor degree also national solidarity but affects least engagement in EU solidarity.

Table 2.10 Engagement in solidarity action at national, European and global level (% participated in some form of action) by political interest

	National	EU	Outside EU
Not at all interested	28.8	14.6	18.0
Not very interested	40.5	18.9	27.4
Quite interested	48.0	21.8	36.2
Very interested	63.8	39.5	51.1
Don't know	21.8	13.8	17.7
Total	46.6	23.3	34.5

Table 2.11 Engagement in solidarity action at national, European and global level (% participated in some form of action) by party attachment

	National	EU	Outside EU
Socialdemokratiet	48.9	22.6	38.2
Dansk Folkeparti	38.5	16.3	22.0
Venstre	42.5	21.6	30.7
Enhedslisten	64.1	41.1	56.2
Liberal alliance	43.8	25.7	33.2
Det Radikale Venstre	57.6	34.2	53.2
Socialistisk Folkepar	63.4	29.2	48.2
Det Konservative folk	38.7	24.2	32.1
Other party	55.8	29.6	47.6
No party	39.3	16.2	26.3
Don't know	38.8	18.5	24.5
Total	46.6	23.3	34.5

From the literature, we would expect that in a consociational democracy, like Denmark, ideological cleavages matter less and that citizens, while aligning with political parties, show similar patterns of solidarity and support for the welfare state (Christoffersen et al. 2013). This is not exactly corroborated by our data where a left-right cleavage in solidarity action is clearly visible (Table 2.11). While supporters of all political parties are involved in forms of solidarity action to some extent, we find that supporters of right and liberal parties are less engaged in solidarity action than supporters of left and social-democratic parties (Giugni and Grasso 2015). The two solidarity poles are marked by citizens who feel attached to the populist *Dansk Folkeparti* (Danish People's Party) (39.4% involved in solidarity action) and citizens who feel close to the left-socialist *Enhedslisten*

Table 2.12 Engagement in solidarity action at national, European and global level (% participated in some form of action) by closeness to political party

	National	EU	Outside EU
Not very close	43.0	18.5	32.3
Quite close	51.0	25.3	37.8
Very close	54.7	35.6	46.9
Don't know	36.6	21.3	28.2
Total	46.6	23.3	34.5

(Red-Green Alliance) (66.4%). This difference between the left and the right is even more pronounced when it comes to engagement with global solidarity with the same poles formed by *Danske Folkeparti* (22.8% involved in global solidarity action) and *Enhedslisten* (57.8%). In the case of solidarity action within the EU, engagement is generally lowest and party differences matter less, but it is interesting to note that the two Eurosceptic parties *Dansk Folkeparti* and *Enhedslisten* form again the poles, with only 16.9% of *Dansk Folkeparti* supporters engaged in EU solidarity action and 42.6% of supporters of *Enhedslisten*.

The closer you feel connected to a political party, the more likely you are to engage in solidarity action; closeness to a political party impacts on solidarity action most in the case of global solidarity and least in the case of solidarity within the EU (Table 2.12). In general, it appears that the contours of the field of EU solidarity action are still blurred, while Danish citizens across all variables prefer to engage in solidarity nationally and to a lower extent invest in global solidarity action (the half-third-fourth model: that is, 50% national, 33% global and 25% EU). While Danes have a generally positive attitude toward the EU, their willingness to invest personally in solidarity action within the EU is low and, in fact, lowest among the supporters of Eurosceptic right-populist parties.

There is a slight positive bias in engagement in solidarity action among those who are more positive about EU membership (Table 2.13). The same thing is true of those who think the country benefited from EU membership (Table 2.14). On the other hand, a substantial number (20.2%) of Danes who think that EU membership is a bad thing still engage in EU solidarity action (compared to 23.3% of the whole population and 27.6% among those who think that EU membership is a good thing).

Table 2.13 Engagement in solidarity action at national, European and global level (% participated in some form of action) by opinion on EU membership

	National	EU	Outside EU
A good thing	51.2	27.6	41.6
A bad thing	46.1	20.2	29.7
Neither good nor bad	47.0	23.8	33.8
Don't know	27.7	12.7	20.6
Total	46.6	23.3	34.5

Table 2.14 Engagement in solidarity action at national, European and global level (% participated in some form of action) by opinion on whether country benefits from EU membership

	National	EU	Outside EU
Benefited	51.4	27.7	40.7
Not benefited	45.7	20.9	31.1
Don't know	36.9	16.8	25.4
Total	46.6	23.3	34.5

Table 2.15 Engagement in solidarity action at national, European and global level (% participated in some form of action) by support for EU debt relief

	National	EU	Outside EU
Strongly disagree	37.5	13.7	23.4
Disagree	44.1	21.0	27.9
Neither	47.2	22.6	34.7
Agree	57.4	32.2	48.5
Strongly agree	65.9	44.5	58.4
Don't know	31.2	14.4	22.8
Total	46.6	23.3	34.5

Moreover, opponents of EU redistribution policies engage less in solidarity action at all levels, which either reflects a general non-solidary attitude or a preference of altruistic forms of solidarity action over redistributive ones (Table 2.15). There does not seem to be a trade-off between solidarity at different levels.

Finally, personal perceptions of justice tend to be linked to a strong focus on engagement in national solidarity action (Table 2.16). Those

Table 2.16 Engagement in solidarity action at national, European and global level (% participated in some form of action) by what the respondent feels they receive relative to others in their country

	National	EU	Outside EU
More than your fair share	51.5	41.9	51.9
Your fair share	49.1	22.7	37.9
Somewhat less than your fair share	49.3	26.7	34.4
Much less than your fair share	47.6	24.0	31.9
Don't know	30.5	13.4	16.7
Total	46.6	23.3	34.5

who thought they received less than their just share would still be willing to invest in national solidarity, and to some extent global solidarity, but are less likely to engage in EU solidarity action. The biggest differences between those who feel they have more or about their fair share and those who feel they get less are in EU and global solidarity.

Our results have shown that a substantial number of Danes who feel strongly attached to their country would still engage in European and global solidarity action. This confirms findings from other studies, which have shown that identities expressed at different levels are not exclusive: people can feel attached to their nations but at the same time feel also belonging to a European and global community (Risse 2010). This difference between attitudinal variables and engagement in solidarity action is weakest in the case of support of EU membership.

'Cosmopolitans' and 'Europeanists' differ to some degree from 'nationalists' but are not fundamentally different in their engagement in transnational solidarity action. Instead, we find a strong partisan division line with supporters of extreme left parties being strongly engaged in transnational solidarity and supporters of extreme right parties weakest. This division is however less visible when comparing supporters of the two center-mainstream parties *Social-Democrats* and *Venstre*, showing very similar patterns of national and European solidarity engagement and only some minor deviation in the case of global solidarity engagement. Left-leaning and right-leaning Danes are thus clearly distinct in their solidarity behavior, while the center-leaning majority displays very similar patterns of solidarity engagement. If polarization happens, this takes place mainly at the fringes of the political spectrum. Given the strong mobilization potential of *Dansk Folkeparti* with a potential to affect the whole population (as in the case of the refugee crisis), such forms of enhanced solidarity contestation still mark an important shift from the consensus orientation that has traditionally characterized Danish society.

Conclusion

In this chapter, we have identified a number of factors that condition solidarity practices in Denmark. By putting to the test the principled universalism of the Danish welfare state, we found that solidarity practices are relatively widespread across the population in Denmark and that Danes in all age groups and independently of gender and residence engage in solidarity above all at the national level but to significant degrees also at global and European level (the half-third-fourth model: that is, 50% national, 33% global and 25% EU). To the extent that a formally universal welfare state is upheld, Danes also continue to be proud of their high-taxed, universal welfare regime, even though in practice many welfare services have become conditional, and criteria of deservingness are applied when deciding about the needs of diverse groups of people. In line with our hypothesis, we can thus conclude that the belief in the value of universal welfare is still deeply ingrained in the Danish mindset, but the question of how to redistribute welfare and cover the needs of specific groups is increasingly contested.

In line with this new conditionality in the implementation of state-centered welfare services, we found that also reported solidarity practices and attitudes distinguish different degrees of deservingness for deciding on the access to welfare. Our findings in this sense rather support our second hypothesis reflecting a reality of conditional solidarity and unequal access to welfare that is justified by criteria such as ethnic belonging or expected contributions of solidarity recipients to Danish society. An instrumental view on conditional solidarity prevails at the level of reported solidarity practices and restrictive attitudes toward specific groups in need (in particular migrants, refugees and long-term unemployed), while in terms of general beliefs, the inclusiveness of universal welfare is still upheld as a counterfactual norm that distinguishes Denmark in Europe and in the world. This new conditionality of solidarity attitudes and practices is partly explained by socio-structural variables such as education and occupational class with less resourceful individuals less likely to engage in different forms of solidarity action. Apart from these socio-structural variables, we also considered a number of attitudinal variables. Among those, identity (as measured through territorial and ethnic belonging) matters less, but party affiliation is found to be a strong predictor for differences in solidarity behavior with adherents of the right-populist Danish People's Party engaged less in solidarity at all levels and the sympathizers of the Red-Green Alliance engaged most. In future analyses, the conditionality of solidarity needs to be also tested with regard to manifestations of solidarity toward different vulnerable groups in society. This would allow for a more systematic identification of conditional factors of solidarity in relation to different levels (national, European, global) and reference groups (unemployed, people with disabilities and immigrants/refugees) which could be developed further in future work.

Notes

1. See, for instance, their statement on 'Europe in the crisis' with an explicit reference to solidarity and welfare in the wider Europe and the world (http://org.enhedslisten.dk/tema/europa-i-krise-fakta-og-muligheder last accessed May 10, 2017).
2. See our overview of most recent policy changes and restrictions in the field of unemployment, disabilities and immigration/asylum in Duru et al. (forthcoming).
3. Comparative GDP per capita indices over the period 2008–2016 are provided by Eurostat (see http://ec.europa.eu/eurostat/tgm/table.do?tab=table&init=1&language=en&pcode=tec00001&plugin=1).
4. http://www.dst.dk/da/Statistik/nyt/NytHtml?cid=22577.
5. http://ec.europa.eu/eurostat/statistics-explained/index.php/Unemployment_statistics#Recent_developments_in_unemployment_at_a_European_and_Member_State_level.
6. https://www.nyidanmark.dk/NR/rdonlyres/D7322BD4-B6ED-43D7-AFEA-00F597BE0800/0/statistical_overview_2013.pdf.
7. Trust in political institutions and impact on the crisis on political attitudes are measured by Standard Eurobarometer (http://ec.europa.eu/commfrontoffice/publicopinion/index.cfm).
8. http://www.humanityinaction.org/knowledgebase/59-the-danish-illusion-the-gap-between-principle-and-practice-in-the-danish-welfare-system.

References

Banting, K., & Kymlicka, W. (2017). *The Strains of Commitment: The Political Sources of Solidarity in Diverse Societies.* Oxford University Press.

Calhoun, C. (2002). Imagining Solidarity: Cosmopolitanism, Constitutional Patriotism, and the Public Sphere. *Public Culture, 14,* 147–171.

Christoffersen, H., Beyeler, M., Eichenberger, R., et al. (2013). *The Good Society: A Comparative Study of Denmark and Switzerland*. Springer Berlin Heidelberg.

Duru, D. N., Spejlborg Sejersen, T., and Trenz, H. J. (forthcoming). The Best Welfare System in the World? The Danish Welfare State, Transnational Solidarity, and Civil Society in Times of Crisis. Basingstoke: Palgrave Macmillan.

English, P., Grasso, M. T., Buraczynska, B., Karampampas, S., & Temple, L. (2016). Convergence on Crisis? Comparing Labour and Conservative Party Framing of the Economic Crisis in Britain, 2008–2014. *Politics & Policy, 44*(3), 577–603.

European Commission. (2014). EU Employment and Social Situation. *Quarterly Review*. Recent Trends in the Geographical Mobility of Workers in the EU. Luxembourg: Publications Office of the European Union. Retrieved January 22, 2018, from http://ec.europa.eu/employment_social/employment_analysis/quarterly/essqr-2014june-sup1mobility.xls.

Giugni, M., & Grasso, M. T. (2015). Environmental Movements in Advanced Industrial Democracies: Heterogeneity, Transformation, and Institutionalization. *Annual Review of Environment and Resources, 40*, 337–361.

Grasso, M. T. (2011). *Political Participation in Western Europe*. D.Phil. Thesis, Nuffield College, University of Oxford.

Grasso, M. T. (2013). The Differential Impact of Education on Young People's Political Activism: Comparing Italy and the United Kingdom. *Comparative Sociology, 12*(1), 1–30.

Grasso, M. T. (2014). Age-Period-Cohort Analysis in a Comparative Context: Political Generations and Political Participation Repertoires. *Electoral Studies, 33*, 63–76.

Grasso, M. T. (2016). *Generations, Political Participation and Social Change in Western Europe*. London: Routledge.

Grasso, M. T. (2017). Young People's Political Participation in Times of Crisis. In S. Pickard & J. Bessant (Eds.), *Young People Regenerating Politics in Times of Crisis*. London: Palgrave Macmillan.

Grasso, M. T., Farrall, S., Gray, E., Hay, C., & Jennings, W. (2017). Thatcher's Children, Blair's Babies, Political Socialisation and Trickle-Down Value-Change: An Age, Period and Cohort Analysis. *British Journal of Political Science*. https://doi.org/10.1017/S0007123416000375.

Grasso, M. T., & Giugni, M. (2016). Protest Participation and Economic Crisis: The Conditioning Role of Political Opportunities. *European Journal of Political Research, 55*(4), 663–680.

Habermas, J. (2013). *Democracy, Solidarity and The European Crisis*. Retrieved from http://www.social-europe.eu/2013/05/democracy-solidarity-and-the-european-crisis-2/.

Hall, P. A. (2017). The Political Sources of Solidarity. In K. Banting & W. Kymlicka (Eds.), *The Strains of Commitment: The Political Sources of Solidarity in Diverse Societies* (pp. 201–233). Oxford: Oxford University Press.

Jensen, P. H., & Torpe, L. (2016). The Illusion of Universalism: The Case of the Danish Welfare State. *Politiche Sociali, 3,* 403–420.

Jöhncke, S. (2011). Integrating Denmark: The Welfare State as a National(ist) Accomplishment. In K. F. Olwig & K. Paerregaard (Eds.), *The Question of Integration, Immigration, Exclusion and the Danish Welfare State*. Newcastle upon Tyne, UK: Cambridge Scholars Publishing.

Jørgensen, M. B., & Thomsen, T. L. (2013). Crises Now and Then—Comparing Integration Policy Frameworks and Immigrant Target Groups in Denmark in the 1970s and 2000s. *International Migration & Integration, 14,* 245–262.

Larsen, J. E., Bengtsson, T. T., & Frederiksen, M. (2015). *The Danish Welfare State*. Basingstoke: Palgrave Macmillan.

Martinsen, D. S. (2005). The Europeanization of Welfare—The Domestic Impact of Intra-European Social Security. *JCMS: Journal of Common Market Studies, 43,* 1027–1054.

Risse, T. (2010). *A Community of Europeans? Transnational Identities and Public Spheres*. New York: Cornell University Press.

Spejlborg Sejersen, T., & Trenz, H. J. (2017). *Transnational Solidarity in Danish Civil Society, in: TransSOL: Integrated Report on Integrated Report on Collective Forms of Solidarity at Times of Crisis*. Work Package 4: Collective Forms of Solidarity at Times of Crisis, 20–42. Retrieved January 22, 2018, from http://transsol.eu/files/2017/12/WP4-Integratedreport-final.pdf.

Stjernø, S. (2004). *Solidarity in Europe: The History of an Idea*. Cambridge: Cambridge University Press.

Strøby-Jensen, C. S. (2011). The Flexibility of Flexicurity: The Danish Model Reconsidered. *Economic and Industrial Democracy, 32*(4), 721–737.

Temple, L., Grasso, M. T., Buraczynska, B., Karampampas, S., & English, P. (2016). Neoliberal Narrative in Times of Economic Crisis: A Political Claims Analysis of the UK Press, 2007–2014. *Politics & Policy, 44*(3), 553–576.

Open Access This chapter is licensed under the terms of the Creative Commons Attribution 4.0 International License (http://creativecommons.org/licenses/by/4.0/), which permits use, sharing, adaptation, distribution and reproduction in any medium or format, as long as you give appropriate credit to the original author(s) and the source, provide a link to the Creative Commons license and indicate if changes were made.

The images or other third party material in this chapter are included in the chapter's Creative Commons license, unless indicated otherwise in a credit line to the material. If material is not included in the chapter's Creative Commons license and your intended use is not permitted by statutory regulation or exceeds the permitted use, you will need to obtain permission directly from the copyright holder.

CHAPTER 3

Solidarity Activism in Germany: What Explains Different Types and Levels of Engagement?

Johannes Kiess, Christian Lahusen, and Ulrike Zschache

Introduction

During the summer of 2015, an unprecedented wave of solidarity with incoming refugees from Syria and other countries of the Middle East, Africa and Asia swept through Germany. Innumerable initiatives and individual citizens committed to what was called the new German "welcoming culture". These initiatives not only engaged in the provision of immediate help (e.g., clothing, food, shelter, language courses and assistance with German administration) but also rallied in support of migrant and refugee rights. The inability of German authorities to handle the inflow of migrants and the growing mobilization of populist, right-wing and xenophobic groups, dampened the "welcoming culture" considerably and boosted conflicts on the correct policies for the German administration to pursue. As a consequence, solidarity became a contested issue. While some rallied for solidarity with all people in need of help—refugees included—and insisted that "we can do this" (Schiffauer et al. 2017), oth-

J. Kiess (✉) • C. Lahusen • U. Zschache
Department of Social Sciences, University of Siegen, Siegen, Germany

© The Author(s) 2018
C. Lahusen, M. Grasso (eds.), *Solidarity in Europe*,
Palgrave Studies in European Political Sociology,
https://doi.org/10.1007/978-3-319-73335-7_3

ers proclaimed the need to refrain from unlimited assistance and instead opt for the exclusive support of Germans, fearing that the multiple crises in the world would eventually hit Germany as well. Consequently, it seems as though solidarity has become a contentious field that separates people with different cultural orientations, political beliefs and social standing.

Given this background, it is important to map the field of solidarity within the German population. For this purpose, we will make use of the survey data provided by the "European paths to transnational solidarity at times of crisis: Conditions, forms, role models and policy responses (TransSOL)" project. Our aim is to answer the following series of questions. How diffused is the disposition to engage for solidarity within the German population, and are there differences in the degree of reported activities when distinguishing between various target groups? What can we say about those people who report being committed to solidarity activities when compared to those indicating they abstain? Are there specific social traits (e.g., socio-demographic characteristics, social standing, attitudinal dispositions or cultural values) that distinguish one group from the other? In order to answer these questions, the chapter will proceed as follows. Firstly, we will briefly introduce previous research on solidarity dispositions and activities in order to identify the core social traits that play a role in distinguishing the "active" from the "inactive". Secondly, we will describe the frequencies of different solidarity actions in regard to various target groups: on the one hand, with reference to spatial entities (people in the respondents' own country, within the EU and outside the EU), and on the other hand, in regard to three issue field specific target groups, namely, refugees, the unemployed and people with disabilities. Thirdly, we will conduct a series of multinominal regression analyses in order to identify the social profile of the "active" and thus to validate the various research assumptions about relevant social, economic or cultural differences between the groups acting and not acting on behalf of others. In this context, we will also deal with issue field specific motivations and beliefs that might explain why people decide to engage for specific target groups. Finally, we will summarize and briefly discuss the core findings of this chapter.

Theories of Solidarity Activism

Our analysis of solidarity in Germany requires a brief summary of previous research findings in order to identify those potential traits that might enable us to distinguish active from the inactive citizens, and thus to identify those social traits that might increase the probability of being engaged in solidarity activities. Relevant insights come from different strands of research because social solidarity touches the study of public support for redistribution and redistributive policies, of social capital and social movements, among others. Many of these studies tend to paint a similar picture of solidarity-related activities. First of all, we know from research on political behaviour and social movements that resources, skills and opportunities do matter (Brady et al. 1995; Verba et al. 1978; Jenkins 1983), which means that the socio-demographic characteristics of citizens determine to a certain extent their readiness to engage in political and social activities. Age, for instance, matters in terms of biographical availability (Beyerlein and Bergstrand 2013), since people might reduce their social and political activities because of personal constraints, for example, due to marriage or family responsibilities. The unequal access to resources and skills (e.g., income and education) impinges on levels of political and civic engagement as well, meaning that socially excluded people might be more affected by a lower degree of social and political engagement (Verba et al. 1978; Kronauer 1998). Finally, we need to look at the effect of migration, because research has shown that migrants might be involved in (cross-national) forms of solidarity in support of ethnic diasporas or communities (Morokvasic 1999; Schulze 2004).

Building on these observations, we might expect—secondly—that social class might be a relevant factor as well (Cainzos and Voces 2010). Following the findings of other studies, we expect the middle classes to be overrepresented in political and social activism, as this reflects their preferences, civic norms and their economic, cultural and social capital (Kriesi 1989; Eder 1993). At the same time, however, we know from studies on the support of redistributional policies that vulnerability and deprivation do impinge positively on solidarity disposition (Iversen and Soskice 2001; Rehm 2009), at least in regard to target groups exposed to similar risks of social exclusion and degradation. In this regard, we thus need to measure the potential effect of several variables that are related to social class and social exclusion. For this purpose, we will also look at subjective class affiliation and feelings of deprivation. Beyond that, we will look at the living situation and international exposure (housing situation and number of friends from different countries) in order to assess whether social isolation and contact with individuals outside one's social group might be related to social solidarity.

A third set of expectations is related to ideational factors, such as feelings of collective identity, political beliefs, religiosity and trust. The social movement literature holds it that cultural and moral resources, in addition to material, organizational and human resources, are important for explaining the successful emergence of collective action (Edwards and McCarthy 2004). In the first instance, we know that individual dispositions to engage in solidarity activities and support redistributive policies are closely related to religiosity, given that religion generally supports the idea of helping others (Stegmueller et al. 2012; Lichterman 2015). Moreover, we assume that solidarity is determined by collective identities, in the sense that feelings of belongingness to certain collectivities might increase the readiness to support members of these (imagined) communities. National identities should thus be interrelated to forms of solidarity with fellow citizens, European identification with solidarity activities in support of people living in other European member states (Bauböck 2017). Additionally, we expect that political preferences and orientations make a difference in regard to solidarity. In general terms, solidarity might be more diffused among respondents with leftist political orientations and preferences for multiculturalism, while xenophobic, right-wing and populist dispositions might be more probable among the inactive, as corroborated in regard to public policies (Likki and Staerklé 2014). However, the latter ideological preferences might be linked to certain forms of group-bound solidarity, for example, within nations or specific target groups (e.g., the unemployed). Finally, solidarity could also be more common among people with higher levels of interpersonal trust, when considering research on social capital that highlights the importance of trust, membership and active participation in civic associations and groups (Putnam et al. 2003; van Oorschot et al. 2006).

A final set of factors to be taken into consideration is related more strictly to specific issue fields. This last group follows the basic idea that solidarity is not necessarily a universal disposition of support related to anybody, that is, to all human beings. Possibly, solidarity is always group-bound, meaning that citizens tend to centre their engagement to certain groups to which they feel particularly attached. This argument puts an emphasis on the fact that solidarity needs to be activated (against potentially detrimental factors such as lack of resources, social exclusion or apathy) and that this is more probable in regard to people to whom one feels personally attached. Feelings of social proximity between oneself and the target groups seem to play a role here (van Oorschot 2006; Stegmueller et al. 2012), which means that empathy with significant others is thus an important "opener" that helps to mobilize support. At the same time, however, this means that solidarity might be—per se—limited to specific groups, a predisposition that has been called philanthropic particularism (Komter 2005). Hence, we expect feelings of attachment towards specific groups and the belief that a fair society implies the inclusion of and assistance to specific groups to increase solidarity activity towards them.

Measurement

Our analysis draws on an original dataset of 2064 respondents (aged 18+) in Germany matched for age, gender, region and education level quotas to national population statistics. Weights were applied in all descriptive analyses and all models control for age, gender and education. Data retrieval was conducted as part of the Horizon 2020 project TransSOL using CAWI method (computer-assisted web interviewing) and took place between December 2016 and January 2017.[1] The dependent variables intend to measure reported solidarity activity on behalf of different groups and on different levels. The questionnaire specifies for all three groups ("Have you ever done one of the following in order to support the rights of…"). We report all variables used for modelling, including recoding procedures, in the Appendix.

Findings

In this section we present findings on solidarity actions in Germany across three levels (national, EU, outside EU) as well as three fields of solidarity, namely, the support of refugees and asylum seekers, of the unemployed and people with disabilities. We begin with descriptive findings along the six dimensions. In the second part, we present findings of multinominal regression analyses identifying socio-structural and ideational factors that influence the probability of people choosing to engage in solidarity actions. In a third subsection, we turn to group specific motifs and beliefs to better explain engagement in solidarity activities.

Frequencies of Solidarity Action: Descriptive Results

Table 3.1 shows two patterns: first, solidarity depends on proximity since engagement is more frequent in support for people and their rights in the respondent's own country than abroad and support for people outside the EU is also quite frequent, but focused on activities like donating money

Table 3.1 Frequencies of engagement over levels and fields of solidarity (in %)

	Attended march	Donate money	Donate time	Buycott/boycott	Passive member	Active member	None	R^2
Support of rights/people in own country	12.7	24.0	19.0	20.7	5.5	10.2	49.0	0.58
Support of rights/people in other EU country	6.5	13.4	8.8	15.0	3.4	4.7	68.6	0.59
Support of rights/people in country outside EU	5.8	20.8	9.3	19.0	3.0	4.1	60.0	0.50
Support rights of asylum seekers/refugees	5.3	15.2	14.1	9.2	2.8	6.3	65.9	0.50
Support rights of unemployed	4.7	8.2	10.2	9.6	2.6	4.9	73.0	0.49
Support disability rights	3.9	26.5	19.0	18.6	5.4	7.5	48.4	0.44
R^2	0.68	0.51	0.74	0.73	0.59	0.67	0.81	

and buycotting/boycotting products. Moreover, our data allows us to distinguish between the support for our three main target groups: asylum seekers/refugees, unemployed and disabled people. Here we observe, overall, the highest frequencies in the field of disability rights. Support of refugees is more limited but still exceeds support of the unemployed. This shows that solidarity is not a generalized disposition or practice but that it is linked to specific issues and target groups drawing a pattern of affinity: in spatial terms people in one's own country receive the most support, as do disabled if we compare between issue fields. In comparison, people in other EU countries and the unemployed receive the least support. In this respect, the findings provide a first hint to the fact that solidarity is shaped by feelings of attachment to particular groups. We will return to this issue in the third part of our analysis.

Beyond descriptive frequencies, we were interested in the connections between different solidarity actions people engage in and also similarities across issue fields (i.e., solidarity towards the unemployed, disabled and refugees). Some types of action may be considered more demanding, for example, in terms of resources, than others. Likewise, some fields may be more prone to attract civil engagement because of current media attention or differently perceived proximity to the target group. Moreover, activists who join certain activities may do so across levels (national, European and outside Europe) and across issue fields.

In a next explorative step and following these considerations, we conducted principal factor analyses for both the issue fields and levels of solidarity (do people in one field engage in multiple activities?) and the activities across fields (do people choosing one activity in one field also chose this in another field?). In regard to the activities within levels and fields, we found—to some surprise—that at no level and in no issue field did the analysis reveal more than one factor[2]: there do not seem to be different types of activists, for example, those who protest on behalf of refugees on the one hand and those who spend time and money on the other hand. In this respect, we may expect variation rather between those opting to engage and those not acting at all. Similarly to the fields of activity, we could not find any differences within action types across fields. This suggests that people who protest or spend money do so with—to this point—no relevant difference in terms of activity chosen across fields. Simple bivariate regression shows, for example, a correlation between protesting for unemployed and protesting for refugees. We may conclude that people protesting for one group are also prone to protest for another.

This does not indicate, however, that the same people are likely to engage in all different types of solidarity action and for all groups at the same time. It is more likely that actions vary enough to disguise specific patterns—other than that solidarity activities in one field and one type are likely to go together with activity in another field and commute with other activities. Moreover and as we will argue below, active people choose their field of activity based on attachment towards specific groups or issues. Before we turn to this, we want to differentiate and compare the intensity of activity in each issue field to complete this descriptive subsection.

Table 3.2 shows the intensity of engagement, thus revealing if and to what extent active persons are engaged in several forms of action.[3] On first sight, the table provides a clear picture with the frequencies declining in parallel with the intensity of engagement. However, we also observe that only a very small minority engages more deeply in either field and on either level of solidarity. If we consider the threshold for engaging in one activity only as relatively low (e.g., it could be a one-time action of donating five euro to an integrative school project with no further involvement and, more importantly, no indication of repetition), the percentage of people engaging considerably in solidarity activities in the population is between 10 and 20%.

Table 3.2 Multiple forms of actions over levels and fields of solidarity (in %)

	None	One activity	Two activities	Three activities	Four activities	Five activities	All six activities
Support of rights/people in own country	49.0	28.1	11.9	6.2	2.7	1.8	0.3
Support of rights/people in other EU country	68.6	19.5	6.4	3.7	1.1	0.5	0.2
Support of rights/people in country outside EU	60.0	25.5	9.4	3.2	1.3	0.4	0.2
Support rights of asylum seekers/refugees	65.9	21.5	8.5	2.7	0.9	0.5	0.1
Support rights of unemployed	73.0	18.1	6.0	1.9	0.7	0.2	0.1
Support disability rights	48.4	32.9	11.8	4.3	1.8	0.8	0.1

These findings led us to choose the summary frequencies in the different solidarity fields as our dependent variable for further analysis[4]: We decided to differentiate between three groups: those not engaging at all, the one-action activists and multiply engaged respondents. Even though different action forms were only moderately interrelated in each of the fields and on each of the levels (with *Cronbach's alpha*'s at only around 0.5, see last column of Table 3.1), the usage of summary variables for each issue field and distinguishing along intensity, while making sure through factor analyses that there are not different dimensions involved, seems to be an acceptable compromise.

Comparing the Active and the Inactive: Socio-structural and Ideational Factors

Following the findings of our descriptive analysis, we opted for multi-nominal regression models. This allows us to compare those who do not engage with the "one-action activists", as well as those who engage in different activities. This was done without assuming linearity of our dependent variable, which might not hold considering the small *Cronbach's alpha*. We will present different models, including different sets of vari-

Table 3.3 Multinominal regression models 1a–1f (socio-economic variables)

		Germany	Other EU	Global	Refugees	Unemplo	Dissabil
One action	Age	−0.169**	−0.217**	−0.164**	−0.236**	−0.224**	0.039
	Income	0.121*	0.139*	0.184**	0.122*	0.114	0.189**
	Education	0.109	0.131*	0.214**	0.092	0.080	0.037
	Male	−0.005	0.137	−0.228*	−0.004	0.150	−0.001
	Migrant	0.008	0.213	0.160	0.088	0.151	0.123
	_Cons	−0.510**	−1.329**	−0.695**	−1.084**	−1.444**	−0.369**
Multiple actions	Age	−0.029	−0.127	−0.179*	−0.103	−0.006	0.166*
	Income	0.115	0.181*	0.242**	0.238**	0.028	0.110
	Education	0.289**	0.190*	0.393**	0.213**	0.174*	0.286**
	Male	−0.067	0.212	−0.330*	−0.165	0.333*	−0.014
	Migrant	0.198	0.388*	0.537**	0.500**	0.556**	0.277
	_Cons	−0.753**	−1.926**	−1.358**	−1.701**	−2.328**	−0.975**
N		1800	1800	1800	1800	1800	1800
Pseudo-R^2		0.0117	0.0151	0.0263	0.0159	0.0130	0.0122

*$p < 0.05$, **$p < 0.01$

ables, and will focus in this subsection on the comparison of the different fields and levels of solidarity. Thus, we calculated each of the models (1–3) separately for the different fields and levels of solidarity (indicated by a–f).

In the first step, we only included socio-economic variables (as well as the country weight). While increasing age may increment opportunities to engage in solidarity activities, income and education can be interpreted as variables indicating resources. Thus higher income and higher education may increase the probability of engagement as well. We include gender as a control variable. Migrant background sometimes comes with additional social capital but also vulnerability. Accordingly, we may expect a positive influence on solidarity activities. As Table 3.3 shows, we find a lot of significant correlations, but there are some differences we will need to point out. First, if we compare those engaging in one activity with those not engaging, age is significant across all fields and levels, excluding the support of disability rights. Moreover, the effect suggests that the younger people are, the more likely they are to engage in one action relative to none. If we compare with those engaging in at least two activities, however, the effect is only significant for engagement for people outside of Europe. In this case, the effect for solidarity with people with disabilities is reversed: those engaging for the rights of this group in various forms are more likely to be older. Income is positively correlated with engagement for both groups, the "one-action" activists and the "multiply active". However, the effect is not significant for both groups concerning the rights of the unemployed. Moreover, education is for "one-action" activists only relevant if they engage on the European or global level. But for the "multiply active", we find that higher education leads to more engagement on all fields and issues relative to non-actives. Gender has a very limited impact overall. Migrant background, finally, has no impact on single-activity engagement, but it increases chances to be multiply active on the European and global level, on behalf of refugees and also on behalf of the unemployed. To summarize, our findings suggest in line with the literature (Brady et al. 1995; Verba et al. 1978; Jenkins 1983) that resources play an important role and the young are more frequently engaged in one action relative to none, but we must also emphasize that the explained variance through these variables is very low. This means that other factors must play a role.

In a second series of calculations, we added further and also subjective socio-structural variables to our model (see Table 3.4). Age remains significant for the one-action activists (with the exceptions of global solidarity and disability rights), and education underlines its importance for all issue fields and solidarity levels. Self-placement in a lower social class reduces only solidarity on the European level for one-action activists—which is in line with current observations in the EU (e.g., Brexit). However, income loses its limited effect almost entirely, and there are no clear effects across fields. Material resources do not seem to play a dominant role, and this observation seems plausible, because the type of activities we asked our respondents to comment on are not particularly costly.

If we turn to the perception of (collective) resources, this changes only on first sight: for one-action activists, positive perception of living conditions in Germany seems to mobilize for solidarity in and beyond Europe as well as for the unemployed and people with disabilities, relative to inactives. However, this result does not hold for our second group, those who engage in multiple activities, relative to inactives. Here, having friends from other countries spurs solidarity towards refugees, disabled people but also people within the country in general. The experience of relative deprivation increases the chances of multiple activism on behalf of the unemployed (and vice versa) but has no effect on other fields of solidarity. Overall, we find that being younger and having German residence generally has a positive effect on having participated at least once relative to never. Education is the most important factor for

Table 3.4 Multinominal regression models 2a–2f—socio-structural determinants

		Germany	Other EU	Global	Refugees	Unemplo	Dissabil
One action	Age	−0.124	−0.182**	−0.101	−0.181**	−0.237**	0.013
	Income	0.047	0.002	0.158	−0.054	0.111	0.084
	Education	0.064	0.126	0.163*	0.086	0.057	0.030
	Male	−0.005	0.084	−0.199	0.037	0.199	−0.053
	Migrant	−0.034	0.259	0.169	0.115	0.086	0.008
	Socialclass	−0.004	−0.229**	−0.025	−0.099	0.046	−0.001
	Reldep	0.012	−0.140	0.031	0.148	−0.111	0.028
	Living in Germany	0.094	0.230**	0.141*	0.137*	0.253**	0.164**
	Friendsdiff	−0.089	−0.060	0.000	0.002	−0.116	0.058
	Live alone	−0.052	−0.062	0.056	−0.192	−0.325	−0.190
	East	−0.222	0.073	−0.041	−0.209	0.159	0.109
	_Cons	−0.359**	−1.239**	−0.634**	−0.967**	−1.387**	−0.197
Multiple actions	Age	−0.018	−0.133	−0.125	−0.090	−0.067	0.140
	Income	0.028	0.068	0.208	0.126	0.010	−0.152
	Education	0.275**	0.200*	0.408**	0.209**	0.211*	0.317**
	Male	−0.121	0.101	−0.403**	−0.218	0.258	−0.116
	Migrant	−0.012	0.279	0.467*	0.349	0.475*	0.033
	Socialclass	−0.082	−0.139	−0.048	−0.120	−0.093	−0.175*
	Reldep	−0.026	−0.084	0.004	0.029	−0.322**	−0.047
	Living in Germany	−0.002	0.076	0.140	0.077	0.094	0.091
	Friendsdiff	0.145*	0.091	0.125	0.178**	−0.055	0.138*
	Live alone	0.140	0.075	0.336	0.403*	−0.203	−0.380*
	East	−0.413*	−0.037	−0.296	−0.579*	−0.494	−0.439*
	_Cons	−0.548**	−1.768**	−1.273**	−1.543**	−2.046**	−0.574**
N		1500	1500	1500	1500	1500	1500
Pseudo-R^2		0.0153	0.0202	0.0287	0.0269	0.0279	0.0190

*$p < 0.05$, **$p < 0.01$

distinguishing between multiple activists and inactives—this confirms resource-based and civic voluntarism theories in the literature (Verba et al. 1995). Moreover, there are specific effects of other variables like social class for helping people in other EU countries, relative deprivation for helping unemployed and having friends from different countries and helping refugees.

In a third series of calculations, we included variables for cultural and ideational factors (see Table 3.5). Religiosity and social trust seem to impact solidarity activity considerably. This is in line with the literature, pointing to cultural and moral resources as grounds for civil society mobilization. In turn, the already limited effects of socio-structural determinants are weakened. For example, the living conditions in Germany are now only a significant factor for solidarity with unemployed and European solidarity, having friends from different countries is not significant anymore and so on. Only the effect of relative deprivation[5] on

Table 3.5 Multinominal regression models 3a–3f—cultural-ideational determinants

		Germany	Other EU	Global	Refugees	Unemplo	Dissabil
One action	Age	−0.128	−0.168*	−0.134	−0.186*	−0.259**	−0.030
	Income	0.053	0.022	0.217*	−0.000	0.048	0.115
	Education	0.004	0.114	0.127	0.034	0.002	−0.025
	Male	0.161	0.085	−0.236	0.030	0.176	−0.035
	Migrant	−0.056	0.256	0.100	0.044	−0.070	−0.154
	Socialclass	−0.088	−0.235*	−0.021	−0.108	−0.046	0.007
	Reldep	−0.144	−0.237*	−0.132	−0.114	−0.248*	−0.134
	Living in DE	0.026	0.225**	0.143	0.065	0.184*	0.054
	Friendsdiff	−0.069	−0.170	0.036	−0.012	−0.089	−0.003
	Live alone	−0.018	−0.033	0.032	−0.210	−0.415	−0.186
	East	−0.153	0.110	−0.135	−0.100	0.178	0.099
	Attached DE	−0.143	−0.229*	−0.116	−0.185	−0.147	0.043
	Attached city	0.156	0.025	0.112	−0.073	0.041	−0.209
	Attached reg	0.074	0.170	−0.044	0.056	0.140	0.175
	Attached EU	0.085	0.269**	0.237*	0.376**	0.284**	0.157
	Attached hu	0.081	0.015	0.006	−0.137	−0.047	0.150
	Social trust	0.196*	0.232**	0.217**	0.261**	0.304**	0.223**
	Religiosity	0.199**	0.300**	0.117	0.265**	0.170*	0.172*
	Identity	−0.017	−0.030	0.092	0.026	0.035	0.079
	Left self	−0.091	−0.094	−0.145	−0.084	−0.158	0.041
	Demsat	0.011	−0.099	−0.056	−0.017	−0.080	−0.012
	Multicult	0.104	0.032	−0.055	0.377**	−0.150	0.118
	Populism	0.041	−0.022	0.070	0.097	0.293**	0.177*
	Xeno_econ	0.039	0.095	0.040	0.057	0.066	0.016
	Xeno_cult	0.044	−0.063	0.243*	0.316*	0.172	−0.002
	_Cons	−1.624**	−2.680**	−1.399**	−1.565**	−2.579**	−0.864

(continued)

Table 3.5 (continued)

		Germany	Other EU	Global	Refugees	Unemplo	Dissabil
Multiple actions	Age	−0.080	−0.165	−0.165	−0.118	−0.128	0.085
	Income	0.118	0.157	0.334**	0.359**	0.052	−0.030
	Education	0.193*	0.119	0.313**	0.129	0.184	0.258**
	Male	0.036	0.183	−0.413*	−0.139	0.312	−0.030
	Migrant	−0.122	0.121	0.206	0.161	0.244	−0.237
	Socialclass	−0.068	−0.091	0.056	−0.054	−0.113	−0.160
	Reldep	−0.209*	−0.365**	−0.164	−0.259*	−0.457**	−0.173
	Living in DE	−0.040	0.052	0.105	0.010	0.017	−0.003
	Friendsdiff	0.113	0.029	0.184*	0.162	−0.041	0.101
	Live alone	0.169	0.040	0.161	0.365	−0.146	−0.393
	East	−0.272	0.147	−0.122	−0.274	−0.355	−0.252
	Attached DE	−0.096	−0.189	−0.168	−0.253*	−0.205	−0.083
	Attached city	0.104	−0.149	−0.139	−0.058	−0.220	−0.053
	Attached reg	−0.024	0.120	0.010	−0.018	0.089	0.008
	Attached EU	0.094	0.071	0.255*	−0.014	0.252	0.028
	Attached hu	0.169	0.25	0.188	0.025	0.020	0.271*
	Social trust	0.183*	0.354**	0.239*	0.265*	−0.013	0.081
	Religiosity	0.348**	0.339**	0.384**	0.576**	0.332**	0.363**
	Identity	0.050	0.077	0.048	0.007	0.168	0.103
	Right self	−0.264**	−0.114	−0.103	−0.346**	−0.089	−0.083
	Demsat	−0.107	−0.066	−0.235*	0.215	−0.057	0.028
	Multicult	−0.008	0.133	0.198	0.366*	−0.046	0.137
	Populism	0.061	0.049	0.087	0.127	0.246*	0.262**
	Xeno_econ	0.220	0.335*	0.353*	0.265	0.464**	0.232
	Xeno_cul	0.159	0.137	0.135	0.398*	−0.046	−0.019
	_Cons	−1.653**	−2.866**	−2.149**	−1.771**	−2.413**	−1.358**
N		1265	1265	1265	1265	1265	1265
Pseudo-R^2		0.0528	0.0789	0.0849	0.1397	0.0709	0.0548

*$p < 0.05$, **$p < 0.01$

solidarity with unemployed is strengthened. If people think they are better off, they are considerably less likely to engage in multiple actions on behalf of the unemployed. But this effect, too, is not significant for one-action activists.

Motifs and Beliefs Explaining Solidarity Actions?

So far, there are only a few variables that seem to be relevant across dimensions. Above all, religiosity and social trust increase the likelihood of people engaging in solidarity actions but also, to some degree, higher levels of education and younger age. Beyond that, there are factors that show significance for specific dimensions, but the patterns are hard to identify. For this reason, we engage in further analyses that include variables that could be relevant per field. In particular, we will focus on issue-specific motifs and beliefs that may increase the likelihood of respondents to have been engaged in solidarity actions on behalf of refugees, unemployed, disabled people and citizens in other European countries.[6] Moreover, we will now switch the mode of presentation and describe the results for the issue fields separately and with comparisons of different models per issue field in order to focus more directly on the explanatory power of individual variables. As the second to last rows of the subsequent tables show, for the following models we used only those cases in our survey that would remain in the least inclusive model (missing in individual variables lead to the exclusion of a case) in order to ensure proper comparison across the models.

Table 3.6 presents the results for solidarity actions at the European level. We included four items that asked for the motivation to grant financial help to other European countries and that aim to measure reciprocity and deservingness as determining factors for this specific type of solidarity. In other words, we wanted to test whether redistributive attitudes are connected to individual solidarity activities. Surprisingly, none of these have a significant effect on actual solidarity activities of people on the micro level. This could be explained by the fact that people actually differentiate between financial aid and redistribution on the macro level and within the EU on the one hand and solidarity actions on behalf of other people living in these other European countries on the micro level on the other hand. What seems to impact European solidarity activities is the agreement on the policy suggestion to "pool funds to help EU countries" ($M = 2.82$, see Appendix). If respondents agree to this statement, they are more likely to engage. However, this effect is not significant for those acting in multiple ways if we control for all other variables introduced above. In the controlled model, the feeling that Germany benefits from its membership in the EU (68% of our respondents believe so, see Appendix) becomes significant. In sum, solidarity actions increase only slightly if people agree on

Table 3.6 Multinominal regression models for European level solidarity

	Model 4c		Model 5c	
	One action	Multiple action	One action	Multiple action
Age	0.836**	0.829**	−0.136*	−0.202**
Income	1.092	1.008	0.0586	0.112
Education	1.158*	1.189*	0.102	0.111
Male	0.966	1.110	0.0402	0.194
Migrant	1.166	1.405	0.168	0.199
EUhelpmotiv_1	0.990	1.363	−0.0966	0.269
EUhelpmotiv_2	0.851	0.957	−0.164	−0.157
EUhelpmotiv_3	0.918	1.099	−0.0833	0.108
EUhelpmotiv_4	0.869	0.893	−0.0185	0.198
EUaid	0.956	1.398***	−0.0648	0.124
EUdebt	1.371***	1.220*	0.216**	0.0877
EU benefits D	0.836	0.797	−0.291	−0.424*
Socialclass			−0.204**	−0.0390
Reldep			−0.200*	−0.368***
Living in DE			0.232***	0.0216
Friendsdiff			−0.163	0.0596
Live alone			0.0304	−0.0423
East			0.148	0.168
Attached DE			−0.161	−0.204
Attached city			0.0250	−0.0800
Attached reg			0.144	0.115
Attached EU			0.244**	0.141
Attached hum			0.00621	0.187
Socialtrust			0.221**	0.388***
Religiosity			0.274***	0.306***
Identity			−0.00269	0.0612
Lrscale			−0.136	−0.149
Demsat			−0.0905	−0.0438
Multicultural			0.0362	0.0957
Populism			−0.0537	0.0343
Xeno_econ			0.118	0.306**
Xeno_cult			−0.145	0.137
Constant	0.426***	0.188***	−2.183***	−2.923***
N	1144	1144	1144	1144
Pseudo-R^2	0.0304	0.0304	0.0828	0.0828

***$p < 0.01$, **$p < 0.05$, *$p < 0.1$

political steps for (fiscal and financial) integration; the two topics—financial transfers on the macro level and solidarity with people on the micro level—seem to be rather disentangled from each other. This could be explained by considering the harsh preconditions that are tied to the "help" for countries in difficulties. This reading is supported by the continued importance of religiosity, social trust but also deprivation as well as the negative impact of economic xenophobia.

In recent years, the influx of large numbers of refugees has challenged German civil society. People organized to help newcomers in many places. Table 3.7 presents two models for this issue field of solidarity action. The feeling of attachment to refugees ($M = 2.74$, see Appendix) seems to play an important role explaining why people are active on their behalf. Again, we can connect this with the importance of religiosity and social trust that increase solidarity activity towards refugees. Education increases only multiple engagements; income correlates positively in the full model (last column). Moreover, satisfaction with the way the government deals with refugees ($M = 3.32$, see Appendix) increases activity, as do beliefs that it is Germany's moral responsibility to accept refugees ($M = 3.35$) and that the government should be supporting them financially ($M = 3.16$). Interestingly xenophobia does not correlate negatively in a significant way with refugee solidarity, perhaps some people still help even though they do not see refugees as enriching the country (culturally or economically), and, vice versa, people may see immigration as a good thing but do not bother to support refugees. This is also why we see the positive correlation of populism as a sign for dissatisfaction with politics (but not with the decision to help the refugees!) rather than anti-democratic sentiment (we may speak of left-wing populism in this case). Moreover, agreeing with the European response to the refugee crisis ($M = 3.80$) is only significant in one model. Given the controversies on the European level on how to deal with refugees, it comes as no surprise that most respondents to our survey were dissatisfied (on a scale from 0 to 10). In the case of solidarity activities supporting refugees, we can conclude to see a clearer picture of why people engage. This is probably due to the fact of the heightened attention the topic had in the months before the survey was conducted.

Table 3.8 presents the results of our regressions with solidarity towards unemployed people as the dependent variable. Again, we seem to get a much better picture if we include variables measuring motivations and

Table 3.7 Multinominal regression models for solidarity with refugees

	Model 4d		Model 5d	
	One action	*Multiple action*	*One action*	*Multiple action*
Age	0.881	0.870	−0.0948	−0.134
Income	1.040	1.142	−0.0306	0.289**
Education	1.092	1.284***	0.0508	0.211**
Male	1.071	0.836	−0.00677	−0.165
Migrant	1.225	1.694**	0.0772	0.252
Attached refu	1.465***	1.813***	0.399***	0.678***
Satgov_refu	1.269***	1.093	0.243**	0.104
Fair_refu	1.199	1.792***	0.198	0.576***
Fair_mig	1.152	0.993	0.114	−0.0554
Refugeesupp	1.107	1.118	0.129	0.140
Refugeemoral	0.906	1.093	−0.122	−0.0733
Refugeecrisis	1.370***	1.038	0.312***	−0.00918
Syrian refugees	0.860	0.812	−0.0856	−0.106
Inclusivity	1.045	1.041	0.00293	−0.0467
Socialclass			−0.147	−0.0922
Reldep			−0.102	−0.224*
Living in DE			0.0296	0.0171
Friendsdiff			0.00440	0.166*
Live alone			−0.241	0.272
East			−0.171	−0.253
Attached DE			−0.144	−0.193
Attached city			−0.116	−0.140
Attached reg			0.0994	0.0774
Attached EU			0.300***	−0.0525
Attached hu			−0.276**	−0.165
Socialtrust			0.223**	0.191*
Religiosity			0.202**	0.536***
Identity			−0.146	−0.248**
Lrscale			−0.00764	−0.246**
Demsat			−0.232**	0.136
Multicultural			0.226*	0.139
Populism			0.144*	0.223**
Xeno_econ			−0.0721	0.108
Xeno_culture			0.122	0.185
Cons	0.312***	0.143***	−0.983*	−1.287*
N	1236	1236	1236	1236
Pseudo-R^2	0.144	0.144	0.1870	0.1870

***$p < 0.01$, **$p < 0.05$, *$p < 0.1$

Table 3.8 Multinominal regression models for solidarity with unemployed people

	Model 4e		Model 5e	
	One action	Multiple action	One action	Multiple action
Age	0.791***	0.887	−0.234***	−0.148
Income	1.102	1.074	0.0579	0.103
Education	1.065	1.278***	0.0260	0.193*
Male	1.191	1.327	0.115	0.293
Migrant	0.937	1.507*	−0.0770	0.252
Attached unemp	1.666***	1.469***	0.483***	0.352***
Satgov_unemp	1.042	0.739***	0.0836	−0.333***
Fairsocietey_jobs	0.910	0.960	−0.0806	−0.00152
Inclusivityunemp	1.020	1.255**	−0.0314	0.173
Socialclass			−0.0553	−0.154
Reldep			−0.217**	−0.382***
Living in DE			0.117	0.0265
Friendsdiff			−0.0531	−0.0257
Live alone			−0.429**	−0.167
East			0.192	−0.325
Attached DE			−0.131	−0.199
Attached city			0.0173	−0.243
Attached reg			0.163	0.101
Attached EU			0.277**	0.282**
Attached hu			−0.0868	−0.0236
Socialtrust			0.278***	−0.0257
Religiosity			0.166**	0.335***
Identity			−0.145	0.0213
Lrscale			−0.139	0.000612
Demsat			−0.144	0.0248
Multicultural			−0.172	−0.0876
Populism			0.268***	0.164
Xeno_econ			0.0727	0.491***
Xeno_cult			0.148	−0.0832
Constant	0.244***	0.119***	−2.445***	−2.361***
N	1261	1261	1261	1261
Pseudo-R^2	0.0503	0.0503	0.0958	0.0958

***$p < 0.01$, **$p < 0.05$, *$p < 0.1$

beliefs. Above the ideational-cultural items already included in previous analysis, in particular deprivation, social trust and religiosity, attachment to unemployed ($M = 2.93$, see Appendix) has a very clear impact on people choosing to act in solidarity as well as dissatisfaction with the government's policies on unemployment ($M = 4.93$). Solidarity activity on behalf of this group can thus be observed more likely when people identify with the unemployed and feel that they are treated unfairly (see also the positive effect of populism and deprivation). To some extent this explains the positive correlation of economic xenophobia, but not cultural xenophobia. The populism index we used includes statements like "Politicians in the parliament need to follow the will of the people" and "Political differences between the elite and the people are larger than among people" (see Appendix) and thus expresses discontent with the political system (not necessarily right-wing populism).

Finally, Table 3.9 summarizes the results of two models calculated to explain variance regarding solidarity actions on behalf of people with disabilities. Education stays a relevant factor in explaining solidarity actions on behalf of disabled. Beyond the already reported variables, we find again the feeling of attachment to the specific group ($M = 3.40$, see Appendix) to be important in explaining solidarity activity. The belief, a fair society should include people with disabilities ($M = 4.24$), is relevant for people active in multiple ways. Overall and in comparison to the other issue fields investigated so far, we confirm that solidarity with disabled people is less contentious. For example, only 2.4% of respondents saw it as "not at all" or "not very" important that people with disabilities are included in public life. Similarly, the attachment (reported mean) is higher than with refugees and the unemployed. Thus, in comparison, questions on refugees and their rights were answered more diversely. Also in regards to correlating variables, solidarity with disabled is closer to solidarity with unemployed than to solidarity with refugees.

Conclusion

Our investigation set out to describe the frequency of solidarity activities in Germany, investigate socio-economic and cultural-ideational determinants and, last but not least, test for issue-specific motifs and political beliefs. First, we compared the relative frequencies of solidarity activities. We found solidarity to depend on geographic proximity, as the way and frequency of people engaging varies across spatial levels, and also to depend on issue fields: solidarity activity with disabled people is more common than activism on behalf of other groups, and, at the moment, the needs of refugees are addressed more often than those of the unemployed through these type of political actions. This suggests that solidarity at the individual level is not universalistic but rather particularistic.

Table 3.9 Multinominal regression models for solidarity with people with disabilities

	Model 4f		Model 5f	
	One action	Multiple action	One action	Multiple action
Age	0.901	0.935	−0.0947	−0.0608
Income_D	1.137*	1.103	0.129	−0.00681
Education	1.026	1.377***	0.00221	0.297***
Male	0.974	0.975	−0.0447	−0.0159
Migrant	0.940	1.127	−0.154	−0.142
Attached disab	1.525***	1.848***	0.430***	0.710***
Satgov disab	1.098	0.906	0.0363	−0.139
Fairsocietey_disa	1.021	1.191*	0.0298	0.189*
Inclusivity disab	1.028	1.091	0.0111	0.0636
Socialclass			−0.00779	−0.197*
Reldep			−0.156*	−0.178
Living in DE			0.0242	−0.00897
Friendsdiff			0.00641	0.0925
Live alone			−0.166	−0.391*
East			0.0872	−0.218
Attached DE			0.0408	−0.0577
Attached city			−0.274**	−0.134
Attached reg			0.188*	0.00900
Attached EU			0.188*	0.0799
Attached hu			0.103	0.178
Socialtrust			0.240***	0.107
Religiosity			0.190**	0.385***
Identity			−0.133	−0.258**
Lrscale			0.0781	−0.00382
Demsat			−0.00601	0.0909
Multicultural			0.104	0.0866
Populism			0.159**	0.194**
Xeno_econ			0.0331	0.250**
Xeno_cult			−0.0557	−0.0869
Constant	0.879	0.438***	−0.577	−1.034*
Observations	1235	1235	1235	1235
Pseudo-R^2	0.0458	0.0458	0.0838	0.0838

***$p < 0.01$, **$p < 0.05$, *$p < 0.1$

Moreover, our results indicate that solidarity depends not only on spatial proximity but also on social proximity.

Second, while we did not find clear socio-economic patterns that held across levels and issue fields, it seems as if the not-engaged are of diverse age, the one-action activists across levels and issues are often of younger age and the multiple activists are older. In addition, higher education seems to increase solidarity activity at least in some respects. Furthermore, across issue fields, higher social trust and religiosity seem to provide people with the motivation and (ideational) resources to engage on the behalf of others. Beyond that, our findings point to issue-specific explanations. For example, we found relative deprivation to increase the support of unemployed people and higher attachment with Europe as well as lower attachment with Germany to increase solidarity with people in other European countries.

Thus, in the third step, we sought to confirm this interpretation by including extra variables for models designed specifically for each specific issue fields, namely, support of other people in Europe, refugees, unemployed and people with disabilities. We confirmed that indeed attachment to specific groups also increased solidarity activity on behalf of them. In this respect, our findings corroborate the idea that solidarity is not a universalist inclination directed to any human being regardless of his or her affiliation or background. Instead, acting in solidarity is rather linked to specific groups to which one feels particularly close or attached. Moreover, attachment to different groups differs: it is highest towards disabled people and lowest, comparing our three issue fields, towards refugees (see means in Appendix). In this respect, feelings of social proximity to and empathy with certain target groups are important prerequisites for solidarity engagement in support of others.

Furthermore, satisfaction with government policies on specific issues might increase or decrease solidarity. For unemployment, people who are dissatisfied with the government are more likely to help those who are unemployed. This further supports our observation that social proximity and empathy help to mobilize support of particular groups because we can assume that people who express discontent with the government's unemployment policies have directly or indirectly (by observation) experienced the impact of these policies themselves and can thus identify with the situation of the unemployed. As for the issue of refugee policies, we observe the opposite relationship. Those who feel empathy with refugees would tend to be those who agree with the German "welcome policy" and also to be the type of individuals who would engage in actions to help refugees. In summary, our analysis has shown how, at least for the case of Germany, across the issue fields that social proximity and empathy with certain groups encourage solidarity behaviours.

Appendix

Variable	Item(s)	Recoding	Distribution
Germany	Have you ever done one of the following in order to support the rights of people/groups in your own country? (six options)	0 = 0, 1 = one activity, 2 = more than one activity	49.2% 27.9% 22.9%
Other EU	Have you ever done one of the following in order to support the rights of people/groups in other countries within the European Union? (six options)	0 = 0, 1 = one activity, 2 = more than one activity	68.7% 19.4% 11.9%
Global	Have you ever done one of the following in order to support the rights of people/groups in countries outside the European Union? (six options)	0 = 0, 1 = one activity, 2 = more than one activity	60.1% 25.4% 14.4%
Refugees	Have you ever done any of the following in order to support the rights of refugees/asylum seekers? (six options)	0 = 0, 1 = one activity, 2 = more than one activity	66.0% 21.4% 12.6%
Unemplo	Have you ever done any of the following in order to support the rights of the unemployed? (six options)	0 = 0, 1 = one activity, 2 = more than one activity	72.9% 18.2% 8.9%
Dissabil	Have you ever done any of the following in order to support disability rights? (six options)	0 = 0, 1 = one activity, 2 = more than one activity	48.5% 32.9% 18.7%
Age	How old are you?	Standardized	$M = 48.4$ ys
Income	What is your household's MONTHLY net income? (ten deciles)	Standardized	–
Education	What is the highest level of education that you have completed? (ISCED-list)	Standardized	–
Male	Are you male or female? 1 = male, 2 = female	0 = female, 1 = male	49.9%
Migrant	Born in other country; parents born in other country	If (parents) not born in Germany = migrant background	17.6%
Socialclass	Which of the following classes do you feel that you belong to?	Standardized	Upper to lower class

Variable	Item(s)	Recoding	Distribution
Reldep	Own current standard of living compared to parents (0–10); economic situation of household compared to five years ago (0–10); financial situation of household in the near future (0–10); your current living conditions (0–10); living conditions of the people in your neighbourhood (0–10); living conditions of your friends (0–10)	Index	(alpha > 0.81)
Living in DE	Still thinking about the living conditions, where would you place each of the following countries? Germany (0–10)	Standardized	M = 5.03
Friendsdiff	How many of your family, friends and/or acquaintances come from a different country?	Standardized	M = 3.96
Live alone	I currently live with…[alone]	–	25.0%
East	Living in an East German *Bundesland*	–	15.9%
Attached DE	Please tell me how attached you fell to Germany? (1–4)	Standardized	M = 3.29
Attached city	Please tell me how attached you fell to your city/town/village? (1–4)	Standardized	M = 3.28
Attached reg	Please tell me how attached you fell to your region? (1–4)	Standardized	M = 3.22
Attached EU	Please tell me how attached you fell to the European Union? (1–4)	Standardized	M = 2.59
Attached hu	How attached do you feel towards all people/humanity? (1–4)	Standardized	M = 2.92
Socialtrust	Most people can be trusted or you can't be too careful (0–10)	Standardized	M = 4.38
Religiosity	How religious would you say you are? (0–10)	Standardized	M = 3.34
Identity	How attached do you feel towards people with the same religion as you? (1–4); how attached do you feel towards people from your social class? (1–4); how attached do you feel towards people from your same ethnic group? (1–4); how attached do you feel towards people from your country of birth? (1–4); how attached do you feel towards people from your same age or generation? (1–4); how attached do you feel towards people from your same gender? (1–4); how attached do you feel towards people from your same sexual orientation? (1–4); how attached do you feel towards all people/humanity? (1–4)	Index	(alpha > 0.88)
Lrscale	People sometimes talk about the left and the right in politics. Where would you place yourself on the following? (0–10)	Standardized	M = 4.60

Variable	Item(s)	Recoding	Distribution
Demsat	On the whole, how satisfied or dissatisfied are you with the way democracy works in Germany? (0–10)	Standardized	M = 5.15
Multicultural	It is a good thing to live in a multicultural society. (1–5)	Standardized	M = 3.37
Populism	Politicians in the parliament need to follow will of the people (1–5); people should make our most important policy decisions (1–5); political differences between the elite and the people are larger than among people (1–5); rather be represented by a citizen than by specialized politician (1–5)	Index	(alpha > 0.76)
Xeno_econ	Would you say it is generally bad or good for the German economy that people come to live here from other countries? (0–10)	Standardized	M = 5.80
Xeno_cult	Would you say that German cultural life is generally undermined or enriched by people coming to live here from other countries? (0–10)	Standardized	M = 5.51
EUaid	The EU provides development aid to assist certain countries outside the EU in their fight against poverty and in their development. How important do you think it is to help people in developing countries? (1–5)	Standardized	M = 3.89
EUdebt	The EU is currently pooling funds to help EU countries having difficulties in paying their debts. To what extent do you agree or disagree with this measure? (1–5)	Standardized	M = 2.82
EUmotiv	There are many reasons to state for or against financial help for EU countries in trouble. Which one of the following best reflects how you feel?	–	–
1	Financial help has also beneficial effects for the own country. (0–1)	–	15.2%
2	It is our moral duty to help other member states that are in need. (0–1)	–	20.5%
3	The European Union member states should help each other, as somewhere along the way every country may require help (0–1)	–	44.6%
4	Financial help should not be given to countries that have proven to handle money badly (0–1)	–	40.3%

Variable	Item(s)	Recoding	Distribution
EU benefits D	Generally speaking, do you think that Germany's membership of the European Union is...? (1–2)	Recode: 0 = not benefiting; 1 = benefiting	68.0%
Attached refu	How attached do you feel towards people who have asked for asylum in this country? (1–5)	Standardized	M = 2.74
Satgov_refu	How satisfied or dissatisfied are you with the way in which the ***NATIONALITY*** government is dealing with the following? Refugee crisis (0–10)	Standardized	M = 3.32
Fair_refu	In order to be considered fair, what should a society provide? Welcoming refugees and asylum seekers (1–5)	Standardized	M = 3.19
Fair_mig	In order to be considered fair, what should a society provide? Welcoming immigrants and migrants (1–5)	Standardized	M = 3.13
Refugeesupp	Government offering financial support to help refugees (1–5)	Standardized	M = 3.16
Refugeemoral	It is the moral responsibility of Germany to accept refugees. (1–5)	Standardized	M = 3.35
Refugeecrisis	How satisfied or dissatisfied are you with the degree of cooperation in the European Union to handle the refugee crisis? (0–10)	Standardized	M = 3.80
Syrian refugees	How do you think Germany should handle refugees fleeing the war in Syria? (1–4)	Standardized	M = 2.56
Inclusivity	How would you feel about having people from a different country/ethnic background as citizens in your country? (happy-not happy) How would you feel about having people from a different country/ethnic background as residents living in your city? (happy-not happy) How would you feel about having people from a different country/ethnic background working alongside you in your job? (happy-not happy) How would you feel about having people from a different country/ethnic background as close kins by marriage? (happy-not happy)	Index	(alpha > 0.91) M = 0.72
Attached unemp	How attached do you feel towards people who are unemployed? (1–5)	Standardized	M = 2.93
Satgov_unemp	How satisfied or dissatisfied are you with the way in which the ***NATIONALITY*** government is dealing with the following? Unemployment (0–10)	Standardized	M = 4.93

Variable	Item(s)	Recoding	Distribution
Fairsocietey_jobs	In order to be considered fair, what should a society provide? Providing jobs for all citizens (1–5)	Standardized	M = 4.21
Inclusivityunemp	How would you feel about having people from families with one or more unemployed people as citizens in your country? (happy-not happy)	Index, standardized	(alpha > 0.88) M = 0.71
	How would you feel about having people from families with one or more unemployed people as residents living in your city? (happy-not happy)		
	How would you feel about having people from families with one or more unemployed people working alongside you in your job? (happy-not happy)		
	How would you feel about having people from families with one or more unemployed people as close kins by marriage? (happy-not happy)		
Attached disab	How attached do you feel towards people who have disabilities? (1–5)	Standardized	M = 3.40
Satgov disab	How satisfied or dissatisfied are you with the way in which the German government is dealing with the following? Disability support (0–10)	Standardized	M = 4.95
Fairsocietey_disa	In order to be considered fair, what should a society provide? Including people with disabilities into public life (1–5)	Standardized	M = 4.24
Inclusivity disab	How would you feel about having people with disabilities as citizens in your country? (happy-not happy)	Index, standardized	(alpha = 0.84) M = 0.90
	How would you feel about having people with disabilities as residents living in your city? (happy-not happy)		
	How would you feel about having people with disabilities working alongside you in your job? (happy-not happy)		
	How would you feel about having people with disabilities as close kins by marriage? (happy-not happy)		

Notes

1. Further information is available at the project website www.transsol.eu.
2. The results were very clear for all analyses conducted. Still, in addition to the principal factor analysis, we also conducted principal component analyses as well as iterated principal factor analyses but did not find any hints for another factor.
3. Nota bene: we did not ask people how often they engaged in the activities. We instead combine the different activities, arguing that engaging in multiple activities equals higher solidarity. This does not mean that one cannot be involved deeply in one activity expressing solidarity in this way. We account for this in the following analyses by including the one-action activists as an extra group.
4. Regressions for single items did not produce clearer patterns.
5. A lower score marks lower self-placement (and thus higher deprivation); a higher score means people feel better off.
6. Since solidarity actions on behalf of people in Germany and on behalf of people in non-European countries are more difficult to isolate, we exclude them from the following analysis.

References

Bauböck, R. (2017). Citizenship and Collective Identities as Political Sources of Solidarity in the European Union. In K. Banting & W. Kymlicka (Eds.), *The Strains of Commitment. The Political Sources of Solidarity in Diverse Societies* (pp. 80–106). Oxford: Oxford University Press.

Beyerlein, K., & Bergstrand, K. (2013). Biographical Availability. In D. A. Snow, D. della Porta, B. Klandermans, & D. McAdam (Eds.), *The Wiley-Blackwell Encyclopedia of Social and Political Movements* (pp. 137–138). New York: Wiley-Blackwell.

Brady, H. E., Verba, S., & Schlozman, K. L. (1995). Beyond SES: A Resource Model of Political Participation. *The America Political Science Review, 89*(2), 271–294.

Cainzos, M., & Voces, C. (2010). Class Inequalities in Political Participation and the 'Death of Class' Debate. *International Sociology, 25*(3), 383–418.

Eder, K. (1993). *The New Politics of Class: Social Movements and Cultural Dynamics in Advanced Societies.* London: Sage Publications.

Edwards, B., & McCarthy, J. D. (2004). Resources and Social Movement Mobilization. In D. A. Snow, S. A. Soule, & H. Kriesi (Eds.), *The Blackwell Companion to Social Movements* (pp. 116–152). Oxford: Blackwell.

Iversen, T., & Soskice, D. (2001). An Asset Theory of Social Policy Preferences. *American Political Science Review, 95*(4), 875–893.

Jenkins, J. C. (1983). Resource Mobilization Theory and the Study of Social Movements. *Annual Review of Sociology, 9*, 527–553.
Komter, A. E. (2005). *Social Solidarity and the Gift*. Cambridge: Cambridge University Press.
Kriesi, H. (1989). New Social Movements and the New Class in the Netherlands. *American Journal of Sociology, 94*(5), 1078–1116.
Kronauer, M. (1998). 'Social Exclusion' and 'Underclass': New Concepts for the Analysis of Poverty. In A. Hans-Jürgen (Ed.), *Empirical Poverty Research in a Comparative Perspective* (pp. 51–75). Aldershot: Ashgate.
Lichterman, P. (2015). Religion and Social Solidarity. A Pragmatist Approach. In L. Hustinx, J. von Essen, J. Haers, & S. Mels (Eds.), *Religion and Volunteering. Complex, Contested and Ambiguous Relationships* (pp. 241–261). Cham: Springer.
Likki, T., & Staerklé, C. (2014). A Typology of Ideological Attitudes Towards Social Solidarity and Social Control. *Journal of Community and Applied Social Psychology, 24*, 406–421.
Morokvasic, M. (1999). La mobilité transnationale comme ressource: le cas des migrants de l'Europe de l'Est. *Cultures et Conflits, 32*, 105–122.
Putnam, R., Feldstein, L. M., & Cohen, D. (2003). *Better Together: Restoring the American Community*. New York: Simon & Schuster.
Rehm, P. (2009). Risks and Redistribution. An Individual-Level Analysis. *Comparative Political Studies, 42*(7), 885–881.
Schiffauer, W., Eilert, A., & Rudloff, M. (Eds.). (2017). *So schaffen wir das—eine Zivilgesellschaft im Aufbruch: 90 wegweisende Projekte mit Geflüchteten*. Bielefeld: transcript.
Schulze, R. (2004). Islamische Solidaritätsnetzwerke: Auswege aus den verlorenen Versprechen des modernen Staates. In J. Beckert, J. Eckert, M. Kohli, & W. Streeck (Eds.), *Transnationale Solidarität. Chancen und Grenzen* (pp. 195–219). Frankfurt a. M: Campus.
Stegmueller, D., Scheepers, P., Roßteuscher, S., & de Jong, E. (2012). Support for Redistribution in Western Europe. Assessing the Role of Religion. *European Sociological Review, 28*(4), 482–497.
van Oorschot, W. (2006). Making the Difference in Social Europe: Deservingness Perceptions Among Citizens of European Welfare States. *Journal of European Social Policy, 16*(1), 23–42.
van Oorschot, W., Arts, W., & Gelissen, J. (2006). Social Capital in Europe. Measurement and Social and Regional Distribution of a Multifaceted Phenomenon. *Acta Sociologica, XLIX*, 149–167.
Verba, S., Nie, N., & Kim, J. (1978). *Participation and Political Equality: A Seven Nation Comparison*. London: Cambridge University Press.
Verba, S., Schlozman, K. L., & Brady, H. E. (1995). *Voice and Equality: Civic Voluntarism in American Politics*. Cambridge: Harvard University Press.

Open Access This chapter is licensed under the terms of the Creative Commons Attribution 4.0 International License (http://creativecommons.org/licenses/by/4.0/), which permits use, sharing, adaptation, distribution and reproduction in any medium or format, as long as you give appropriate credit to the original author(s) and the source, provide a link to the Creative Commons license and indicate if changes were made.

The images or other third party material in this chapter are included in the chapter's Creative Commons license, unless indicated otherwise in a credit line to the material. If material is not included in the chapter's Creative Commons license and your intended use is not permitted by statutory regulation or exceeds the permitted use, you will need to obtain permission directly from the copyright holder.

CHAPTER 4

Pulling Together or Pulling Apart? Solidarity in the Post-Crisis UK

Tom Montgomery, Simone Baglioni, Olga Biosca, and Maria Grasso

INTRODUCTION

The importance of solidarity can hardly be underestimated in contemporary Britain. The UK has weathered the financial crisis, witnessed the impact of austerity in public services and local economies, and experienced a highly divisive European referendum which has not only polarised British society and transformed the political landscape but also reconfigured relations with European neighbours and reopened internal divisions regarding the constitutional future of the UK (Temple and Grasso 2017). In this context, this chapter seeks to uncover the reality of solidarity in British society by analysing data from a novel survey data set examining various aspects of solidarity—including its correlate political behaviours in support of various beneficiary groups residing within and outside one's country. Our aim is to analyse the various dimensions of solidarity as well as which

T. Montgomery (✉) • S. Baglioni • O. Biosca
Yunus Centre, Glasgow Caledonian University, Glasgow, UK

M. Grasso
Department of Politics, University of Sheffield, Sheffield, UK

© The Author(s) 2018
C. Lahusen, M. Grasso (eds.), *Solidarity in Europe*,
Palgrave Studies in European Political Sociology,
https://doi.org/10.1007/978-3-319-73335-7_4

factors lead to its political behavioural practice. In what follows, we analyse which groups in society are the most solidaristic and which groups can rely on others' solidarity the most. First, however we analyse the relevant literature that has addressed these theoretical questions in the past.

The concept of solidarity has been long established in social science and has been the subject of key works (Durkheim 1893) including those focused on the UK context (Thompson 1963). While the introduction to this volume has offered a conceptual discussion, this chapter focuses on examining the practical behavioural manifestations of solidarity understood as a range of actions that people deploy in support of potentially vulnerable groups and individuals, namely, the disabled, the unemployed, and migrants and refugees. Our focus on solidarity in terms of practiced forms of active engagement in favour of vulnerable groups has political connotations. This is because such activities imply either claims in support of these groups in relation to civil or human rights and social policy entitlements vis-à-vis the state or because they challenge negligence or refusal to support such rights and entitlements that have been promised through policy but still lack actual enforcement.

Furthermore, the political connotations of our conceptualization of solidarity are related to two highly contentious issues: (a) how to fund the enforcement of rights and (b) whether the same level of access to the implementation of rights should be granted on an equal basis to all those in need. In other words, our understanding of solidarity implies answering politically relevant questions such as should the costs of implementing rights be equally shared among members of the community or should those directly benefiting from implementation bear the costs? And if the costs should be pooled from general taxation—as happens in most Western European welfare states—should public funds provide universal support equally across groups in need, or should solidarity be made conditional upon meeting given criteria?

These are fundamental questions at the heart of democratic debate today. The ultimate contemporary relevance of these questions today further illustrates how solidarity lies at the heart of a contentious domain, given that individuals and groups have different and sometimes opposing opinions about whether we should and to what extent help others in need. Indeed this question lies at the very heart of the fundamental ideological debate between left and right which has been at core of democratic politics at least since the French Revolution. Whereas the post-war social democratic consensus was characterised by strong support for universalist welfare states across Western Europe, the neo-liberal break of the late 1970s challenged the idea that society should provide safety nets to help vulnerable groups and insisted on the principles of self-interested market competition as incentivising individuals to contribute towards society (English et al. 2016; Grasso et al. 2017; Temple et al. 2016). Other than ideological factors, earlier studies have also suggested that the willingness of people to express solidarity with others is mediated by several other important factors, some of which pertain to perceived characteristics of those being helped and their ascribed deservingness, while others are linked to the characteristics of those providing help or with the socio-economic and political characteristics of the contexts where people live.

Among those factors considered to be influential for the willingness of people to help others are the perceptions of:

1. the degree of control those in need have over their own 'neediness' (the less responsible for their situation they are perceived to be, the more inclined are people to help);
2. their level of need (people with greater needs are seen as more deserving);
3. their identity (cultural proximity facilitates deservingness);
4. their attitude (conforming to 'standards' fosters solidarity), and
5. reciprocity (people that have 'earned' support through their contribution to the community and its pool of funds in earlier periods are more deserving of being helped). (van Oorschot 2006: 26)

Moreover, earlier studies have also argued that a disposition towards solidarity depends upon individual characteristics such as age, level of education, socio-economic position and political-ideological orientation, as well as levels of life satisfaction (Dunn et al. 2014; Grasso 2013, 2016). These studies had shown that the solidarity of older, less well-educated, less well-off, less-satisfied, and more right-wing individuals is more conditional on the beneficiaries meeting precise criteria with in particular the perceived degree of control that beneficiaries have over their needs as well their identity being the most powerful 'conditionality' drivers (ibid.). The reasons behind such a high degree of conditionality among older, less well-educated, less well-off, less-satisfied, and more right-wing people have been shown to cluster around two main factors: personal interests and ideology. People that feel themselves to be in a relatively more insecure social position consider the solidarity provided to those in need as providing competition for their own needs, thus diminishing their support for solidarity. Other aspects preventing solidarity from developing or making it more conditional are linked to ideas people have of 'otherness' such as, for example, a negative attitude towards migrants preventing solidarity for asylum seekers or refugees and more generally a lack of trust in others and narrow views of social embeddedness (inhibiting wider social solidarity) (van Oorschot 2006).

Nevertheless, research reveals that the willingness of people to help others is also influenced by the type of country they live in: welfare regimes play a crucial role in institutionalising solidarity and are relevant in fostering or mitigating social solidarity. For example, residual welfare regimes tend to increase conditionality as fewer resources are available to meet a range of needs, and also national policies and policy discourses should be considered since one would imagine a national policy environment supporting solidaristic attitudes will mitigate claims for conditionality among its citizens, while a general policy discourse emphasising prejudices against those in need would create the opposite—a more greatly conditional attitude (Blekesaune and Quadagno 2003; van Oorschot and Arts 2005).

To summarise this discussion, solidarity implies a dynamic, interactive process of constant renegotiation of social citizenship boundaries, which is per se in essence a political phenomenon. In this chapter we are interested in understanding how people living in the UK are part of this process, the extent to which solidaristic activities are practised, whether solidarity activities are germane to a conditionality approach, and also if solidarity is practised at different levels between people living in the various geographic areas of the country, and finally whether such differences could be explained by taking into consideration both individual characteristics and local contexts. The chapter unfolds as follows. We next present our hypotheses and then move on to illustrate data and methods, and finally we discuss our results and their wider implications.

Hypotheses

Building on the extant literature, we explore solidarity through the prism of five main hypotheses related to either the individual or contextual levels of analysis. Starting with the latter, we focus on the role that national policies and discourses play in generating solidaristic (or anti-solidaristic) attitudes and hypothesise that solidarity will be unevenly distributed across the constituent nations of the UK. We expect that it will be more vibrant in those areas which have a tradition of progressive and solidaristic approaches to social issues and where the effects of the Conservative-led government anti-statist, neo-liberal policies have been mitigated by devolved authorities with a different policy orientation (viz. Northern Ireland and Scotland). Secondly, we also hypothesise that in such different contexts, we will find a varying degree of conditionality attached to solidarity: thus we will have a lower degree of conditionality in the more progressive and 'policy solidaristic' constituent nations (Northern Ireland and Scotland) than in others (England and Wales).

To understand why we hypothesise that solidarity can diverge across the constituent nations of the UK requires an appreciation of the historical context and the political cultures which have developed in devolved nations. Firstly, in terms of Scotland, we can see that there is a longstanding argument in the literature on the development of 'policy autonomy' (Midwinter et al. 1991) or indeed a distinctive political culture (Kellas 1989). The debate regarding a distinctively Scottish political culture and its extent is ongoing and to some extent has been integrated into the seemingly unresolved question of the future of Scotland in the UK following the 'No' vote which took place in the 2014 Scottish independence referendum (Torrance 2013; Macwhirter 2014) and the rise of the SNP as the dominant force in Scottish politics (Johns and Mitchell 2016). Another dimension to that debate is whether or not the Scottish sociopolitical context can be considered more egalitarian than its counterparts in England (Mooney and Poole 2004).

Northern Ireland can also be seen to have a distinctive political context where the divisions between the nationalist and unionist communities continue to be a fault line through society. Nevertheless, following the common experience of 'the Troubles' which saw a great loss of life over a period of 30 years, the peace process (Mallie and McKittrick 1996) cemented by the Good Friday Agreement (Tonge 2000; Bew 2007) has developed alongside an emphasis on equality (McCrudden 1998) between the previously conflicting communities and the centrality of consociationalism (McGarry and O'Leary 2004) in overcoming divisions (Lijphart 2012). Therefore, to some extent we can hypothesise that the proliferation of discourses, legislation, and indeed the very governance of Northern Ireland (Tonge 2002) may contribute towards the construction of a more fertile environment for solidarity to be practised.

Considering the individual level, following earlier studies, we hypothesise that younger, more educated, more socially connected people (Giugni and Grasso 2015; Grasso and Giugni 2016) and people with a higher level of satisfaction with their overall life will be more likely to take action in favour of disabled people, the unemployed, migrants and refugees. In addition to these considerations, we are also controlling for the exposure of individuals to specific media discourses building from research that has identified newspaper readership as a factor which shapes attitudes towards each of our three vulnerable groups (Golding and Middleton 1982; Greenslade 2005; Briant et al. 2011). Consistent with this literature, we hypothesise that reading more right-wing and prejudicial newspapers (e.g. tabloids) will likely be associated with lower inclination to solidarity in comparison to progressive newspaper readership. Moreover, building upon the findings of earlier studies that 'identity sharing' is a factor facilitating solidarity, we also control for direct exposure to vulnerability and hypothesise that those who are more directly exposed to vulnerability through being in one of our vulnerable categories (disabled, unemployed, migrants, or refugees) will likely be more solidaristic than those who are not. In the following section, we briefly present our data set, variables, and methods.

Data

This chapter uses cross-sectional data from an original survey, described in greater detail in the introduction of this book conducted in the context of the TransSOL European collaborative project in the winter months of 2016/2017 to examine solidarity at the individual level in eight European countries. Information was gathered on citizens' solidarity practices, attitudes and behaviours, as well as on socio-demographic characteristics, political attitudes, and cultural orientations. In this study, we use the UK-based sample with age, gender, region, and education quotas matched for nationally representative statistics of 2083 UK-based survey respondents. Survey weights were included in all analyses.

The variables used for this analysis are presented in Table 4.1 and further details of the original survey questions and any relevant recodings are provided in Appendix. The dependent variables of solidarity practices used indicate if respondents have supported, in the last 12 months, the rights of particular people/groups through various forms of political actions including more contentious as well as more

Table 4.1 Descriptive statistics

	Mean	Std. dev.	Obs.
Supported rights of people/groups in own country	38.4	0.49	2083
Supported rights of people/groups in other countries within the EU	18.9	0.39	2083
Supported rights of people/groups outside Europe	25.4	0.44	2083
Supported the rights of refugees/asylum seekers	21.7	0.41	2083
Supported the rights of the unemployed	18.8	0.39	2083
Supported disability rights	34.6	0.48	2083
Age	47.32	16.58	2083
Female	51.3	0.50	2083
Higher education	29.9	0.47	2083
Intermediate education	33.8	0.47	2083
Unemployed	5.1	0.22	2083
Disabled	17.3	0.38	2044
Born in UK	90.2	0.30	2083
Daily Mail	21.2	0.41	2083
The Sun	12.2	0.33	2083
The Times	9.5	0.29	2083
The Guardian	10.6	0.31	2083
Daily Mirror	8.0	0.27	2083
Other newspapers	15.4	0.36	2083
Met friends at least once a month	73.9	0.44	2083
Life satisfaction	6.45	2.15	2032
Scotland	8.5	0.28	2083
Wales	4.8	0.21	2083
Northern Ireland	2.8	0.16	2083

Note: Age is measured in years. Life satisfaction is measured by a 10-point Likert-style response scale where a higher number represents higher life satisfaction. The remainder of the variables are percentages. Base category for education variable is lower education. Base category for newspaper variable is 'Not reading any newspaper regularly (3+ days a week).' Base category for constituent country variable is England

conventional types: attended a march, protest, or demonstration; donated money; donated time; bought or refused to buy products; engaged as passive member of an organisation (pay cheque membership); engaged as an active member of an organisation (volunteering in an organisation). A further question asked was if respondents participated in any of the above actions: through a process of recoding, binary variables were created that took the value of one if respondents reported participating in any of these solidarity actions and zero if they said otherwise. These binary variables resulted in six dependent variables for this analysis indicating if individuals said they had been involved in any of the listed political activities (1) in support of the rights of people/groups in one's own country, (2) in support of the rights of people/groups in other countries within the EU, (3) in support of the rights of people/groups outside Europe, (4) in support of the rights of refugees/asylum seekers, (5) in support of the rights of unemployed people, and finally (6) in support of the rights of disabled persons.

Geographies of Solidarity: Findings from the Constituent Nations and Regions of the UK

Our analysis begins by considering if the data supports our hypothesis concerning the expectation of diverse degrees of solidarity between the constituent nations of the UK. We do so by comparing answers to three questions which asked respondents whether, in the last 12 months, they had engaged in various political actions in support of the rights of people living in the UK, living in Europe, and those living outside of Europe. Findings in Table 4.2 reveal supportive evidence for our hypothesis about divergent patterns of solidarity across the UK constituent nations: although with small margins, our respondents from Scotland and Northern Ireland report stronger solidarity than people living in England or Wales. This is true not only of solidarity activities undertaken for UK-based beneficiaries but also with respect to beneficiaries based elsewhere. With the caveat of their being small numbers in our sub-UK level sample—which are however

Table 4.2 Solidarity practices in different geographical areas by constituent country in the UK

Country	N	Supported rights in own country (%)	Supported rights in Europe (%)	Supported rights outside Europe (%)
England	1761	38.0	18.7	25.1
Scotland	177	44.7*	20.9	29.6
Wales	97	38.2	14.5	20.8
Northern Ireland	48	31.2	25.1	27.0
Total UK	2083	38.4	18.9	25.4

Notes: ***$p < 0.01$, **$p < 0.05$, *$p < 0.1$. For definition of the variables, see Table 4.1

representative of the different demographic weights of the UK constituent nations—our findings provide a unique contribution to the debate on divergence between the constituent nations of the UK by focusing on practices of solidarity, and our results do suggest that there is indeed a divergence between these contexts within the UK.

Our findings also reveal the uneven distribution of solidarity practices in terms of the groups towards which support is directed (still holding across the constituent nations of the UK). Contrary to our hypothesis, in fact, the vibrancy of solidarity practices is not equal across people in need: some groups appear more 'deserving' of help than others. Our results indicate that for the most part, the practice of solidarity is aimed at protecting the rights of those within the UK. Further, longitudinal research could reveal if this inward-looking tendency is a constant within British society or whether these feelings have intensified towards UK beneficiaries following the financial crisis and the ensuing austerity measures. Regardless, our analysis shows that the focus is primarily on practising solidarity within the UK. In turn, this may be reflecting a narrowing of the scope of solidarity during periods of financial downturn and the retrenchment of public services, or alternatively this trend could predate the current crisis. Indeed, we can see that in terms of transnational solidarity, practices are more geared towards supporting those who are outside of Europe rather than our European neighbours. We can speculate that the issue of prioritising deservingness may have a role to play here. In other words, those engaged in solidarity practices may consider that those outside of Europe require the most assistance. We can further speculate that this may be driven by responses to emergencies such as the Syrian refugee crisis.

Still concerning the hypothesis about the existence of a 'solidarity ladder' where different categories of people and groups occupy different positions, our findings appear to confirm earlier studies (van Oorschot 2000, 2006). Table 4.3 reveals an uneven distribution of solidarity across the three vulnerable groups: people with disabilities, unemployed people, and migrants/refugees. The group which attracts the greatest degree of solidarity are people with disabilities. In fact, disabled people are the group with the greatest degree of solidaristic support across all four constituent nations of the UK. However, again we also find an uneven distribution with the highest levels of solidarity to be found in Northern Ireland and Scotland.

Table 4.3 Solidarity practices with vulnerable groups (refugees, unemployed, disabled) by constituent country in the UK

Country	N	Support refugees (%)	Support unemployed (%)	Support disabled (%)
England	1761	20.8*	18.0**	33.2***
Scotland	177	28.6*	27.5***	44.9***
Wales	97	18.5	16.5	33.9
Northern Ireland	48	30.9*	18.7	48.0**
Total UK	2083	22.7	18.8	34.6

Notes: ***$p < 0.01$, **$p < 0.05$, *$p < 0.1$. For definition of the variables, see Table 4.1

Our findings that solidarity is more targeted towards people with disabilities may indicate that in the UK this group is deemed the most deserving out of our three vulnerable groups, although this heavier distribution of solidarity towards disabled people deserves a more nuanced analysis. For example, we can speculate that this could be driven by a more paternalistic attitude towards people with disabilities. The perception of people with disabilities as being somehow helpless or indeed tragic figures who require support from others has been strongly opposed by disability campaigners who since the 1970s in the UK have sought to contrast those narratives of disabled people as victims. This is illustrated, for example, through those social movements and activists who adopt the 'social model of disability' which understands the challenges faced by people with disabilities as being constructed by a 'disabling society' and rejects deservingness but instead demands equal treatment as citizens (Oliver et al. 2012). Therefore, although our findings make for positive reading in terms of the solidarity targeted towards people with disabilities, our analysis requires a much more cautious approach and fine-grained understanding of the perceptions of disabled people which may be driving this solidarity especially when considered alongside the solidarity professed for the other vulnerable groups.

Our findings outlined in Table 4.3 reveal that the group with the next highest share of solidarity practices are refugees and that these practices are again unevenly distributed across the constituent nations of the UK. We can see how the support for refugees is highest in Northern Ireland and Scotland with a visible gap between them and England and Wales. From previous research, we can see that there has been, for a considerable time, a proliferation of negative policy discourses aimed at those seeking refuge and asylum in the UK and indeed at migrants more generally (Sales 2002; Statham and Geddes 2006; Squire 2008). Our findings confirm that there is certainly a section of the population which stands in stark contrast to the 'racist public' thesis, and their practices point towards a current of solidarity suggested by extant research (Squire 2011). Nevertheless, there has been, across governments of different political orientations, a drive towards policies which are far more focused on border control than solidarity when it comes to refugees arriving in the UK (Squire 2016). Given that immigration and asylum policy is reserved to Westminster control and there are few avenues for devolved administrations to pursue alternative approaches, this perhaps only leaves space for rhetorical divergence.

Moreover, our findings reveal that among our three groups, it is unemployed people in the UK who are supported by the lowest number of solidarity participation practices. Any analysis of why the unemployed are the least supported group should be caveated by the fact that most support for the unemployed in the UK has traditionally been delivered by the welfare state through support with basic subsistence such as Jobseeker's Allowance (JSA) and with the cost of rent through Housing Benefit (HB). It is, however, worth noting that both of these benefits have been at the centre of a welfare reform agenda pursued in the aftermath of the financial crisis by the Conservative and Liberal Democrat coalition government elected in 2010 and articulated through their policy document *Welfare in the Twenty-First Century* which highlighted concerns of a 'culture of worklessness' in the UK. Moreover, ever since the break with the post-war consensus initiated by Margaret Thatcher and followed through by both Conservative and New Labour prime ministers, support for unemployed people has been under attack with those out of work increasingly characterised as lazy and as undeserving of public support. Rather than unemployment being understood as a social, political, and structural problem emerging from the limits of capitalist production, it has now been fully recast as an individual-level problem resulting from the deficient personalities of certain people. Indeed, such policies reflected this ideological process of transformation of poverty and unemployment from market failure to personal failure (Wiggan 2012). Indeed this has been shown as a consistently strong trope in austerity Britain, even impervious to contrary evidence (MacDonald et al. 2014a, b), and offers some context as to why the unemployed are the group viewed as least deserving among the three vulnerable groups we have focused upon here.

Our findings in Table 4.3 also reveal that there is variation in solidarity practices towards the unemployed across the UK, with a much greater distribution of solidarity evident in Scotland than anywhere else in the UK. These findings in Scotland support our hypothesis of policy divergence across the constituent nations across the UK and add weight to the argument that Scotland has a more social democratic outlook which in turn may lead to a greater degree of solidarity with those out of work, particularly given the common experience of deindustrialization in high-density population centres such as in the Central Belt. Nevertheless, we should be cautious in our approach to understanding this greater tendency towards solidarity practices in Scotland as extant research suggests an alignment between Scotland and England in social attitudes in terms of what are the causes of unemployment (Sinclair et al. 2009).

Therefore, to summarise the key results from this section, our findings reveal, as shown in both Tables 4.2 and 4.3, the existence of a hierarchy of solidarity in the UK. Firstly, British people express more solidarity towards those living in the UK (Table 4.2), and this confirms earlier research pointing towards the role that 'identity' plays in issues of deservingness. Indeed, people have been shown to be more inclined to adopt a solidaristic attitude towards those that are perceived as more similar or sharing identity-related features with them. Considering variations across the vulnerable groups, solidarity towards the unemployed is the least strong of the three and may suggest that policy discourses and media narratives which have stigmatised the unemployed may be cutting through to British society. Moreover, it could be that the British public in general views unemployed people as the most responsible for their condition compared to people with disabilities and refugees/asylum seekers. In the middle of this hierarchy are refugees, who we may have expected to be the primary target for solidarity activities among our three groups, not only because of the sense of urgency regarding the Syrian refugee crisis but also because our earlier findings suggested that transnational forms of solidarity are more geared towards those outside of Europe.

The group at the apex of our hierarchy, namely, the disabled, can be understood to occupy that position for two main reasons. On the one hand, it may be that they have been a group more visible in terms of the impact of austerity upon them, not only through the reassessments of

Fig. 4.1 The hierarchy of solidarity in the UK

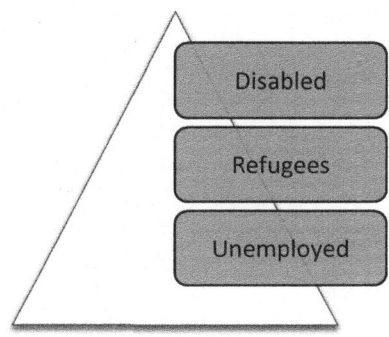

eligibility for welfare support such as Employment and Support Allowance[1] (ESA) but also policies such as the 'bedroom tax'.[2] On the other hand, the high degree of solidarity directed towards people with disabilities could be understood as being reflective of long-standing stereotypes seeing them as victims of their illness rather than equal citizens who have been at the sharp end of austerity measures. Therefore, the 'hierarchy of solidarity', found in our results and illustrated in Fig. 4.1 serves to remind us of the uneven distribution of solidarity towards vulnerable groups and it requires a more careful understanding of the factors which may be driving solidarity such as the continued attempts by the UK government since the onset of the crisis and the ensuing austerity measures to distinguish between deserving and undeserving groups.

Results for the Individual-Level Variables

As we shall discover, our findings suggest that although the hierarchy of solidarity outlined earlier may provide a broad understanding of the distribution of solidarity across each group, a more nuanced analysis reveals the fluidity of these hierarchies when considering a range of different variables. In order to test our hypotheses, we used a logit model (Table 4.4) to analyse the relationship between our dependent variables of solidarity practice across different geographies (inside the UK, outside the UK but inside the EU, and outside the EU) and vulnerabilities (refugee/asylum seekers, the unemployed, and the disabled) and a number of independent variables relevant to our underlying hypotheses. As discussed in the introductory and data sections, these include socio-demographic

Table 4.4 Solidarity practices to support the rights in different areas and groups

	Inside the UK	In the EU, outside UK	Outside the EU	Refugees and/or asylum seekers	Unemployed	Disabled
Age	−0.03	−0.08***	−0.06***	−0.11***	−0.08***	−0.04*
	(0.02)	(0.02)	(0.02)	(0.02)	(0.02)	(0.02)
Age squared	0.00	0.00*	0.00**	0.00***	0.00**	0.00
	(0.00)	(0.00)	(0.00)	(0.00)	(0.00)	(0.00)
Female	−0.18*	−0.14	−0.24**	0.04	−0.44***	−0.13
	(0.10)	(0.13)	(0.12)	(0.12)	(0.13)	(0.10)
Education (ref.: low education)						
Intermediate education	0.09	0.05	0.12	0.25	0.09	0.07
	(0.12)	(0.17)	(0.14)	(0.16)	(0.16)	(0.12)
Higher education	0.32**	0.33*	0.69***	0.74***	0.35**	0.23*
	(0.13)	(0.17)	(0.15)	(0.16)	(0.16)	(0.13)
Unemployed	0.10	0.45	0.23	0.38	0.21	0.32
	(0.25)	(0.28)	(0.27)	(0.29)	(0.30)	(0.25)
Disabled	0.55***	0.31*	0.47***	0.34**	0.54***	0.84***
	(0.13)	(0.17)	(0.15)	(0.16)	(0.16)	(0.13)
Born in UK	−0.10	−0.43**	−0.62***	−0.14	−0.20	−0.35**
	(0.17)	(0.19)	(0.17)	(0.19)	(0.20)	(0.17)
Newspaper readership						
Daily Mail	0.18	0.14	0.13	0.01	0.27*	0.29**
	(0.12)	(0.15)	(0.13)	(0.14)	(0.15)	(0.12)
The Sun	0.23	0.56***	0.43***	0.44**	0.69***	0.53***
	(0.15)	(0.18)	(0.17)	(0.18)	(0.17)	(0.15)
The Times	0.67***	1.00***	0.73***	0.92***	1.11***	0.78***
	(0.17)	(0.18)	(0.17)	(0.18)	(0.18)	(0.17)
The Guardian	1.09***	0.95***	0.91***	1.10***	0.60***	0.45***
	(0.17)	(0.17)	(0.16)	(0.17)	(0.18)	(0.16)
Daily Mirror	0.37**	0.41*	0.43**	0.66***	0.62***	0.36*
	(0.18)	(0.22)	(0.20)	(0.21)	(0.21)	(0.19)
Other newspapers	0.10	−0.14	−0.02	−0.27	−0.09	−0.25*
	(0.14)	(0.19)	(0.16)	(0.18)	(0.18)	(0.14)
Met friends once month	0.40***	0.25	0.23*	0.25*	0.25	0.31***
	(0.12)	(0.16)	(0.14)	(0.15)	(0.16)	(0.12)
Life satisfaction	0.06***	0.03	0.04	0.10***	0.09***	0.08***
	(0.03)	(0.03)	(0.03)	(0.03)	(0.03)	(0.03)
Region (ref.: England)						
Scotland	0.33*	0.28	0.31*	0.56***	0.73***	0.60***
	(0.17)	(0.22)	(0.19)	(0.20)	(0.20)	(0.17)
Wales	0.13	−0.04	−0.07	0.05	0.16	0.22
	(0.23)	(0.32)	(0.27)	(0.29)	(0.30)	(0.23)

(*continued*)

Table 4.4 (continued)

	Inside the UK	In the EU, outside UK	Outside the EU	Refugees and/or asylum seekers	Unemployed	Disabled
Northern Ireland	−0.30 (0.34)	0.42 (0.39)	0.02 (0.37)	0.65* (0.36)	0.01 (0.42)	0.52* (0.32)
Constant	−0.76 (0.50)	0.48 (0.63)	−0.02 (0.56)	−0.28 (0.59)	−0.51 (0.62)	−0.63 (0.51)
Pseudo R^2	0.07	0.16	0.11	0.13	0.12	0.07
N	1996	1996	1996	1996	1996	1996

Notes: Coefficients of the logit model are shown. Standard errors are in parentheses. ***$p < 0.01$, **$p < 0.05$, *$p < 0.1$. For definition of the variables, see Table 4.1

variables (e.g. age, education), but we also look at the significance of being born in the UK, which we regard as an important variable given the importance that identity issues have on solidarity and deservingness, as discussed earlier. We also examine variables encompassing the vulnerability of the respondent (e.g. disability or unemployment) to gauge if exposure to such vulnerability at a time of crisis and austerity has an effect on the practice of solidarity by these groups; social embeddedness has also been a long-standing focus of literature on solidarity (van Oorschot 2006) as well as on political participation (Putnam 2001; Maloney et al. 2000; Hall 1999). Life satisfaction is a variable deployed to reveal whether practices of solidarity are the purview of those who feel happy with their quality of life; as anticipated in the hypotheses, we will also control for how readership of different types of newspapers influence solidarity attitudes (we hypothesise that readers of more conservative and populist-oriented newspapers will be less inclined towards solidarity); and as per one of our key hypotheses, we look at the residency of the respondent (e.g. living in Scotland, Wales, Northern Ireland) to identify divergences in the practice of solidarity across the constituent nations of the UK where devolution has empowered assemblies and parliaments. The results from the regressions we conducted are set out below.

When analysing our individual-level variables, our hypothesis was that the practice of solidarity would depend on a range of factors, including a higher level of education. Our education hypothesis builds upon established research on solidarity but also on political participation and civic engagement that education provides the necessary resources for an individual to become engaged in societal and political issues (Verba et al. 1995). Furthermore, we hypothesised that those with a higher level of education had more material resources to engage in solidarity. When examining our findings in Table 4.4, we can see that our hypothesis is confirmed by a significant and positive relationship between being disposed towards actions of solidarity and being in higher education. Consequently, we find confirmation of our hypothesis that those with higher education are better resourced to engage in practices of solidarity than those with fewer resources (Grasso 2017).

A classic socio-demographic variable—age—presents us with interesting results confirming our hypothesis. What can be seen in Table 4.4 is that age is negative and significantly associated with solidarity with each of the vulnerable groups as well as each geographic area with the sole exception of those inside the UK. Therefore the younger you are in the UK, the more predisposed you are towards engaging in practices of solidarity. The implications of these findings can be seen to some extent in the vote which took place in the 2016 EU referendum for the UK to leave the EU, where older voters were more predisposed towards voting leave (Hobolt 2016). Nevertheless, our findings suggest that the negative relationship between solidarity and age extends to anyone who is 'other' than within the UK. These findings also shed some light on how policies which are restrictive towards refugees, austerity policies affecting the disabled, and policies characterised by sanctions and compulsion towards the unemployed can be sustained given the higher propensity for older people to turn out at elections in the UK and reinforce the urgency for more young people to become politically engaged before any change in direction could take place (Gardiner 2016).

Our findings regarding social embeddedness support our hypothesis that the practice of solidarity depends on exposure to social networks and social interaction. In this case, social embeddedness is defined as 'meeting socially with friends during the last month' and, as we can see in Table 4.4, is positively and significantly associated, from a geographic perspective, with offering solidarity to those within the UK and those outside the EU as well as a similar relationship in terms of solidarity with refugees and the disabled. The importance of social capital in building social cohesion is well established in the literature (Putnam 2001; Li et al. 2005), and our findings in the UK resonate with these works. In terms of implications for policymaking, another of our findings may be acutely relevant towards understanding how to develop solidarity in the UK. Given the significant association between higher life satisfaction and solidarity with others within the UK, as well as each of our vulnerable groups, suggests that policies geared towards individual well-being may have a positive impact in terms of engendering solidarity in the UK.

When considering our results in terms of gender, what we can see in Table 4.4 is the negative and significant relationship between being female and practising solidarity, specifically with groups within the UK and those outside the EU as well as there being a similar relationship with solidarity and the unemployed. Further still, more qualitative research may unpack the specificities of the gender dimension of solidarity (or in this case non-solidarity). Extant research suggests that women have been at the forefront of the austerity cuts and as a consequence may have few resources, in either money or time, to divert to solidarity practices (O'Hara 2014). In addition to this, it is important to note that despite steps closer towards equality, women continue to perform many of the caregiving tasks across UK households, not only in terms of looking after children but also caring for sick or disabled members of the family, which research suggests has an impact on retaining employment (Carmichael et al. 2008).

One hypothesis underpinning our analysis of the practice of solidarity is the exposure to information and, despite the rise of online media, newspaper readers continue to be courted by policymakers in the UK and thus retain an important place in shaping and reflecting policy discourses and the political agenda. Firstly, we discover a positive and significant relationship between reading *The Times*, *The Guardian*, or the *Daily Mirror* and practices of solidarity in comparison to not reading any newspapers. However, Table 4.4 presents a result falsifying our hypothesis regarding the influence of tabloid readership on the lack of solidarity: there is a positive and significant association between reading *The Sun* and the practice of solidarity with each vulnerable group, except for those within the UK. Moreover, reading the *Daily Mail* is positively associated with solidarity towards the unemployed and the disabled. These results are surprising given the conservative leaning history of both publications; consequently, there is perhaps some scope to consider that although content of course matters, our findings suggest the difference between reading and not reading a newspaper appears to be the key determinant in mobilising solidarity in the UK. Given the migration of much political debate in recent years from the analogue world of newspapers to the digital world of social media, with research indicating that even newspapers themselves are utilising social media as a resource for political news gathering (Broersma and Graham 2012), we can speculate, as an avenue for further research, that it is through online media that we may find associations between specific media preferences and asymmetric distributions of solidarity towards vulnerable groups.

Concerning our hypothesis of direct exposure or experience of vulnerability, in Table 4.4 we see that that the disabled are positively and significantly associated with solidarity practices across each of the geographic areas and all other vulnerable groups. The exposure of disabled people to multidimensional forms of discrimination and inequalities may provide a cross-societal insight into the hardships suffered by different groups (EHRC 2017). We can speculate that the importance of rights-based discourses among disabled people's organisations and in a similar way with disability charities in the UK may create the conditions for intersectionality between the disabled and other groups seeking rights, protection, and indeed solidarity. Moreover, the 'social model of disability' (Oliver et al. 2012) embraced by a number of disabled people's organisations has frequently recognised injustices and inequalities in society which impact upon groups other than the disabled. Subsequently, our findings regarding the disposition of the disabled towards supporting other groups may open an avenue to consider an alternative explanation as to why the disabled are viewed as most deserving, as outlined earlier in this chapter, but instead of paternalistic attitudes through a sense of reciprocity. This may seem a less convincing argument for explaining attitudes towards the disabled in the UK, but our findings require us to consider it in the scope of our interpretation.

Still on the individual-level characteristics, Table 4.4 confirms our hypothesis about level of satisfaction with life as a factor being positively related with solidarity: the happier about her/his life conditions a person is, the more she/he will likely be ready to support less fortunate people and vice versa (Borgonovi 2008). Therefore, life satisfaction acts as a pro-altruism factor that discourages people from considering those in need as potential competitors for services and state support.

Looking at the other findings of our regressions in Table 4.4, we can see that the divergences of solidarity between the different constituent nations in the UK outlined earlier in this chapter are confirmed by our regressions. Our results indicate that living in Scotland, in comparison to living in England, is positively and significantly associated with expressing greater solidarity with others within the UK and those living outside the EU. Moreover, we can see that living in Scotland compared to England is also positively and significantly associated with solidarity towards each of our three vulnerable groups. Furthermore, our results indicate that living in Northern Ireland in comparison to England also renders a significant and positive association with undertaking solidarity practices towards refugees and the disabled. Therefore, our regressions do provide further evidence of a significant divergence in the disposition of individuals to engage in practices of solidarity. Consequently, we can hypothesise that these divergences will stay in place should devolved administrations remain sensitive to the support evident within their constituent nations and have the potential to grow wider should policies and discourses at the Westminster level increasingly contrast with these solidaristic dispositions and become more antagonistic towards vulnerable groups. As Keating (2003) points out, the use of values can be central in the construction of identity, and he argues that territorial solidarity was more effective in confronting Thatcherism than class solidarity. Therefore, should a post-Brexit Britain continue to travel down a road of welfare retrenchment and discourses distinguishing between the deserving and undeserving, there may be irreversible constitutional consequences for the UK. This is particularly relevant for Scotland where research has indicated the potential for social policy divergence to open opportunities to reconfigure solidarity and shared values around a (Scottish) national identity of 'difference' rather than the solidarity of a retrenched British welfare state (McEwen 2002) and where the Scottish government has, post-Brexit, called for a second referendum on independence.

Finally, we need to consider another finding relating to the role of identity in solidarity. In fact, being born in the UK is another variable which yields the type of findings which have strong implications for the composition of solidarity in the UK. As we can see in Table 4.4, there is a significant and negative relationship between those individuals who are born in the UK and solidarity with those groups from outside the UK, whether in the EU or not. Such findings suggest that solidarity among those who are British born tends to be inward looking and that policies towards refugees that emphasise border control rather than welcoming asylum do have a constituency in the UK. Thus, our findings perhaps represent the other side of the coin when we are considering those initiatives which are geared towards offering sanctuary to those seeking asylum. Perhaps somewhat surprisingly however, among that same group—those born in the UK—there is also a significant and negative association with solidarity with the disabled. This stands in sharp contrast to the hierarchy of solidarity we set out earlier in this chapter, but we can speculate that those born in the UK may be more likely to view support for the disabled as the remit of the welfare state. If this is the explanation, then it is concerning because as austerity measures have affected the benefits which disabled people have been entitled to, public services have also come under budgetary pressures and, as a consequence, there is the potential for the hardship experienced by disabled people to be somewhat overlooked by those born in the UK who believe that the welfare state would act as a safety net, reinforced by the stigma experienced by disabled benefit claimants who retreat from social circles in order to avoid 'revealing' that they are claiming benefits (Garthwaite 2015). A further consideration based on our finding is that those who are not born in the UK may be more solidaristic towards the disabled and we can speculate that, particularly given the discourses of border control in the UK, those not born in the UK may empathise with others who are cast as 'outsiders' by discourses and policy.

Conclusions

In this chapter we have sought to uncover how solidarity, through active engagement in support of specific groups of people in need, is practised in contemporary Britain. What the analysis of our data reveals is that solidarity is unevenly distributed in terms of geography and the vulnerabilities of different groups. Our findings resonate to some extent with existing research (van Oorschot 2006), suggesting deep-rooted patterns of deservingness and established hierarchies across Europe when considering solidarity with vulnerable groups such as the disabled, refugees, and the unemployed. As such, our findings offer a further contribution to this body of literature, but they also present a contemporary and novel insight into how solidarity is distributed across the constituent nations of the UK, where we have observed some divergence, but also how policies and discourses in post-crisis, post-Brexit Britain may be shaping attitudes towards the three vulnerable groups and thus play a role in constructing the hierarchy of solidarity we have set out in Fig. 4.1. Nevertheless, when we factor in our independent variables, a more complex picture emerges, one that does not disprove the existence of our hierarchy of solidarity but suggests that the hierarchy is less static than we may imagine and is made more malleable when we introduce our independent variables. The findings which then emerge point towards talking not only of hierarchies of solidarity but fluid hierarchies of solidarity which can change shape and reflect a more diverse distribution of solidarity than our initial findings suggest. This fluidity is underpinned by the asymmetric significance of our variables which reveal that access to information (through newspaper readership), exposure to vulnerability (through disability), the experience of higher education, and the interaction with others through social networks are key determinants of solidarity in the UK. As a consequence, we can confirm our hypothesis that the distribution of solidarity is determined by the exposure of an individual to vulnerabilities similar to those experienced by those categories, to their degree of exposure to opportunities of socialisation and information sharing (social networks), as well as to their interest in societal and political issues.

In terms of the distribution of solidarity practices across the UK, our findings confirm our hypothesis of the existence of sub-national divergences. Such divergences suggest a more nuanced understanding of the variegated impact of discourses of deservingness and their commensurate policies beyond traditional welfare regime analysis. This opens the possibility for a renewed research agenda on regional and sub-national distinctiveness across Europe in terms of social solidarity. Any divergences will be relevant to developing a more fine-grained analysis across each context, but perhaps such an approach, as we have outlined in this chapter, is currently most relevant in the UK where such divergences may prove critical in determining the constitutional future of the British state, particularly given our findings that solidarity is most evident in two constituent nations which voted to remain part of the EU: Scotland where there are renewed calls by the SNP for another independence referendum and Northern Ireland where Sinn Fein have called for a poll on a united Ireland. Therefore, understanding solidarity towards vulnerable groups offers an insight not only into the nature of solidarity in contemporary Britain but also provides an indication of the challenges faced by the UK government elected in June 2017.

APPENDIX

Original survey question and coding	Recoding of variable	% distributions in the sample
Have you ever done one of the following in order to support the rights of people/groups in your own country? supotherc_7: none of the above	Individual has done at least one of the following (i.e. some form of political action) in order to support the rights of people/groups in your own country (1/0) supotherc11 = 1: at least one of the above	0 = 61.74 1 = 38.26
Have you ever done one of the following in order to support the rights of people/groups in other countries within the European Union? supEU_7: none of the above	Individual has done at least one of the following (i.e. some form of political action) in order to support the rights of people/groups in other countries within the European Union supEU11 = 1: at least one of the above	0 = 81.52 1 = 18.48
Have you ever done one of the following in order to support the rights of people/groups in countries outside the European Union? supoutsideEU_7: none of the above	Individual has done at least one of the following (i.e. some form of political action) in order to support the rights of people/groups in countries outside the European Union? supoutsideEU11 = 1: at least one of the above	0 = 74.94 1 = 25.06
Have you ever done any of the following in order to support the rights of refugees/asylum seekers? refsup_7: none of the above	Individual has done at least one of the following (i.e. some form of political action) in order to support the rights of refugees/asylum seekers? Refsup11 = 1: at least one of the above	0 = 78.59 1 = 21.41
Have you ever done any of the following in order to support the rights of the unemployed? unemprights_7: none of the above	Individual has done at least one of the following (i.e. some form of political action) in order to support the rights of the unemployed? unemprights11 = 1: at least one of the above	0 = 81.47 1 = 18.53
Have you ever done any of the following in order to support disability rights? dissup_7: none of the above	Individual has done at least one of the following (i.e. some form of political action) in order to support disability rights dissup11 = 1: at least one of the above	0 = 65.63 1 = 34.37
Age	Age2: age squared	

Original survey question and coding	Recoding of variable	% distributions in the sample
Are you male or female?	0 = male	0 = 48.74
	1 = female	1 = 51.26
Education level	0 = higher education	0 = 29.95
	1 = intermediate education	1 = 33.84
	2 = lower education	2 = 36.20
In what region of the UK do you live?	1 = England	1 = 84.54
	2 = Scotland	2 = 8.50
	3 = Wales	3 = 4.66
	4 = Northern Ireland	4 = 2.30
What you have been doing for the past seven days?	Unemployed = 1 if main act = 5–6	0 = 95.01
		1 = 4.99
Would you consider yourself to have a disability?	0 = not disabled	0 = 82.73
	1 = disabled	1 = 17.27
Were you born in the UK?	0 = no	0 = 9.84
	1 = yes	1 = 90.16
How do you keep yourself informed about current events?		
Daily Mail	0 = no	0 = 78.75
	1 = yes	1 = 21.25
The Sun	0 = no	0 = 87.79
	1 = yes	1 = 12.21
The Times	0 = no	0 = 90.55
	1 = yes	1 = 9.45
The Guardian	0 = no	0 = 89.36
	1 = yes	1 = 10.64
Daily Mirror	0 = no	0 = 92.04
	1 = yes	1 = 7.96

Original survey question and coding	Recoding of variable	% distributions in the sample
Other papers	0 = no 1 = yes	0 = 84.60 1 = 15.40
I don't read any newspaper regularly (three plus days a week)	0 = no 1 = yes	0 = 54.06 1 = 45.94
Met socially with friends during the past month	0 = less than once this month 1 = at least once this month	0 = 25.97 1 = 74.03
How satisfied or dissatisfied are you with your life?	Likert scale where: 0 = completely dissatisfied 10 = completely satisfied	0 = 1.66 1 = 1.50 2 = 2.77 3 = 3.67 4 = 6.41 5 = 13.55 6 = 12.90 7 = 23.77 8 = 19.33 9 = 9.35 10 = 5.10

NOTES

1. This involved a national reassessment process that was piloted in 2010 and rolled out in 2011 with the objective of reassessing all claimants for ESA (formerly known as Incapacity Benefit) through a 'Work Capability Assessment' by Spring 2014 which resulted in 750,000 assessments being conducted in 2013 alone (see Baumberg et al. 2015).
2. A reduction applied to the Housing Benefit of social housing tenants (14% if they have one spare bedroom and 25% if they have two or more spare bedrooms) that disproportionately affected disabled people despite measures introduced ('discretionary housing payments') to mitigate the impact (See Gibb 2015; Wilcox 2014).

REFERENCES

Baumberg, B., Warren, J., Garthwaite, K., & Bambra, C. (2015). *Rethinking The Work Capability Assessment*. London: Demos.

Bew, P. (2007). *The Making and Remaking of the Good Friday Agreement*. Dublin, Ireland: Liffey Press.

Blekesaune, M., & Quadagno, J. (2003). Public Attitudes Toward Welfare State Policies: A Comparative Analysis of 24 Nations. *European Sociological Review*, *19*(5), 415–427.

Borgonovi, F. (2008). Doing Well by Doing Good. The Relationship Between Formal Volunteering and Self-Reported Health and Happiness. *Social Science & Medicine*, *66*(11), 2321–2334.

Briant, E., Watson, N., & Philo, G. (2011). *Bad News for Disabled People: How the Newspapers Are Reporting Disability*. Project Report. Strathclyde Centre for Disability Research and Glasgow Media Unit, University of Glasgow, Glasgow, UK.

Broersma, M., & Graham, T. (2012). Social Media as Beat: Tweets as a News Source During the 2010 British and Dutch Elections. *Journalism Practice*, *6*(3), 403–419.

Carmichael, F., Hulme, C., Sheppard, S., & Connell, G. (2008). Work–Life Imbalance: Informal Care and Paid Employment in the UK. *Feminist Economics*, *14*(2), 3–35.

Dunn, A., Grasso, M. T., & Saunders, C. (2014). Unemployment and Attitudes to Work: Asking the 'Right' Question. *Work, Employment, and Society*, *28*(6), 904–925.

Durkheim, E. (1893 [2014]). *The Division of Labour in Society*. Simon and Schuster.

English, P., Grasso, M. T., Buraczynska, B., Karampampas, S., & Temple, L. (2016). Convergence on Crisis? Comparing Labour and Conservative Party

Framing of the Economic Crisis in Britain, 2008–2014. *Politics & Policy, 44*(3), 577–603.

Equality and Human Rights Commission. (2017). *Being Disabled in Britain: A Journey Less Equal.*

Gardiner, L. (2016). *Votey McVoteface: Understanding the Growing Turnout Gap Between the Generations.* London: Resolution Foundation.

Garthwaite, K. (2015). 'Keeping Meself to Meself'—How Social Networks Can Influence Narratives of Stigma and Identity for Long-Term Sickness Benefits Recipients. *Social Policy & Administration, 49*(2), 199–212.

Gibb, K. (2015). The Multiple Policy Failures of the UK Bedroom Tax. *International Journal of Housing Policy, 15*(2), 148–166.

Giugni, M., & Grasso, M. T. (2015). Environmental Movements in Advanced Industrial Democracies: Heterogeneity, Transformation, and Institutionalization. *Annual Review of Environment and Resources, 40*, 337–361.

Golding, P., & Middleton, S. (1982). *Images of Welfare: Press and Public Attitudes to Poverty.* Oxford: Robertson.

Grasso, M. T. (2013). The Differential Impact of Education on Young People's Political Activism: Comparing Italy and the United Kingdom. *Comparative Sociology, 12*(1), 1–30.

Grasso, M. T. (2016). *Generations, Political Participation and Social Change in Western Europe.* London: Routledge.

Grasso, M. T. (2017). Young People's Political Participation in Times of Crisis. In S. Pickard & J. Bessant (Eds.), *Young People Regenerating Politics in Times of Crisis.* London: Palgrave Macmillan.

Grasso, M. T., & Giugni, M. (2016). Protest Participation and Economic Crisis: The Conditioning Role of Political Opportunities. *European Journal of Political Research, 55*(4), 663–680.

Grasso, M. T., Farrall, S., Gray, E., Hay, C., & Jennings, W. (2017). Thatcher's Children, Blair's Babies, Political Socialisation and Trickle-Down Value-Change: An Age, Period and Cohort Analysis. *British Journal of Political Science.* https://doi.org/10.1017/S0007123416000375.

Greenslade, R. (2005). *Seeking Scapegoats: The Coverage of Asylum in the UK Press.* Institute for Public Policy Research.

Hall, P. A. (1999). Social Capital in Britain. *British Journal of Political Science, 29*(3), 417–461.

Hobolt, S. B. (2016). The Brexit Vote: A Divided Nation, a Divided Continent. *Journal of European Public Policy, 23*(9), 1259–1277.

Johns, R., & Mitchell, J. (2016). *Takeover: Explaining the Extraordinary Rise of the SNP.* London: Biteback.

Keating, M. (2003). Social Inclusion, Devolution and Policy Divergence. *The Political Quarterly, 74*(4), 429–438.

Kellas, J. G. (1989). *The Scottish Political System.* Cambridge University Press.

Li, Y., Pickles, A., & Savage, M. (2005). Social Capital and Social Trust in Britain. *European Sociological Review, 21*(2), 109–123.

Lijphart, A. (2012). *Patterns of Democracy: Government Forms and Performance in Thirty-Six Countries*. Yale University Press.

MacDonald, R., Shildrick, T., & Furlong, A. (2014a). In Search of 'Intergenerational Cultures of Worklessness': Hunting the Yeti and Shooting Zombies. *Critical Social Policy, 34*(2), 199–220.

MacDonald, R., Shildrick, T., & Furlong, A. (2014b). 'Benefits Street' and the Myth of Workless Communities. *Sociological Research Online, 19*(3), 1.

Macwhirter, I. (2014). *Road to Referendum*. Glasgow: Cargo Publishing.

Mallie, E., & McKittrick, D. (1996). *The Fight for Peace*. London: Heinemann.

Maloney, W., Smith, G., & Stoker, G. (2000). Social Capital and Urban Governance: Adding a More Contextualized 'Top-Down' Perspective. *Political Studies, 48*(4), 802–820.

McCrudden, C. (1998). Mainstreaming Equality in the Governance of Northern Ireland. *Fordham Int'l LJ, 22*, 1696.

McEwen, N. (2002). State Welfare Nationalism: The Territorial Impact of Welfare State Development in Scotland. *Regional & Federal Studies, 12*(1), 66–90.

McGarry, J., & O'Leary, B. (2004). *The Northern Ireland Conflict: Consociational Engagements*. Oxford University Press on Demand.

Midwinter, A., Keating, M., & Mitchell, J. (1991). *Politics and Public Policy in Scotland*. London: Macmillan.

Mooney, G., & Poole, L. (2004). A Land of Milk and Honey? Social Policy in Scotland After Devolution. *Critical Social Policy, 24*(4), 458–483.

O'Hara, M. (2014). *Austerity Bites*. Policy Press.

Oliver, M., Sapey, B., & Thomas, P. (2012). *Social Work with Disabled People*. Palgrave Macmillan.

van Oorschot, W. (2000). Who Should Get What, and Why? On Deservingness Criteria and the Conditionality of Solidarity Among the Public. *Policy & Politics, 28*(1), 33–48.

van Oorschot, W. (2006). Making the Difference in Social Europe: Deservingness Perceptions Among Citizens of European Welfare States. *Journal of European Social Policy, 16*(1), 23–42.

Putnam, R. D. (2001). *Bowling Alone: The Collapse and Revival of American Community*. Simon and Schuster.

Sales, R. (2002). The Deserving and the Undeserving? Refugees, Asylum Seekers and Welfare in Britain. *Critical Social Policy, 22*(3), 456–478.

Sinclair, S., McKendrick, J. H., & Kelly, P. (2009). Taking the High Road? Media and Public Attitudes Toward Poverty in Scotland. *Scottish Affairs, 67*(1), 70–91.

Squire, V. (2008). Accounting for the Dominance of Control: Inter-Party Dynamics and Restrictive Asylum Policy in Contemporary Britain. *British Politics, 3*(2), 241–261.

Squire, V. (2011). From Community Cohesion to Mobile Solidarities: The City of Sanctuary Network and the Strangers into Citizens Campaign. *Political Studies, 59*(2), 290–307.

Squire, V. (2016). *The Exclusionary Politics of Asylum*. Springer.

Statham, P., & Geddes, A. (2006). Elites and the 'Organised Public': Who Drives British Immigration Politics and in Which Direction? *West European Politics, 29*(2), 248–269.

Temple, L., & Grasso, M. T. (2017). Austerity, Politics, and Partisanship in the UK. In M. Giugni & M. T. Grasso (Eds.), *Citizens and the Crisis: Perceptions, Experiences, and Responses to the Great Recession in Europe*. London: Palgrave Macmillan.

Temple, L., Grasso, M. T., Buraczynska, B., Karampampas, S., & English, P. (2016). Neoliberal Narrative in Times of Economic Crisis: A Political Claims Analysis of the UK Press, 2007–2014. *Politics & Policy, 44*(3), 553–576.

Thompson, E. P. (1963 [2016]). *The Making of the English Working Class*. Open Road Media.

Tonge, J. (2000). From Sunningdale to the Good Friday Agreement: Creating Devolved Government in Northern Ireland. *Contemporary British History, 14*(3), 39–60.

Tonge, J. (2002). *Northern Ireland: Conflict and Change*. Pearson Education.

Torrance, D. (2013). *The Battle for Britain*. London: Biteback Publishing.

Van Oorschot, W., & Arts, W. (2005). The Social Capital of European Welfare States: The Crowding Out Hypothesis Revisited. *Journal of European Social Policy, 15*(1), 5–26.

Verba, S., Schlozman, K. L., & Brady, H. E. (1995). *Voice and Equality: Civic Voluntarism in American Politics*. Harvard University Press.

Wiggan, J. (2012). Telling Stories of 21st Century Welfare: The UK Coalition Government and the Neo-Liberal Discourse of Worklessness and Dependency. *Critical Social Policy, 32*(3), 383–405.

Wilcox, S. (2014). *Housing Benefit Size Criteria: Impacts for Social Sector Tenants and Options for Reform*. York: Joseph Rowntree Foundation.

Open Access   This chapter is licensed under the terms of the Creative Commons Attribution 4.0 International License (http://creativecommons.org/licenses/by/4.0/), which permits use, sharing, adaptation, distribution and reproduction in any medium or format, as long as you give appropriate credit to the original author(s) and the source, provide a link to the Creative Commons license and indicate if changes were made.

The images or other third party material in this chapter are included in the chapter's Creative Commons license, unless indicated otherwise in a credit line to the material. If material is not included in the chapter's Creative Commons license and your intended use is not permitted by statutory regulation or exceeds the permitted use, you will need to obtain permission directly from the copyright holder.

CHAPTER 5

Solidarity Practices in Poland and Their Social Capital Foundations

Anna Kurowska and Maria Theiss

INTRODUCTION

Poland is a country where the idea of solidarity is primarily associated with the "Solidarity" social movement which had a substantial influence on political change and democratization (Krzemiński 2010; Staniszkis 2010). However, while "Solidarity" as a movement and as a value was very important in the times of the fall of the communist system, the subsequent transformation period is often perceived as a "defeat of Solidarity" (Ost 2006), both in the institutional and attitudinal dimensions of public life. A significant literature points to low levels of social solidarity in Poland which is often linked to a relatively weak civic tradition and faint social capital, in particular trust (Giza et al. 2000; Czapiński 2006; Gliński 2006; Szymczak 2008).

The mentioned bulk of literature and its findings refer to the societal and, foremostly, the civic aspect of social transformation in Poland shortly after the fall of communism. However, contemporary political and economic changes both in Poland and other EU countries call for newer insights into the problems of solidarity in Poland. The economic crisis of

A. Kurowska • M. Theiss (✉)
Institute of Social Policy, University of Warsaw, Warsaw, Poland

© The Author(s) 2018
C. Lahusen, M. Grasso (eds.), *Solidarity in Europe*,
Palgrave Studies in European Political Sociology,
https://doi.org/10.1007/978-3-319-73335-7_5

2008, the influx of refugees to Southern European countries and the relocation policy of the EU, as well as political changes in Poland create a new context for solidarity attitudes and practices. Moreover, the conservative government of Law and Justice, which has been governing since 2015, manifestly uses the rhetoric of solidarity limited exclusively to Polish compatriots, combined with little charity for people suffering in conflicts abroad. As Bartkowski (2014) shows, although deterioration of international solidarity and rise of political egocentric attitudes are Europe-wide, they manifest in Poland intensively. His study provides evidence that solidarity within close family ties and within national polity has recently strengthened in Poland, on the contrary to transnational solidarity. Thus, both Polish specificity which encompasses traditionally low level of social trust (Domański 2009: 142–175), relatively weak social capital measured by density of civil society organizations and associations, and recent political narratives pose significant tensions to solidarity nowadays. This refers in particular to transnational solidarity—the solidarity action with people living abroad.

In this chapter, adding to the literature on political solidarity (rather than to the dominant discussion on social solidarity within institutions of welfare state), we make an insight into three types of solidarity practices and we investigate their geographical scope. We show the frequency of *protesting, donating time* and *donating money* in order to support the rights of the three different groups of addressees: *the compatriots, the people in other EU member states* and *the people in countries outside the EU*. We look at these aspects with the lens of three basic socio-demographic characteristics: gender, age and education. Further, we also make an analytical insight into the area of relations between individuals' social capital in Poland and these solidarity practices. Since Poland has been portrayed in scholarly literature as a country of low "civic" social capital and of strong familialistic bonds (Guasti 2016; Jakubowska and Kaniasty 2014; Czapiński 2014), as well as a country focused on in-group solidarity (Gliński 2006), we pose a question whether this specific post-communist legacy of social capital affects solidarity practices of Poles. In particular, we explore the role of bonding and bridging social capital in shaping solidarity behaviors in general, specifically its impact on transnational solidarity action.

In the first section of this chapter, we present understanding of solidarity as individuals' practice and discuss its linkages to the types of social capital in the context of a post-communist country. In the second section, the operationalization of transnational solidarity and social capital is presented. The third section of the chapter provides the overview of solidarity practices in its mentioned forms, toward three basic groups of addressees. In the fourth section, we present results of the logistic regression analysis with the use of which we aim to explain how generalized and transnational solidarity are related to diverse aspects of social capital. We conclude in the last section of the chapter emphasizing specific constellations of bonding and bridging social capital which contribute to solidarity practices in Poland

STRUCTURAL AND NORMATIVE SOURCES OF SOLIDARITY ACTION: THE CASE OF A POST-COMMUNIST COUNTRY

Despite the variety of meanings attributed to solidarity—of moral value, societal ideal, individual attitude or collective behavior—researchers tend to agree that its core understanding refers to the type of action. For example, Kolers (2012) notices that solidarity is fundamentally neither sentiment nor attitude but a type of action which is associative and teleological: it means working with others for common political aims. Given the multidimensionality of solidarity and various traditions of its understanding, it is useful to provide an analytical definition of solidarity practice. According to Sangiovanni (2015), solidarity differs from other types of collective action in regard to five aspects. Firstly, A acts in solidarity with B when A and B *share the goal to overcome some significant adversity*, although no joint agency of A and B is obligatory. Secondly, both *ways of A and B to achieve the goal mesh*. Thirdly, a *commitment of A and B to the goal is needed* which means that if A is involved in activity only for financial reasons, it may not be acknowledged as solidarity practice. This criterion, however, does not exclude pragmatic concerns of solidarity. Fourthly, A and B are *disposed to incur significant costs* to realize the goal. This assumes that A's action may not be meaningless to A to be recognized as a solidarity practice. And finally, features of action of A and B are not a common knowledge, which undertakes that *A and B may act "in parallel"* not knowing about each other; A's action is not conditioned upon what B does. Although Sangiovanni's definition is coined for the sake of welfare state analysis, it seems that so defined solidarity practice may be applied to various circumstances and may take a form of either *robust solidarity (solidarity with a group)* or *expressional solidarity (solidarity toward a group)*. The first one is perceived as moving people toward a collective action, as it is based on multidirectional relationships and includes joint interest, identification with a group and disposition to empathy. It is close to a notion of *social solidarity* (Bang 2015). The latter is founded on unidirectional relationship and entails action toward distant others and resembles *political solidarity* which is rather connective than collectivist in its nature (Bang, ibid.). Taylor (2015) interprets this form of solidarity as coherent with Gould's (2007) account of transnational solidarity meaning "supportive relations we can come to develop with people at a distance" these relations being "aimed at supporting people in overcoming oppression" (Taylor 2015: 129).

Since solidarity as a practice needs to be understood and analyzed within a broader cultural, political and economic setting (Bartkowski 2014; Lahusen 2016), in this chapter we locate solidarity action within specific meso-level social feature of the society, namely, *social capital*. In the subsequent section of the chapter, we propose a method of how to measure it. In general, we understand it as a set of social networks (or more broadly: social structures) and norms which may result in solidarity action(s). Thus, our account of social capital follows classical approaches which point to the role of its structural and normative components (Coleman 1988; Grootaert and van Bastelaer 2002; Putnam 2002: 9). In theory, the structural component of social capital entails relations and individuals' memberships in formal and informal social networks. The normative element of social capital includes values, beliefs and attitudes of a person, such as generalized trust, openness, a custom to act with others in a reciprocal manner, moral obligation to help the people in need, and so on. Both components may mutually reinforce—for example, the more various social contacts one has, the more she or he can be trusting others, and consequently the more prone to solidarity action he/she can be (Grootaert and van Bastelaer 2002; Narayan and Cassidy 2001).

The reasons for employing social capital perspective in this chapter are, firstly, of theoretical manner and, secondly, related to scientific discourse about the communist heritage in Poland which is considered to be harmful for social capital.

The theoretical connection between social capital and solidarity has already been acknowledged in the scientific literature[1] (Portes 1998; Putnam 2000). As Lahusen (2016: 5) emphasizes, the analysis of solidarity can benefit from studies on social capital, which converge on the conviction that social capital is a necessary "glue" of social cohesion and thus essential for understanding the conditions and structures of solidarity. More specifically, from social capital scholarship, two stances emerge which are relevant for research on solidarity. We label the first one as a thesis about the *consequences of the level of social capital*. According to this argument, the more dense and diverse the social networks of an individual are, as well as the more trusting a person is, the more prone he or she is to get involved in cooperative behavior (Coleman 1988) and—consequently—in solidarity action.

The second stance may be labeled as a thesis on the *consequences of the type of social capital*. It assumes that the type of structural and normative elements of social capital affects individual's propensity to engage in solidarity action. Two types of social capital are differentiated in this context. The so-called bonding or thick social capital is based on relatively homogenous relations with family and friends. It entails strong norms of mutual support and thus might be exclusive. It is claimed that, for example, closed self-help groups may be based on this type of social capital and due to the effects of this form of social capital is named by some authors an "inward-looking" social capital. Extreme form of this asset is close to traditional familialism (Banfield 1967; Portes 1998). On the other hand, the so-called bridging social capital, based on horizontal, crosscutting social networks and values of openness and generalized trust, positively contributes to social cooperation and public good at a systemic level (Putnam et al. 1994; Granovetter 1973).

When explaining causal mechanism which constitutes relation between social capital and solidarity action, a more general framework of its role in shaping political participation may be referred to. Following van Stekelenburg and Klandermans (2013), three mechanisms arising from diverse components of social capital may be pointed to in this regard. Firstly, the *structural element* of social capital refers to whom people can reach in actions of political participation. For example, engaging time to support the rights of refugees living in the camp in one's country may result from personal networks to volunteers already engaged in helping this group. Secondly, the *relational component* of social capital refers to informational, physical and emotional incentives toward solidarity action. Thus, the bigger and more diverse one's personal network is, the more information one has about, for example, significant adversity that other people are experiencing, methods of action to engage in help, possibilities to pool resources for action. Finally, the *cognitive element* encompasses shared representations, interpretations, systems of meaning—it may lead to consciousness raising or shaping one's political beliefs. This aspect of social embeddedness contributes to individuals' beliefs about whose and which rights may primarily need support and what kind of broader societal goals need to be achieved thanks to solidarity action.

Combining mentioned mechanisms with the *type* of social capital suggests each of them, comprising specific structures and societal values, is a trigger of different forms of solidarity action. Thus, homogenous personal ties, including strong bonds to family members and friends, accompanied by norms of involvement in the issues of family and/or close community which constitute bonding social capital would rather result in *solidarity with a group*. On the contrary, a diversified social network, including one's connections to people of different class, origins, both with disabilities and able-bodied, which provide knowledge about various forms of significant adversity which other people may experience would have a different effect. These structures and values representing Putnamian ideal would rather bring about *solidarity toward a group*, including transnational solidarity.

Clearly, the sketched framework serves only as a theoretical reference point. Empirical studies speak for much more nuanced relations between social structure, values and solidarity practices. They include, for example, Segall's (2005) study challenging positive impact of political participation on solidarity or Bang's (2004) claim to revise Putnamian approach of political participation being anchored in political virtues, since in everyday lives of contemporary citizens, "lighter" version of political engagement in building and running various governance networks comes to the fore. However, as noted, social capital perspective seems specifically relevant to research of solidarity in the Polish context. Both societal and academic debate about systematic transformation of Poland after the fall of communism tends to emphasize the "social capital problem" in Poland (Giza et al. 2000). Namely, it has been argued that civic participation and generalized trust in Poland are very low although typical of post-communist country (see e.g. Guasti 2016; Jakubowska and Kaniasty 2014; Czapiński 2014). This stance has been recently challenged, though. Firstly, it is claimed that vibrant examples of social capital have been overlooked due to methodological Occidentalism of dominant civil society studies (Jacobsson and Korolczuk 2017; Tworzecki 2008). Secondly, it is emphasized that on the contrary to Putnamian model, church-related activism does not result in withdrawal from public engagement and depicts important form of political participation in Poland (Żukowski and Theiss 2009). Thirdly, recent massive protests against populist and conservative turn in Polish public policy after Law and Justice came into power in 2015 prove high potential of massive political mobilization in Poland (see Karolewski 2016).

Thus, we follow "bonding" and "bridging" social capital distinction in a somewhat provocative manner, rather referring to debate which emphasizes high level of familialism (bonding social capital) in Poland than assuming that mentioned dichotomy may be regarded as justified social sciences category. Against this backdrop, our focus is to differentiate between the structures and social norms which are labeled as "bonding" social capital and the structures, actions and values referred as to "bridging" social capital. Our research questions focus on the impact of these two phenomena on solidarity behaviors both in general and specifically at transnational level. As noted, in particular we aim at explaining the relation between structures and values inherent in different types of social capital and different scopes of solidarity action. Central to our investigation are the questions: which social networks and values contribute to solidarity actions in general? But foremost—which contribute to solidarity with people abroad? Building on the presented literature, we hypothesize that (1) bonding social capital (based on family and friendship ties) has a negative impact on solidarity with addressees of international scope and (2) bridging social capital (generalized trust and civic engagement) has positive impact on solidarity behaviors, in particular in regard to behaviors with international scope of addressees.

Measuring Individual Transnational Solidarity: Methods and Data

The sample used for our analysis consists of 2119 respondents from Poland, gathered in an international survey carried out within the framework of TransSOL project (for more details about the survey—see the Introduction to this book). The basic socio-demographic characteristics of this group are provided in Table 5.1. The sample is representative for all age groups. Each age group consists of over 200 respondents, which exceeds 10 percent of the total population. The largest group consists of respondents aged between 55 and 64 years old, and the smallest group consists of the youngest group of adults below 25 years old. The educational structure of the Polish population of adults (people 18 years old and older) is also closely reflected in our sample. It is presented with the account of a very detailed set of categories. These categories are similar to

Table 5.1 Socio-demographic characteristics of Polish respondents in TransSOL survey

	Number of respondents	% in the weighted sample
Gender		
Female	1107	47.7
Male	1012	52.3
Age groups		
18–24	221	10.4
25–34	395	18.6
35–44	402	19.0
45–54	336	15.9
55–64	514	24.2
65 and older	252	11.9
Education		
Primary education or less	33	1.5
Lower secondary education	42	2.0
Vocational upper secondary education	432	20.4
Post-secondary education with access to tertiary	1048	49.5
Post-secondary-non-tertiary	172	8.1
Short-cycle (3–4 years) tertiary education	40	1.9
Long-cycle (4+ years) tertiary education	111	5.2
Master's equivalent education	232	11.0
Doctoral or equivalent level	9	0.4

Notes: Frequencies and percentages are calculated with the use of variable: weight_country. This applies to all the tables in this chapter

the ISCED (International Standard Classification of Education) seven categories of education levels (UNESCO 1997).

According to the twofold goal of this chapter, its first section has a descriptive character and aims at presenting the frequency of three different types of solidarity behaviors/practices toward three groups of addressees in detail, that is, among groups identified on the base of the distributions of three basic socio-demographic variables such as gender, age and education. In order to present these frequencies, we use three responses for three questions from the TransSOL survey. All the questions were formulated similarly—"Have you ever done one of the following in order to support the rights of people/groups in …?"—but ended up referring to three different groups of addressees of the support, that is, people/groups in respondent's own country, in other countries within the EU and in countries outside the EU. The responses which we conceptualize as three different types of solidarity behaviors/practices were (a) attended a march, protest or demonstration, (b) donated money and (c) donated time.

The second section of this chapter explores the role of these sociodemographic determinants, as well as the role of two types of social capital based on close family and friendship ties (bonding social capital) and on civic-associational ties (bridging social capital), on the propensity of Poles to engage in mentioned solidarity practices. As a *generalized solidarity* behavior, we label *any* form of the three researched solidarity activities (i.e. protest activity, time donation and money donation) to support the rights of people in *any* location (in respondent's country, other EU countries or in other countries outside the EU). In this section we also explore the impact of the same determinants for the propensity of solidaristic Poles (the subgroup that had engaged in any form of solidarity behavior) to engage specifically in transnational solidarity. As *transnational solidarity*, we understand the support either for people from other EU countries or (and) other countries outside EU. In order to achieve both aims, we estimate two separate logistic regression models. The first model uses the full sample of Polish respondents, and the second model is run on the subsample of Poles who engage in any form of solidarity behavior.

In order to operationalize the two types of social capital as explanatory variables, we use a series of questions included in TransSOL survey which we divide into two blocks, according to the type of social capital. In the group of indicators of "bonding social capital", we include four indicators. Firstly, *contacts with friends*—a quasi-continuous variable, based on the survey question: "During the past month, how often have you met socially with friends not living in your household?" The answers included four frequencies to choose from: less than once this month (1); once or twice this month (2); every week (3); almost every day (4). Secondly, *contacts with family*—a binary variable based on the survey question: "Please say if each of the following do or do not apply to you: I have seen a family member over the last six months (other than my parents or children)?" The answers included yes (1)/no (0) option only. Thirdly, *formalized family ties*—which was created on the base of marital status variable in the survey, from which we identified respondents who were married or in civil/legally registered union as being in a formalized relationship (1). And finally, *receiving help in community*—a quasi-continuous variable, based on the question: "In the past 12 months, how often did you get help such as getting a lift with someone, help in looking after children, having shopping done, having something repaired at your house etc.?" The answers included four frequencies to choose from: less than once this month (1); once or twice this month (2); every week (3); almost every day (4).

In the group of "bridging social capital", we included five variables: *membership in civil society organization(s)* (any type of membership[2] in any organization from the list provided in the TransSOL survey[3]). Secondly, a *generalized trust level*—a quasi-continuous variable which was based on the survey question: "Generally speaking, would you say that most people can be trusted, or that you can't be too careful in dealing with people?" to which the answers included an 11-point scale where 0 indicated an attitude "You can't be too careful" and 10 "Most people can be trusted". Thirdly, *political participation in the form of voting*—a binary variable which was based on the question: "Did you vote in the national election October 25, 2015?" The answers included yes (1)/no (0) option only. Furthermore, we included—*local attachment*, which we understood as an aspect of local citizenship—a binary variable which was constructed on the base of the answers "very attached" to the question: "Please tell me how attached you fell to your country/city/town/village?" Finally we also added *interest in politics*—a binary variable which was created based on the survey question: "How interested, if at all, would you say you are in politics?" The answers included five options, from which we identified "very" and "quite" interested responses and coded them as "1", and other answers, including don't know option, we coded as "0".

The Table 5.2 presents basic statistics for the main explanatory variables used in both models.

Table 5.2 Explanatory variables—frequencies, means and standard deviations

Ordinal (binary) variables	Percent of values = 1	
Formalized family ties	59	
Contacts with family	77.7	
Membership in organizations	30.3	
Interest in politics	72.8	
Political participation	75.2	
Local attachment	62.3	
Continuous variables	Mean	Standard deviation
Contacts with friends	2.33	(0.87)
Receiving help in community	1.51	(0.83)
Generalized trust level	3.76	(2.72)

Notes: Means for binary variables indicate the percentage of respondents with variable value equal to 1

Solidarity Behaviors in Poland: Three Types of Support for Different Groups of Addressees According to the Geopolitical Proximity

The frequency of solidarity behaviors in Poland varies significantly between types of activity and between geopolitical scopes of addressees. As shown in Table 5.3, 16.3 percent of Polish respondents report they have ever taken part in a march, protest or demonstration in order to support the rights of people in Poland.[4] A slight overrepresentation of men in protest activity, but nothing statistically significant can be seen. Although some studies on political participation in Western societies prove protest behavior to be only form of political participation in which women are more active than men (Burns et al. 2001: 246), our finding is consistent with previous research, for example, by Domański (2009: 227) who showed men are more likely to protest in Poland than women. Similarly to his study and the general pattern (e.g. Pattie et al. 2004: 85), the higher education level turned to coincide with more frequent experience of participation in protest activities, ranging from 12.2 percent among respondents who have completed vocational upper secondary education to 22.0 percent among those who have obtained a MA title. In regard to age groups, a U-shaped relationship is present: the youngest respondents (age 18–24 years), as well as the oldest (above 65 years) subpopulation, reveal the highest rates of protest participation. This may be explained by co-occurrence of two features: typical for the EU higher propensity of younger generations to involve in protests, mainly due to higher tolerance level of youth and a higher level of membership in trade unions among the older generations, which act as a mobilization force for the members (Domański 2009; Żuk and Żuk 2015). Moreover, since we have asked if respondent has ever taken part in protest activity, we can see a cumulative effect of political experiences among older generations.

The share of Poles who participate in protest activities to support the rights of people in other countries in the EU is only 6 percent (see Table 5.3), that is, by more than half smaller than the support for the compatriots. Gender, education and age composition of this group are similar to the group of those respondents who have stand for Poles' rights.

Table 5.3 Participation in march, protest or demonstration in order to support the rights of people: in respondent's country, in other countries in the EU and in countries outside the EU

	In the country		Other countries in EU		Other countries outside EU	
	n	%	n	%	n	%
Total	346	16.3	127	6	118	5.6
By gender						
Men	171	16.9	69	6.8	61	6
Women	175	15.8	58	5.2	58	5.2
By education						
Primary education or less	0	0	0	0	2	6.9
Lower secondary education	4	9.6	1	1.8	2	4.2
Vocational upper secondary education	53	12.2	30	7	29	6.6
Upper secondary with access to tertiary	180	17.2	55	5.3	47	4.5
Post-secondary education	25	14.4	11	6.5	10	5.9
Short-cycle (3–4 years) tertiary education	6	14.7	5	11.3	2	5.7
Long-cycle (4+ years) tertiary education	25	22.6	6	5.5	7	6.6
Master's equivalent education	51	22	19	18.1	19	8
Doctoral or equivalent level	2	24.1	0	0	1	8
By age groups						
18–24	39	17.6	6	2.8	15	6.9
25–34	68	17.2	27	7	32	8.2
35–44	51	12.7	25	6.3	23	5.7
45–54	47	13.9	14	4.2	17	5.8
55–64	87	16.9	35	6.9	16	3.2
65 and older	54	21.5	19	7.6	15	5.8

Notes: Frequencies and percent are waged according to the country wage
Qs: Have you ever done one of the following [item: attended a march, protest or demonstration] in order to support the rights of people/groups in your own country/in other countries within the EU/in other countries outside the EU?

A similar share (5.6 percent) of the Polish population has the experience of protesting with an aim to support the rights of people in other countries outside the EU. Although this share is only slightly lower than in the case of protests which are aimed to support other EU countries' citizens, it needs to be noticed that only a limited overlap of both groups of protestors

Table 5.4 Donating time in order to support the rights of people in respondent's country, in other countries in the EU and in countries outside the EU

	In the country		Other countries in EU		Other countries outside EU	
	n	%	n	%	n	%
Total	511	24.1	266	12.5	241	11.4
By gender						
Men	244	24.1	128	12.7	109	10.8
Women	267	24.2	137	12.4	131	11.9
By education						
Primary education or less	6	17.1	1	3.6	1	3.6
Lower secondary education	12	27.3	3	7.8	4	9.6
Vocational upper secondary education	83	19.1	67	15.5	50	11.6
Upper secondary with access to tertiary	241	23	112	10.7	110	10.5
Post-secondary education	47	27.4	21	12.3	15	8.5
Short-cycle (3–4 years) tertiary education	8	20	4	9.5	6	14.7
Long-cycle (4+ years) tertiary education	34	30.9	16	14.2	11	10
Master's equivalent education	76	32.7	40	17.3	41	17.6
Doctoral or equivalent level	5	55	2	16.4	3	31.2
By age groups						
18–24	65	29.7	34	15.3	31	14.1
25–34	105	26.7	55	13.9	45	11.3
35–44	70	17.5	42	10.5	38	9.6
45–54	87	26	44	13.1	38	11.4
55–64	119	23.1	63	12.2	59	11.4
65 and older	64	25.5	23	11.1	29	11.7

Qs: Have you ever done one of the following [item: donate time] in order to support the rights of people/groups *in your own country*/in other countries within the EU/in other countries outside the EU?

has been observed. 36.2 percent of Polish citizens who have attended the protests supporting EU citizens have also protested for rights of non-EU citizens.

Not surprisingly donating time in order to support others' rights is a much more frequent solidarity action in Poland than protesting (see Table 5.4). As much as 24.1 percent of Polish society has devoted time to support the rights of some groups in the country. Given that other studies on activism in Poland reveal that 20 percent of respondents claim to engage in unpaid work for some societal goals in the previous year (CBOS 2016:10), it seems that a narrow understanding of supporting rights of compatriots was present in our sample. A similar pattern in regard to education and age may be observed among those who donated time for compatriots as among those who were engaged in protests. The propensity to donate time grows with educational level and follows a U-shaped relationship with age, as it was in case of protests.

Similarly to the mentioned protesting behavior, the share of Poles who donated their time to support others' rights falls with the geographical scope of the addressees. 12.5 percent of Polish respondents report to have been engaged in donating time to support the rights of people in other countries of the EU. The same activity aimed at supporting people outside the EU has been reported by 11.4 percent of Polish respondents. It may be hypothesized that the younger subgroups are slightly more likely to be engaged in this type of solidarity behavior, although, as noted, the small numbers of cases do not allow us for far-reaching interpretations. According to other surveys conducted in Poland, 27 percent of Poles devotes some time in the year to services to people outside the family or for organizations, and 15 percent claims to engage in voluntary work (Czapiński 2015: 345). We can see that only a relatively small share of these activities is solidarity in our understanding—that is, supports rights of others.

Consistent with international studies in the field (e.g. Marien et al. 2010: 196) which prove donating money to be one of the most frequent political participation forms, it turned out to be the most frequent solidarity behavior in our study. As presented in Table 5.5, 29.6 percent of Polish respondents reveal that they have donated money to support compatriots. Both higher education level and age improve the chances of being engaged in donating money. Financial support to the EU citizens living in other countries is, again, over twice less frequent; 13.2 percent of respondents have been active in this manner, whereas the educational and age composition of this group resembles similar to the previous one which might be explained by a significant overlap of these two groups. Over 61 percent of Poles who donate money to support other EU countries' inhabitants also financially support Polish citizens.

It should be noticed that on the contrary to protest activities devoting one's own time to support others, donating money to support people outside the EU is more widespread in Polish society than financial help to

Table 5.5 Donating money in order to support the rights of people in respondent's country, in other countries in the EU and in countries outside the EU

	In the country		Other countries in EU		Other countries outside EU	
	n	%	n	%	n	%
Total	627	29.6	280	13.2	381	18
By gender						
Men	283	28	133	13.1	188	18.6
Women	345	31.1	147	13.2	193	17.4
By education						
Primary education or less	3	10.1	1	3.5	2	6.4
Lower secondary education	10	24.3	4	9.7	7	16.9
Vocational upper secondary education	109	25.2	53	12.2	75	17.3
Upper secondary with access to tertiary	329	31.4	146	13.9	195	18.6
Post-secondary education	51	29.9	23	13.2	27	15.9
Short-cycle (3–4 years) tertiary education	13	32.7	8	19.2	8	20.6
Long-cycle (4+ years) tertiary education	28	25.1	12	11.1	20	18
Master's equivalent education	79	34	31	13.5	43	18.5
Doctoral or equivalent level	5	55.9	2	16.7	4	39.5
By age groups						
18–24	39	17.5	15	6.8	30	13.7
25–34	103	26	34	8.5	43	11
35–44	100	24.8	44	10.8	56	13.9
45–54	111	33	56	16.5	67	20
55–64	187	36.5	95	18.4	120	23.4
65 and older	88	35.1	37	14.8	65	25.6

Qs: Have you ever done one of the following [item: donate money] in order to support the rights of people/groups *in your own country*/in other countries within the EU/in other countries outside the EU?

EU inhabitants. Eighteen percent of the respondents claim they have donated money to support other people not living in the EU. Only 39.9 percent of them also financially support EU inhabitants. As in the case of other mentioned types of financial help, also in case of extra-EU financial support, higher education and age (with exception of people aged more than 65 years) coincide with more frequent solidarity behavior.

To sum up, out of the researched political acts of solidarity, the most frequent is donating money to support the rights of other people. Secondly, engaging one's own time is practiced. If our respondent is seen by us as being solidarity with some geographical group, it most probably means she or he donates money and/or time to support others' rights. It is much less likely that he or she has participated in the protests with a similar goal. It should be noticed that in the case of some researched activities, we have observed particular patterns of engagement across subpopulations. In regard to gender, we see men are involved in protests and money donation, whereas women are rather engaging their own time (e.g. as volunteers). With regard to age groups, transnational solidarity in the form of protesting is more frequent in the group of people aged 25–34, whereas the older generation (55–64 years) rather donates money. Educational attainment, as in any time of political activity, is positively correlated with engagement in all three solidarity practices.

Table 5.6 shows the frequency of generalized solidarity behaviors (i.e. any form from the three analyzed solidarity practices) toward different combinations of addressees. Almost 40 percent of Polish respondents declared having no experience of participation in solidarity practices, no matter the geopolitical scope of the addressees. The remaining 60.3 percent of respondents—which, as specified earlier, undertake generalized solidarity practices (solidaristic respondents)—can be divided into two groups. The first group (21.3 percent of all respondents, i.e. 35.3 percent of the "solidaristic respondents") includes respondents who were solidaristic in supporting the rights of compatriots only. The second group (39 percent of all respondents, i.e. 64.7 percent of the "solidaristic respondents") participated (also) in solidarity action in order to support the rights of people in other countries. Table 5.6 provides information on the

Table 5.6 Solidarity practices in Poland with different scopes of beneficiaries

	Frequency	% of all respondents
No solidarity practice at any level	842	39.7
Solidarity practices, including	1277	60.3
Solidarity action(s) only at the country level	450	21.3
Solidarity actions at the country and EU level	147	6.9
Solidarity actions at the country and outside EU level	185	8.7
Solidarity actions at all levels	292	13.8
Solidarity action(s) only at the supranational level (EU or outside EU)	63	3

Notes: Frequencies and percent are waged according to the country wage more detailed subgroups. For example, almost 14 percent of all respondents reported being engaged in at least one supportive practice at all geopolitical levels.

The findings on differences in geographical scope of solidarity action are consistent with earlier study of Bartkowski (2014) who argues that after economic crisis of 2008, solidarity attitudes toward neighbors and compatriots have grown and that, however, readiness to help people living abroad and in particular outside the EU has fallen, widening the gap between in-group and out-group solidarity. The mentioned study, however, refers to attitudes, whereas our investigation is focused on factual solidarity behaviors. Although only 2.4 percent of Poles declare "they are concerned about the Europeans to a very high extent" and 12.4 confirm "they are concerned to some extent" (years 2005–2009 data based on EVS and WVS surveys), our research shows that 36 percent of Poles has participated in some activity to support the rights of people living in the EU. As further discussed in the last section of this chapter, we may hypothesize that even for some respondents who are not necessarily concerned about the EU as a polity and its members, there are other incentives to support specific rights of citizens living in other EU countries.

BONDING AND BRIDGING SOCIAL CAPITAL AND THEIR IMPACT ON (TRANSNATIONAL) SOLIDARITY BEHAVIOR

Table 5.7 presents the results of the estimated logistic regressions. As expected, we find diverging results for both models, the one for propensity to engage in solidarity practices among general population and the other for propensity to engage particularly in transnational solidarity among the subgroup of "solidaristic" Poles. On the one hand, we find that such bridging capital indicators as membership in organizations and generalized trust level positively impact both the propensity to engage in solidarity practices in general and toward transnational solidarity action among the "solidaristic" Poles. Polish respondents who declared to be members of at least one civic organization had over four times higher propensity to engage in any solidarity practice than Poles not being members of any organization. Furthermore, solidaristic Poles, who declared to be members of civic organization(s), had again almost two times higher propensity to engage in transnational solidarity practices than the rest of the "solidaristic" Poles.

Table 5.7 Logistic regression results (expβ) for the model of *general solidarity* and model of *transnational solidarity*

	General solidarity	*Transnational solidarity*
	Model 1	*Model 2*
Socio-demographic factors		
Gender (ref. male)	1.09	1.02
Age	1	1.01**
Education	1.06*	1.03
Income	1.02	0.94**
Bonding social capital		
Formalized family ties (1)	0.95	1.12
Contacts with family	1.09	1.08
Contacts with friends	1.19***	0.96
Receiving help in community	0.98	1.52
Bridging social capital		
Membership in organizations (1)	4.57***	1.97***
Generalized trust level	1.04*	1.06**
Voting (1)	1.55***	0.96
Local attachment (1)	1.07	0.79*
Interest in politics (1)	1.59***	0.88
Constant	0.17***	0.95
N	1818	1138

Notes: The level of significance are described by number of stars: ***$p \leq 0.01$, **$p \leq 0.05$, *$p \leq 0.1$

On the other hand, we find that local attachment (to the country or to the city/town of the respondent) proves to be negatively correlated only with transnational type of solidarity practice. The impact of local attachment on solidarity behavior in general is positive, although in our analysis this relationship does not prove to be statistically significant. Furthermore, we find that electoral participation as well as interest in politics positively and significantly impact involvement in solidarity practices in general.

People who declared they are quite or very interested in politics have, on average, nearly 60 percent higher propensity to declare being involved in any form of solidarity behavior. People who declared that they participated in the last parliamentary elections in Poland (in 2015) were 55 percent more likely to be involved in such activity. These aspects of bridging social capital do not prove to have significant impact on propensity to engage in transnational solidarity practices among "solidaristic" Poles.

Most of the indicators of bonding social capital did not prove to have significant impact on solidarity behaviors. However, the frequency in contact with friends proved to be positively related to the engagement in solidarity behaviors in general. Its impact on the propensity of "solidaristic" Poles to engage in transnational solidarity practices was found to be negative, although this effect was not statistically significant in our model.

Both models also point at the insignificant role of gender in solidarity behaviors. Men are as likely as women to undertake solidarity actions and among these participate in actions with a transnational scope. The positive impact of age was found to be statistically significant only in model for transnational solidarity and positive education only for model for general solidarity (although the differences in the impact between both models were very small). Finally, income showed significant and negative impact only for transnational solidarity practices among "solidaristic" Poles.

Individual Transnational Solidarity: Beyond Bridging-Bonding Divide? Discussion and Conclusion

Our findings provide evidence that partially supports our hypotheses on the relationships between social capital and solidarity practices outlined in the theoretical section. Firstly, we have observed that such element of bonding social capital, as frequent contacts with friends, positively affects general solidarity. Following van Stekelenburg and Klandermans (2013), we may interpret that the structural, relational and cognitive elements of social capital—based on contacts with friends—enhance individuals' propensity to take action aimed at supporting someone's rights. Thus, radical assumptions about the role of family ties (Putnam et al. 1994) and their impact on solidarity have not been confirmed in our study. We have not observed any negative impact of strong family bonds on involvement in solidarity action.

Secondly, a strong, positive impact of bridging social capital on solidarity practices, both in general and in regard to people living abroad, has been confirmed. Such aspects of social capital increase likelihood of engagement in any solidarity action, as membership in civil society organization, high level of generalized trust and attitudes of engagement in public issues which manifest in declared interest in politics and participation in elections. Membership in civil society organizations and trusting unknown others turn out to positively affect transnational solidarity action, too.

Thus, our analysis confirms that both types of solidarity practices result from social embeddedness of a person. However, we can clearly see that the linkages between two types of social capital and two types of solidarity practices are nuanced and that specific pattern of causal relation emerges. Namely, it seems that classic Putnamian (Putnam et al. 1994) ideal of social capital is at least partly a bedrock for generalized solidarity practice, which according to our conceptualization encompasses also robust solidarity (solidarity in a group). Moreover, apart from such social norms as interest in politics and voting, it is also high education level which contributes to this type of solidarity. All these triggers taken together, it can be seen that general solidarity action in Poland stems from a relatively "elitist" social resources. This is consistent with previous studies on civil activism in Poland which was described as dispersed and confined within societal structures hardly accessible for broader citizenry (Kościański 2016: 236). However, transnational solidarity practice turned out to be embedded in different types of social capital. Surprisingly, these are relatively older and less affluent Poles who are not interested in politics, but trusting others and strongly attached to locality, who are more likely to get involved in transnational solidarity action.

Relating our findings to the above-mentioned discussion about the unfavorable communist legacy of Polish civic practices (Guasti 2016; Jakubowska and Kaniasty 2014; Czapiński 2014), even if we assume that familialism and low interest in public sphere are a part of this heritage, it turns out to be a less dismantling transnational solidarity action than one may thought. As noted—spending time with family does not have a negative effect on solidarity action, whereas spending time with friends has only a positive effect. Moreover, we can see that transnational solidarity cannot be explained in terms of low interest in public issues or scarcity of financial assets and thus may be hardly seen as a result of civic virtues being destroyed by communism. It rather seems that a specific pattern based on combination of high trust, refraining from politics and glocal perspective on others' rights comes into the fore.

Thus, we may hypothesize that this type of civic activism is relatively immune to contemporary political narratives of Poland which suggest the need protect itself from "foreign values". Paradoxically, a tradition of acting out of the state's structures or even against them, practised during communist time in Poland, may be the heritage which some "transnationally solidaristic" Poles may refer to. This mechanism is supported by recent studies which prove that contemporary anti-Law and Justice demonstrations (Karolewski 2016) and transnational solidarity action of civil society organizations (Chimiak 2016) follow tradition of "Solidarity" values and its civil resistance action. Hence, in times when solidarity might be endangered "from above", the heritage of civic action form communist time may be a source to refer to when getting involved in solidarity action "from below".

Appendix

Variables in the models	Recoding from original variables
Continuous variables	
Age	*age*—no recoding needed
Education	*education*—no recoding needed
Income	*income*—no recoding needed (999 = missing values)
Contacts with friends	*metfriends*—no recoding needed
Receiving help in community	*help*—no recoding needed
Generalized trust level	*socialtrust*—999 = 5; else was copied
Ordinal variables	
Gender (ref. male)	*gender*—no recoding needed
Formalized family ties	*mamarsts*—3 and 6 recoded as 1; else = 0
Contacts with family	*deprivepices_8*—no recoding needed
Interest in politics	*polint*—3 and 4 recoded to 1; else = 0
Keeping informed about public issues	*news_12*—no recoding needed
Voting	*votenat_PL*—3 recorded as 1; else = 0
Local attachment	*attachcountry_city*—4 recoded as 1; else 0

Notes

1. It needs to be noticed that in significant part of relevant literature, the relation between social capital and solidarity is conceptualized in a different way than in this chapter. Solidarity is commonly understood only as specific attitude which leads to cooperation (social capital) (Portes 1998). This is also a result of frequent conceptualization of solidarity as a moral value and not a practice.
2. Active (belong and volunteer/unpaid work for) or passive (belong to only).
3. The list included such organizations as political party, trade union, labor union, human/development rights organization, civil rights/liberties organization, environment/anti-nuclear organization, peace/anti-war organization, occupy/anti-austerity organization, anti-capitalist, anti-globalization

organization, anti-racist/migrant rights organization, disability rights organization, unemployment organization and refugees or asylum seekers organization.
4. According to 2014 ESS data, the percentage of people who report they have *taken part in lawful public demonstration* equals 2.8 in Poland. The response to TransSOL survey question—*There are different ways of trying to improve things or help prevent things from going wrong. When have you LAST done the following?—Attended a demonstration, march or rally* (item: 12 months)— equals 11.7 percent. Due to a generally low level of participation in demonstrations in Poland (Domański 2009), we have decided to include in the analysis a question on long-term individual protest experiences.

REFERENCES

Banfield, E. (1967). *The Moral Basis Of a Backward Society*. New York: Free Press.
Bang, B. H. P. (2004). *Everyday Makers and Expert Citizens: Building Political not Social Capital*. Working Paper, 1–32.
Bang, H. P. (2015). Between Democracy and Governance. *British Politics, 10*(3), 286–307.
Bartkowski, J. (2014). Solidarność społeczna i kryzys. Zmiany wartości w Europie i w Polsce w warunkach kryzysu. *Acta Universitatis Lodzienis Folia Sociologica, 48*(2014), 19–34.
Burns, N., Schlozman, K. L., & Verba, S. (2001). *The Private Roots of Public Action: Gender, Equality, and Political Participation*. Cambridge: Harvard University Press.
CBOS. (2016). Potencjał społecznikowski oraz zaangażowanie w pracę społeczną. Komunikat z badań, 15/2016.
Chimiak, G. (2016). From Solidarność to Global Solidarity? The Engagement of Polish Civil Society in Development Cooperation. *Studia Socjologiczne, 3*(222), 165–198.
Coleman, J. (1988). Social Capital in the Creation of Human Capital. *American Journal of Sociology, 94*, S95–S120.
Czapiński, J. (2006). Polska—państwo bez społeczeństwa. *Nauka, 1/2006*, 7–26.
Czapiński, J. (2014). Kapitał społeczny. Diagnoza Społeczna 2013, Warunki i Jakość Życia Polaków – Raport, 320–334.
Czapiński, J. (2015). Stan społeczeństwa obywatelskiego. Diagnoza Społeczna 2015, Warunki i Jakość Życia Polaków - Raport. Contemporary Economics, 9/4, 332-372.
Domański, H. (2009). *Społeczeństwa europejskie. Stratyfikacja i systemy wartości*. Warszawa: Scholar.
Giza, A., Marody, M., & Rychard, A. (2000). *Strategie i system. Polacy w obliczu zmiany społecznej*. Warszawa: IFiS PAN.
Gliński, P. (2006). *Style działań organizacji pozarządowych w Polsce. Grupy interesu czy pożytku publicznego?* Warszawa: IFiS PAN.

Gould, C. (2007). Transnational Solidarities. *Journal of Social Philosophy, 38*, 148–164.
Granovetter, M. S. (1973). The Strength of Weak Ties. *American Journal of Sociology, 78*(6), 1360–1380.
Grootaert, C., & Van Bastelaer, T. (Eds.). (2002). *Understanding and Measuring Social Capital: A Multidisciplinary Tool for Practitioners* (Vol. 1). World Bank Publications.
Guasti, P. (2016). Development of Citizen Participation in Central and Eastern Europe After the EU Enlargement and Economic Crises. *Communist and Post-Communist Studies, 49*(3), 219–231.
Jacobsson, K., & Korolczuk, E. (2017). *Civil Society Revisited. Lessons from Poland*. New York: Berghahn Books.
Jakubowska, U., & Kaniasty, K. (2014). Post-Communist Transformation in Progress: Poles' Attitudes Toward Democracy. *Communist and Post-Communist Studies, 47*(3–4), 399–407.
Karolewski, I. P. (2016). Protest and Participation in Post-Transformation Poland: The Case of the Committee for the Defense of Democracy (KOD). *Communist and Post-Communist Studies, 49*(3), 255–267.
Kolers, A. H. (2012). Dynamics of Solidarity. *Journal of Political Philosophy, 20*(4), 365–383.
Kościański, A. (2016). Partycypacja obywatelska a syndrom zmiany orientacji życiowych w społeczeństwie polskim. In *Przemiany kulturowe we współczesnej Polsce*. IFIS PAN.
Krzemiński, I. (2010). *Wielka Transformacja. Zmiany Ustroju w Polsce po 1989*. Oficyna Łośgraf.
Lahusen, C. (2016). *Transnational Solidarity within the European Union: Towards a Framework of Analysis*. Paper presented at the 8th Pan-European Conference on the European Union. "The Union's Institutional and Constitutional Transformations: Stress or Adaptation?", Trento, 15–18 June 2016.
Marien, S., Hooghe, M., & Quintelier, E. (2010). Inequalities in Non-Institutionalised Forms of Political Participation: A Multi-Level Analysis of 25 Countries. *Political Studies, 58*(1), 187–213.
Narayan, D., & Cassidy, M. (2001). A Dimensional Approach to Measuring Social Capital: Development and Validation of a Social Capital Inventory. *Current Sociology, 49*, 59–102.
Ost, D. (2006). *The Defeat of Solidarity: Anger and Politics in Postcommunist Europe*. Cornell University Press.
Pattie, C., Seyd, P., & Whiteley, P. (2004). *Citizenship in Britain: Values, Participation and Democracy*. Cambridge: Cambridge University Press.
Portes, A. (1998). Social Capital: Its Origins and Applications in Modern Sociology. *Annual Review of Sociology, 24*(1), 1–24.
Putnam, R. D. (2000). *Bowling Alone: The Collapse and Revival of American Community*. New York: Simon & Schuster.

Putnam, R. (2002). *Democracies in Flux. The Evolution of Social Capital in Contemporary Society*. New York: Oxford University Press.
Putnam, R., Leonardi, R. & Nanetti, R. (1994). *Making Democracy Work: Civic Traditions in Modern Italy*. Princeton University Press.
Sangiovanni, A. (2015). Solidarity as Joint Action. *Journal of Applied Philosophy*, 32(4), 340–359.
Segall, S. (2005). Political Participation as an Engine of Social Solidarity: A Skeptical View. *Political Studies*, 53, 362–378.
Staniszkis, J. (2010). *Samoograniczająca się rewolucja*. Gdańsk: Europejskie Centrum Solidarności.
van Stekelenburg, J., & Klandermans, B. (2013). The Social Psychology of Protest. *Current Sociology*, 61(5–6), 886–905.
Szymczak, W. (2008). Zaufanie społeczne i kondycja społeczeństwa obywatelskiego w Polsce. In A. Kościański & W. Misztal (Eds.), *Społeczeństwo obywatelskie między ideą a praktyką*. Warszawa: IFIS PAN.
Taylor, A. E. (2015). Solidarity: Obligations and Expressions. *Journal of Political Philosophy*, 23(2), 128–145.
Tworzecki, H. (2008). A Disaffected New Democracy? Identities, Institutions and Civic Engagement in Post-Communist Poland. *Communist and Post-Communist Studies*, 41(1), 47–62.
UNESCO. (1997). International Standard Classification of Education-ISCED 1997: November 1997. UNESCO.
Żuk, P., & Żuk, P. (2015). *O kulturze protest jako rdzeniu tradycji europejskiej*. Warszawa: IW Książka i Prasa.
Żukowski, T., & Theiss, M. (2009). Islands of Civic Engagement. Differences in the Level of Civic-Associational Social Capital. *International Journal of Sociology*, 39(4), 65–87.

Open Access This chapter is licensed under the terms of the Creative Commons Attribution 4.0 International License (http://creativecommons.org/licenses/by/4.0/), which permits use, sharing, adaptation, distribution and reproduction in any medium or format, as long as you give appropriate credit to the original author(s) and the source, provide a link to the Creative Commons license and indicate if changes were made.

The images or other third party material in this chapter are included in the chapter's Creative Commons license, unless indicated otherwise in a credit line to the material. If material is not included in the chapter's Creative Commons license and your intended use is not permitted by statutory regulation or exceeds the permitted use, you will need to obtain permission directly from the copyright holder.

CHAPTER 6

The Social and Political Dimensions of Solidarity in Italy

Nicola Maggini

Introduction

This chapter explores the social and political dimensions of solidarity in Italy, measuring solidarity practices in their various aspects and explaining them with reference to core socio-demographic and attitudinal factors. Understanding the spread and the triggers of solidarity practices in the Italian context is a goal that deserves scholars' attention due to the various crises that have affected the country since 2008. Indeed, the global financial crisis and the austerity measures which followed have resulted in drastic cuts to public services, heavy job losses, and reduced incomes. The impact of the crisis on the most vulnerable sectors of society, such as people with disabilities, was particularly tough. In this regard, the most evident and tangible outcome of the crisis was the cut in the "National Fund for the Non-Self-Sufficient". Reduced by 75% due to budget cuts in 2011, the Fund was not financed at all in 2012. While governmental action has focused on fiscal containment and consequent public service retrenchment, societal needs have not only intensified (as the number of people in need has increased) but also diversified (due to socio-demographic changes

---

N. Maggini (✉)
University of Florence, Florence, Italy

© The Author(s) 2018
C. Lahusen, M. Grasso (eds.), *Solidarity in Europe*,
Palgrave Studies in European Political Sociology,
https://doi.org/10.1007/978-3-319-73335-7_6

and global socio-economic processes). Within the gap of a few years, the refugee crisis overlapped with the economic crisis, strongly affecting a country positioned at the centre of several migration routes in the Mediterranean Sea. According to UNHCR estimates, from January until December 2014, the total number of sea arrivals reached 170,000, almost one-third of whom were rescued by the operations "Mare Nostrum"[1] and/or "Frontex's Triton". A new record was registered in 2016, when the total number of sea arrivals reached 181,000: an 18% increase compared with 2015 (154,000). Several thousands of people perished at sea. Solely in 2016, the number of people who lost their lives was 5022. Finally, 2016 data also highlight Italy's record for the number of landings in the Mediterranean: half of more than 361 thousand migrants arriving by sea into Europe landed on the Italian coast, 48% of the landings occurred in Greece (174,000 arrivals), while 8826 migrants landed in Spain. The increased inflow of refugees from Syria and other regions affected by wars and the inability of the EU institutions and its member states to establish a coordinated asylum policy and mechanisms of admission and integration have raised the concerns that solidarity between EU member states is severely at risk.

In such a difficult landscape, solidarity is under pressure. Indeed, the economic and refugee crisis are international challenges that call for joint action and mutual solidarity at the supra-national level. Yet, economic hardships, social inequalities, and lack of collaboration between national governments on the migration issue can increase nationalist sentiments and populist reactions, as shown by the success of populist parties, the Brexit vote, and the mobilisation of Eurosceptic and xenophobic protests across Europe. All this has raised further concerns about not only the weakening of solidarity between member state governments but also the deterioration of solidarity at the level of the European citizenry, especially in a country like Italy that faced multiple crises and therefore can be considered a relevant case study to explain factors which inhibit and/or strengthen solidarity actions. Unmet needs can take two main paths: disenchantment and resentment, deliberately exploited by political entrepreneurs, and resilience and social ingenuity, deployed through a range of civil society organisations, social movements, and social innovations. Do these paths mirror the current situation in Italy? How strongly is solidarity rooted at the individual level, both in terms of attitudes and practices, and how much are Italians engaged in solidarity-related activities? Is solidarity limited to specific target groups, or do we detect also a universalist or cosmopolitan philanthropy dimension? And which factors seem to trigger (or inhibit) solidarity practices? Public debate continues to address these solidarity issues, but we have had very little empirical evidence on which to draw to inform this debate to date. We are in need of empirical evidence in order to answer these research questions. This chapter makes this possible by drawing on data generated from an online individual survey conducted in November–December of 2016 (2087 cases for Italy).

The ultimate goal of this study is to enlarge and deepen knowledge on solidarity in Italy by providing new data and analyses on solidarity practices with respect to three target groups which have been particularly affected by the crises (the disabled, the unemployed, and refugees) and to explain such solidarity actions with reference to social traits of the respondents, their beliefs, and their political preferences. Previous research has not addressed these issues in any systematic manner, contrasting facts and observations have been taken into account, but a review of previous studies is important to comprehend the phenomenon under investigation by detecting relevant dimensions and aspects and by stressing explanatory factors that might affect solidarity practices.

First, previous research is conceptually important to start with a definition of "solidarity". In this regard, we agree with a strong strand of research that defines solidarity as the preparedness to share one's own resources with others (Stjernø 2012, p. 2). This definition emphasises the importance of attitudes and dispositions, which have received much attention in the social sciences. In fact, most surveys are primarily interested in measuring the readiness of citizens to share some of their resources with others. Moreover, survey-based studies measure solidarity by the citizens' approval of redistributional policies and, thus, by the readiness to allocate some of their taxes or contributions to the needy (Svallfors 1997; Fong 2001; Amat and Wibbels 2009; Rehm et al. 2012). Nonetheless, this focus on redistributional preferences is not without problems. Taxes and contributions to social security programmes are compulsory, and, therefore, support for social policies might not automatically bring up the readiness to commit individually in support for others. Furthermore, social psychology has stressed how attitudes and dispositions are not equivalent to actual practices (Blumer 1955; Festinger 1964; Ajzen and Fishbein 2005). Through our own survey, we aimed more explicitly to measure reported solidarity activities in order to get a more reliable picture about the extent to which Italian citizens are committed to supporting others, conceiving solidarity as practices of help or support towards others in struggle or in need, be that by personal contributions or by active support of activities of others, within informal and/or institutionalised communities.

Second, scholars have tended to privilege the charitable dimension of solidarity by focusing on the (financial) help to the needy. While this aspect is significant, it does not consider the political dimension of solidarity. In fact, people reveal solidarity with other needy persons when participating in collective actions (e.g. political protests, public claims making, lobbying, communication campaigns) that aims to improve the situation of these groups by mobilising public support, lobbying stakeholders, and/or changing public policies on their behalf (Giugni and Passy 2001).

Finally, previous studies are an important source of inspiration in order to identify factors that can influence solidarity practices. First, scholars have highlighted the importance of socio-demographic factors and social traits (e.g. age, gender, education, social class) for grasping the conditions, structures, and dynamics of solidarity (Hechter 1988). Some studies (Neill and Gidengil 2006; Valentova 2016) have shown that voluntary engagement tends to replicate the public/private divide by focusing especially on male-dominated and "public" activities. It has been revealed that younger and older citizens are more active in social movements, because of different levels of "biographical availability" in the life course (Beyerlein and Bergstrand 2013). Furthermore, different levels of commitment in solidarity actions can be patterned by citizens' differentiation in terms of personal resources and skills, such as income and education, by the respondents' social status and affiliation to social class (Verba et al. 1978; Cainzos and Voces 2010).

Second, education and subjective class position are also a measure of social centrality, usually linked to social capital, and previous research has shown that social capital measures are particularly important for our topic (Putnam et al. 2003; Jenkins 1983; Bourdieu 1986). In particular, we wish to highlight the role of interpersonal trust, informal networks, and social relations. The assumption is that social capital is the necessary "glue" of social cohesion (Chan et al. 2006; Jeannotte 2000; Delhey 2007), and it is tightly associated with values such as trust in others and with frequency of social connections. Several studies have shown that trust in others is associated with a wide range of positive outcomes in areas such as personal wellbeing (Helliwell and Wang 2010), crime rates, and even mortality rates (Lochner et al. 2003). Also, social trust can determine how much people in a society are willing to cooperate with one another, thus fostering solidarity actions. Similarly, having a good frequency of social connections fosters higher levels of life satisfaction and happiness (Lelkes 2010) but can also give people access to a wider range of possible support in times of need, producing positive outcomes at a community level (Halpern 2005).

Third, research on political behaviour in general, and on social movement and protest participation in particular, can help to answer the question of whether solidarity is determined by political factors. Indeed, we aim to identify the interrelation between political orientations on the one side and solidarity practices on the other. In this regard, studies agree on the fact that solidarity is also highly patterned by political preferences and ideological orientations (Blekesaune and Quadagno 2003; Amat and Wibbels 2009; Likki and Staerklé 2014). Among political factors, it is also important to consider political involvement in terms of interest in politics and party attachment because they are often associated with civic engagement (Scrivens and Smith 2013). The latter is another element that can help individuals to develop their skills and social values (such as trust in others), and, consequently, it can foster solidarity (Putnam et al. 1994).

Finally, we want to explore the role of ideational and cognitive factors, too. In particular, scholars have shown the importance of charitable dispositions linked to religiosity (Abela 2004; Stegmueller et al. 2012; Lichterman 2015) to explain different levels of solidarity. At the same time, we need to take into account that solidarity is attached not only to abstract universal communities—that is, humankind according to Arendt's political theory (Arendt 1972)—but also to specific reference groups. In particular, specific acts of solidarity seem to be conditional and thus tied to specific issues and target groups. In this regard, previous research has shown that perceptions of reciprocity, conditionality, and deservingness can play an important role as regards solidarity among the public (Oorschot 2000, 2006).

Based on these insights, the research is grounded on the hypotheses that social capital, political factors, religiosity, and perceptions of deservingness influence solidarity practices. In particular, we argue that there could be a distinction between triggers of solidarity towards specific target groups and triggers of solidarity in general. As regards the latter, we hypothesise that regardless of the target group, (a) the more an individual is socially embedded and trustworthy of others (the more her/his social capital), the more she/he will support people in need; (b) the more religious one is, the more she/he supports others in a "charitable" esprit; (c) the more a person perceives a group to be deserving of support, the more she/he will be disposed towards solidarity with that group. As regards group-specific triggers of solidarity, the refugee crisis has arisen innumerable initiatives not only to provide immediate help for refugees (e.g. clothing, food, shelter, language courses) but also to rally for migrant and refugee rights, sharing a universalistic and unconditioned notion of solidarity. The increasing inability of Italian authorities to handle the inflow of migrants and the growing mobilisation of populist, right-wing, and in part xenophobic groups boosted conflicts about the correct policies for the Italian government to pursue. Because of these conflicts, solidarity towards refugees became a contested issue. In this regard, scholars (Mudde 2011) have stressed how migrants-related issues are divisive issues that are strongly politicised by right-wing populist parties in order to gain votes (e.g. the Northern League in Italy). Consequently, solidarity towards refugees apparently has become a contentious field that separates people with different political orientations. Unemployment is another sector that can be characterised by a certain degree of contentiousness (Baglioni 2010). The economic crisis and the resulting austerity measures have mobilised Italian trade unions and social movements in defence of the interests and rights of people in economic difficulties, including the unemployed. Disabled persons' organisations mobilised against cuts, too. However, most disability organisations in Italy are composed of disabled people and/or their families and have tended to represent fragmented subsets of people with disabilities (Schianchi 2014), without clear ideological-political connotations.

On the basis of all these, we hypothesise that:

1. political factors do not matter for solidarity towards the disabled, whereas they matter for solidarity towards refugees and the unemployed;
2. the more an individual is involved in politics and characterised in terms of leftist political orientations and libertarian values, the more she/he will support refugees;
3. the more an individual conceives solidarity in universalistic terms without perceptions of reciprocity and conditionality, the more she/he will support refugees.

In order to test these research hypotheses, the following variables will be included in the analysis: socio-demographic characteristics (age, gender, education, income, social class) and social traits (social capital measures), political factors (interest in politics, party attachment, self-placement on the left-right dimension, libertarian vs. authoritarian values, voting intentions), and religiosity and social beliefs (evaluations on deservingness, reciprocity, conditionality). The chapter will first provide a general picture of a variety of solidarity practices in Italy with respect to our target groups (the disabled, the unemployed, and the refugees), looking at the interrelations between attitudes and behaviours in order to comparatively assess the specificities of each target group. Secondly, through multivariate regression models, it will provide pertinent explanation to investigate the (different) determinants of solidarity activities among the three target groups. Findings show that the most important factors fostering solidarity practices in Italy are social capital, religiosity, cognitive political involvement, and perceptions of deservingness. There are also group-specific triggers of solidarity: political factors play a more important role for support towards the unemployed and (especially) refugees compared to support for the disabled; solidarity towards refugees is clearly an unconditioned form of solidarity.

ITALIANS AND SOLIDARITY: AN OVERALL PICTURE

Answering the research questions we presented in the introduction and testing our hypotheses require outlining the profiles of Italians engaged in solidarity with our specific target groups (the refugees, the unemployed, and the people with disabilities), taking into account their sociodemographic characteristics, social traits, political attitudes, ideologies and voting intentions, social beliefs, and cultural orientations. Prior to this discussion, we need to contextualise solidarity practices in the general picture of solidarity in Italy through the analysis of the dependent variables of the study: reported solidarity practices towards refugees, the unemployed, and people with disabilities. Our survey includes a battery of questions that allow comparing levels of solidarity with various reference groups and painting a differentiated picture of diverse practices (donating time or money, passive and active membership, buying products, protest participation) that help to mirror both the philanthropic and political dimension of solidarity (see Table 6.1).

The results show that around half of respondents have been engaged in solidarity activities involving people with disabilities (including donating money or time, protesting, and engaging in voluntary associations), whereas 35.5% engage in solidarity activities with the unemployed and

Table 6.1 Type of reported solidarity activities in favour of three target groups (in %)

	Refugees	Unemployed	Disabled
Attended a march, protest, or demonstration	5.8	11.6	8.4
Donating money	11.0	11.3	26.5
Donating time	7.5	9.0	13.7
Bought or refused to buy products in support to the goals	8.1	11.1	14.5
Engaged as passive member of an organisation	3.5	4.9	6.1
Engaged as active member of an organisation	5.6	6.2	8.3
Total	*27.6*	*35.5*	*49.4*
N	*576*	*741*	*1030*

Table 6.15 in Appendix presents the original wording of the survey's questions used for all tables in this chapter

Table 6.2 Reported solidarity activities in order to support the rights of people/groups in different contexts (in %)

	Italy
In your country	46.7
In a country in the EU	31.7
Outside the EU	32.8
Total N	*2087*

At least one of the following actions was named: protest, donate money or time, bought or boycotted goods, passive or active membership

27.6% with refugees.[2] The disability field is the most "crowded" field in terms of solidarity engagement. If we look at the different types of solidarity practices, political protest-oriented activities are carried out especially in favour of the unemployed (11.6%), whereas the other two fields seem to be less contentious. Conversely, charity behaviour definitely characterises solidarity actions towards the disabled: 26.5% donate money (compared to 11% of those who donate money for refugees or the unemployed), and 13.7% donate time. Similar patterns can be found regarding the active involvement in volunteering, with around 6% volunteering in favour of refugees or the unemployed and 8% in favour of people with disabilities. Regarding solidarity towards refugees, after donating money, the most frequent activity (8.1%) is a relatively more political one, that is, buying or refusing to buy products in favour of refugees.

Looking at solidarity practices oriented to people/groups in Italy and abroad (see Table 6.2) makes the picture more interesting.

Table 6.3 Importance of development aid from the EU to assist certain countries outside the EU in their fight against poverty and in support of their development (in %)

	Italy
Not at all	3.5
Not very	6.9
Neither	18.3
Fairly important	45.6
Very important	25.7
Total	*100*
N	*2087*

Table 6.4 Evaluations of solidarity-based public policies (in %)

		Italy
Importance of eliminating big inequalities in income between citizens	Not at all important	1.4
	Not very important	3.0
	Neither	14.9
	Fairly important	40.0
	Very important	40.7
	Total	100
	N	*2087*
Agreement on EU pooling funds to help EU countries	Strongly disagree	5.2
	Disagree	11.2
	Neither	17.6
	Agree	47.4
	Strongly agree	18.7
	Total	100
	N	*1928*

Around half of the Italian sample reports having been engaged in solidarity activities for people in their country, whereas Italian citizens are less inclined to support European and transnational solidarity. One-third of respondents have engaged in activities in support of the rights of people in other EU countries or outside the EU.

Moving to describe the attitude towards helping people in developing countries, data show that a strong majority of respondents in Italy supports the attempts of the EU to help countries outside Europe in fighting poverty and promoting development, with 72% supporting and only 11% opposing these measures (see Table 6.3).

Finally, it is interesting to look at public support of redistributive policies and of fiscal solidarity among EU member states (see Table 6.4), which have been taken as a measure for "vertical solidarity" (Alesina and

Giuliano 2011), and thus for the readiness of people to finance and endorse public programmes sharing wealth with the needy. It can be argued that people with redistributional preferences might be more likely involved in solidarity practices. Italian citizens strongly support solidarity-based (redistributive) public policies with 81% considering the reduction of big income inequalities as an important goal. In other words, the traditional European social model is definitely not questioned by our interviewees. Italians are inclined also to support solidarity-based policies among EU member states, even if to a lesser extent. A large majority supports fiscal solidarity measures towards countries with public debts (65% vs. 16%), with 18% undecided respondents, probably because Italy has the second largest public debt in the EU. Therefore, this might be also a self-interested solidarity attitude.

Against this general picture, we focus the analysis on the relationships between solidarity actions and the aforementioned set of individual characteristics: (1) socio-demographics and social traits, (2) political attitudes and behaviours, and (3) social beliefs and religiosity.

Solidarity Actions, Socio-demographic Characteristics, and Social Traits

Regarding basic socio-demographic characteristics (see Table 6.5), we can observe a difference in terms of age between support for refugees and the unemployed (where there is an over-representation of the youngest age groups—18–35 years old—with respect to the sample's average) on the one hand and support for the disabled on the other hand (where the distribution of age groups is substantially in line with the average). Regarding gender, most people engaged in solidarity activities (in all fields) are male, whereas in the whole sample most respondents are female. This result confirms findings of some studies, which unveil that voluntary engagement tends to replicate the public/private divide by centring on male-dominated activities (Neill and Gidengil 2006; Valentova 2016). The male over-representation is accentuated within the unemployment field (54.3%), while the disability field is the most gender balanced (50.7% male).

Considering educational attainment, in all the fields, almost half of respondents have a low education level. Nonetheless, higher level of education makes it more likely that people show solidarity. This is true

Table 6.5 Solidarity actions towards target groups by basic socio-demographic characteristics (in %)

		Refugees support	Unemployed support	Disabled support	Total
Age	18–24 years	9.2	8.2	6.6	7.2
	25–34 years	18.4	17.0	13.2	14.3
	35–44 years	18.3	19.8	17.2	17.5
	45–54 years	14.7	17.6	18.6	18.9
	55–64 years	22.5	22.0	24.6	23.7
	65 years and older	17.0	15.6	19.8	18.3
	Total	100	100	100	100
	N	576	741	1030	2087
Gender	Male	51.7	54.3	50.7	48.9
	Female	48.3	45.8	49.3	52.9
	Total	100	100	100	100
	N	576	741	1030	2087
Education	Higher education	17.6	15.8	13.7	12.3
	Intermediate education	33.4	34.9	36.6	35.2
	Lower education	49.1	49.3	49.7	52.5
	Total	100	100	100	100
	N	576	741	1030	2087

especially in solidarity activities concerning refugees and the unemployed. Indeed, the percentage of respondents with higher education is around 18% among people supporting refugees (vs. 12.3% of the total population) and around 16% among people supporting the unemployed.

Table 6.6 reports solidarity actions towards target groups by monthly income level (in euro) and subjective social class. Respondents with the highest income level (3781 euro or more per month) are over-represented among people supporting refugees with respect to the average (9% vs. 6%), whereas respondents with the lowest income level (0–1305 euro) are under-represented (24% vs. 28%). This pattern is less pronounced in the unemployment and disability fields. Quite interesting patterns emerge if we take "social centrality" into examination, as measured by perceived class belonging. Results confirm the specificity of solidarity activities in favour of refugees. Among people supporting refugees, the lower class and, above all, the working class are under-represented compared to the total population, whereas the upper middle class is over-represented.

Table 6.6 Solidarity actions towards target groups by income level and subjective social class (in %)

		Refugees support	Unemployed support	Disabled support	Total
Income	0–1305 euro	24.0	27.4	25.5	28.1
	1306–1920 euro	27.7	25.6	24.6	26.2
	1921–2665 euro	21.7	24.6	24.6	22.9
	2666–3780 euro	17.5	15.4	17.7	16.6
	3781 euro or more	9.1	7.0	7.6	6.2
	Total	100	100	100	100
	N	522	677	922	1803
Subjective social class	Upper class	0.2	0.2	0.3	0.2
	Upper middle class	7.9	5.4	5.8	4.3
	Middle class	42.1	40.4	42.0	40.4
	Lower middle class	28.9	28.5	28.7	27.2
	Working class	10.6	13.4	12.4	15.9
	Lower class	9.2	11.2	10.0	11.5
	Other class	1.1	1.0	0.8	0.5
	Total	100	100	100	100
	N	562	730	1008	2016

Finally, our survey includes some specific questions regarding social capital framework. According to the framework adopted by the OECD (Scrivens and Smith 2013), there are several dimensions of social capital. We focus here just on two aspects: social trust and personal relationships. The first refers to the measure based on the standard question: "Generally speaking, would you say that most people can be trusted or that you need to be very careful in dealing with people?" Trust is measured on a scale of 0 (minimum trust) to 10 (maximum trust). In order to make cross-tabulations more readable, we have recoded this variable by considering values between 0 and 4 as absence of trust in others, 5 as neutral position, and, finally, those between 6 and 10 as trust in others.

The second aspect of social capital refers to the "structure and nature of people's personal networks" (Scrivens and Smith 2013, p. 21) and is concerned with whom people know and what they do to establish and maintain

Table 6.7 Solidarity actions towards target groups by social capital (in %)

		Refugees support	Unemployed support	Disabled support	Total
Social trust	People cannot be trusted	38.8	46.3	46.7	51.2
	Neutral	18.3	18.1	18.6	20.0
	People can be trusted	42.8	35.6	34.7	28.8
	Total	100	100	100	100
	N	570	736	1021	2041
Frequency of meetings with friends	Less than once this month	22.1	23.5	27.3	33.3
	Once or twice this month	35.4	36.9	36.1	34.4
	Every week	35.1	32.7	30.6	26.9
	Almost every day	7.5	6.9	6.0	5.4
	Total	100	100	100	100
	N	576	741	1030	2087

their personal relationships. Meeting socially with friends at least once a week is a well-established measure of this phenomenon (e.g. European Social Survey).

Results seem to confirm the relevance of social capital for solidarity actions (see Table 6.7). As for solidarity actions towards all target groups, people who trust others are clearly over-represented compared to the total population. Indeed, on average 29% of the sample trust in others, whereas this percentage increases at 35% among people supporting the disabled, at 36% among people supporting the unemployed, and at 43% among people supporting refugees. In the latter case, more people trust in others than do not trust in others. It follows that solidarity towards foreigners is strongly associated with a generalised trust in human beings.

A similar pattern is depicted by the second measure of social capital related to the frequency of social connections. Among people engaging in solidarity activities in favour of all target groups, those meeting socially with friends at least every week are strongly over-represented compared to the total population, whereas those who meet less than once a month are strongly under-represented (especially among those supporting refugees and unemployed).

Solidarity Actions and Political Factors

Previously, we mentioned that solidarity has not only a philanthropic dimension but also a political one. Therefore, it is important to look at the relationship between solidarity actions and politics, in particular looking at respondents' attitudes towards politics, their self-placement along the left-right spectrum and along the libertarian-authoritarian dimension, and their voting intentions.

The respondents' attitudes towards politics are derived from their interest in politics and party attachment (see Table 6.8). The level of cognitive political involvement of respondents can be measured on a four-point scale by their interest in politics. On average, those that are very or somewhat interested in politics are 64%. This percentage remarkably increases among people who are engaged in solidarity practices: 74% as for refugees, 75% as for the unemployed, and 70% as for the disabled. Another measure of involvement in politics is the psychological feeling of attachment towards a party, which is also an important explanatory variable of voting behaviour (Campbell et al. 1960). Results strengthen what we have previously seen: political involvement seems to be associated with engagement in solidarity actions. Indeed, on average those who say they are close to a party are 76%. Among people engaging in solidarity actions, this percentage increases, ranging from 81% within the disability field to 85.5% within the unemployment field. Research has stressed the linkage between cognitive involvement in politics and political participation. For instance, low levels of cognitive engagement in politics and the withdrawal from political parties

Table 6.8 Solidarity actions towards target groups by political involvement (in %)

		Refugees support	Unemployed support	Disabled support	Total
Political interest	Not at all interested	6.0	6.4	7.0	11.5
	Not very interested	20.0	18.4	22.7	24.5
	Quite interested	46.8	47.9	45.8	43.7
	Very interested	27.2	27.2	24.6	20.3
	Total	100	100	100	100
	N	565	730	1011	2024
Party attachment	No party	15.7	14.5	19.0	23.9
	Close to a party	84.3	85.5	81.0	76.1
	Total	100	100	100	100
	N	537	690	967	1911

are important factors explaining young people's lower involvement in institutional (and non-institutional) political participation (García-Albacete 2014). Political interest is also an important explanatory factor of young people's voting behaviour (Maggini 2016). Our data show that political involvement is also associated with civic engagement through solidarity activities. This is not surprising, given that civic engagement refers to "actions and behaviours that can be seen as contributing positively to the collective life of a community or society" (Scrivens and Smith 2013, p. 28), including activities such as political participation.

At this point, what about the relationship between political self-placement on the left-right scale and solidarity actions in favour of different target groups? The political self-placement of respondents has been measured from 0 to 10, with the value of 0 corresponding to the far left and the value of 10 corresponding to the far right. Consequently, we have considered values between 0 and 4 as "centre left", 5 as "centre", those between 7 and 10 as "centre right", and, finally, missing values as "not self-placed" (see Table 6.9). These data show that the ideological character of people supporting the disabled is very similar to the total population's. There is a substantial equilibrium between centre-left and centre-right people. Conversely, centre-left people are over-represented among people supporting the unemployed (37% vs. 33% of the whole sample) and, especially, among people supporting refugees (41% vs. 33%).

Table 6.9 Solidarity actions towards target groups by left-right self-placement and libertarian-authoritarian index (in %)

		Refugees support	Unemployed support	Disabled support	Total
Left-right self-placement	Centre left	40.7	37.0	35.5	35.4
	Centre	17.9	16.3	17.0	15.6
	Centre right	31.1	34.1	34.4	33.0
	Not self-placed	10.4	12.6	13.0	18.0
	Total	*100*	*100*	*100*	*100*
	N	*576*	*741*	*1030*	*2087*
Libertarian-authoritarian index	Authoritarian	34.1	39.5	41.1	42.1
	Neutral	25.3	22.6	23.9	22.3
	Libertarian	40.6	37.9	35.0	35.7
	Total	*100*	*100*	*100*	*100*
	N	*490*	*626*	*871*	*1726*

This confirms our hypothesis that disability is not a divisive issue in political terms, whereas solidarity engagement in the other two fields is more related to political-ideological elements. Once again, the field of refugees is singled out for its specificity: here, centre-left people are by far the largest category. Finally, it is worth noting that people not self-placed on the left-right scale are under-represented in all fields, signalling again the positive linkage between political involvement and civic engagement in solidarity actions.

Table 6.9 shows the relationship between the libertarian-authoritarian index and solidarity actions, too. Electoral studies have highlighted that new political issues linked to the libertarian-authoritarian dimension have become salient for voters (Thomassen 2005), besides the traditional lines of political contestation (left-right and religion). In our survey, there are several questions connected to a broader libertarian-authoritarian divide, as confirmed by a factor analysis.[3] Consequently, we created an additive index linked to a unique factor component. This index is an indicator of libertarian values, and we recoded it classifying values between 0 and 4.4 as "authoritarian", values between 4.6 and 5.4 as "neutral", and values between 5.6 and 10 as "libertarian". Findings confirm that disability is not a divisive issue in political terms, whereas solidarity engagement in the unemployment field and, above all, in the refugees field is more related to political values. Indeed, in the latter field people with libertarian values are by far the largest category, whereas within the whole sample people with authoritarian values are the largest category.

Focusing on voting behaviour (see Table 6.10) confirms previous analysis: a difference between centre-left and right-wing parties' voters emerges only among people carrying out solidarity activities in favour of refugees. Indeed, people who vote for centre-left parties (Democratic Party and radical left parties) are over-represented compared to the total population, whereas right-wing voters of Northern League are under-represented. This is in line with our expectation. Regarding the Five Star Movement, its voters are over-represented among people engaging in solidarity actions. According to several studies, indeed, the Five Star Movement is a web-populist party (Corbetta and Gualmini 2013) appealing for direct democracy and cross-cutting the traditional left-right dimension (Maggini 2014; Tronconi 2015). This also means that among its voters there are people with left-wing values (pro-refugees) as well as right-wing people (anti-migration). The Five Star Movement is the most over-represented among people supporting the unemployed. This is

Table 6.10 Solidarity actions towards target groups by voting intentions (in %)

	Refugees support	Unemployed support	Disabled support	Total
Italian left (SI/SEL)	3.0	3.3	2.9	2.3
Democratic Party	20.6	16.8	19.1	18.0
Five Star Movement	26.7	30.8	26.2	23.9
Popular area	3.1	2.6	2.2	1.3
Forward Italy	6.4	6.3	6.5	5.9
Northern League	8.3	10.1	10.6	10.6
Brothers of Italy	3.5	4.1	3.5	3.2
Communist Refoundation Party	2.9	2.9	1.8	1.5
Other party	4.4	3.6	3.7	3.2
Do not know	21.1	19.6	23.6	30.2
Total	*100*	*100*	*100*	*100*
N	*576*	*741*	*1030*	*2087*

consistent with the over-representation of this party among the unemployed, especially young people. Radical left parties are also over-represented in this field, but centre-right voters are in line with the average. Conversely, Democratic Party voters are under-represented. Thus, in the unemployment field, there is not a clear distinction in terms of left and right but a more contingent distinction between voters of opposition parties and voters of the main governing party.[4] Finally, there is no significant pattern in terms of voting choices regarding solidarity actions towards the disabled.

Solidarity Actions, Social Beliefs, and Religiosity

In order to provide a complete picture of people engaged in solidarity, it is necessary to also take into account respondents' social beliefs and religiosity.

Conditionality and deservingness can play an important role regarding solidarity among the public (Oorschot 2000, 2006). Previously we have seen that a large majority of Italians support fiscal solidarity measures towards countries with big public debts. Table 6.11 presents the reasons for fiscal solidarity: 52% of respondents subscribe the idea of reciprocity and deservingness. According to these views, solidarity within the EU is an exchange relation of giving and receiving help; moreover, groups receiving help need to show that they are worth being helped.

This vision is shared by people engaging in solidarity actions, with no substantial differences among target groups. Only a minority of 20% claims that it is a moral duty to help other member states in need. Noticeably, this unconditioned form of solidarity is more widespread among people involved in solidarity activities, especially among those helping refugees (27%).

As shown in Table 6.11, this conditionality is confirmed regarding migrants. Only a minority of 8% is in favour of granting migrants access to social benefits and services immediately on arrival. This is a lower share compared to those who would never grant migrants access to social benefits and services (12%). Hence, access is conditional on two aspects: they should have worked and paid taxes (38%) and they should become citizens of the country (36%). A minority (6.5%) is more generous, granting migrants access more easily after one year staying in Italy (having worked or not). Conditionality decreases among Italians involved in solidarity activities, especially those active in the field of refugees (as it was predictable). In fact, among people supporting refugees, 28% show the most generous attitudes compared to 14.2% among the total population (22% among people supporting the unemployed and 18% among those helping the disabled). Symmetrically, those who say "never" are under-represented in all fields. In addition, among people supporting refugees, those who claim the requisite of citizenship are around 10 percentage points below average. Noteworthy, the largest category remains "after have worked and paid taxes for one year", even in the pro-refugees solidarity field (40%). To sum up, according to our interviewees, solidarity definitely entails entitlements and mutual obligations; this conditioned solidarity prevails even among those helping people who are not part of the national community as refugees.

In our survey, we asked respondents to name the specific group they would choose for charity donation among the following ones: unemployed people, people with disabilities, migrants, refugees/asylum seekers, and children. We can consider this variable as a proxy for deservingness, arguing that people are more likely to choose as preferred group for charity donation the group they consider more deserving of help. Results show (see Table 6.11) that children are by far the most preferred group for charity donation (49%), followed by the disabled (24%) and the unemployed (21%). For Italian citizens, refugees and migrants are definitely the groups less deserving (4% and 2%, respectively). Of course, these percentages increase among those supporting refugees, but, even in this case, the

Table 6.11 Solidarity actions towards target groups by social beliefs: reciprocity, conditionality, and deservingness (in %)

		Refugees support	Unemployed support	Disabled support	Total
Reason to state for financial help for EU countries in trouble	It is our moral duty to help other member states that are in need	26.8	24.5	23.4	20.2
	Total N	576	741	1030	2087
	EU member states should help each other; every country may require help someday	50.6	52.0	54.3	51.8
	Total N	576	741	1030	2087
Conditionality: when should migrants obtain rights to social benefits and services?	Immediately on arrival	13.3	10.2	8.5	7.7
	After living one year (worked or not)	14.9	11.5	9.7	6.5
	After worked and paid taxes one year	40.3	39.3	41.0	38.3
	After citizenship	26.5	31.2	33.5	35.7
	Never	5.0	7.8	7.2	11.8
	Total	100	100	100	100
	N	576	741	1030	2087
Preferred charity group for donation	Unemployed	20.5	25.8	18.7	20.9
	People with disabilities	22.5	23.3	27.4	23.8
	Migrants	6.2	4.5	3.5	2.4
	Refugees	8.1	5.0	4.9	3.8
	Children	42.6	41.4	45.5	49.1
	Total	100	100	100	100
	N	543	708	979	1898

children, the disabled, and the unemployed are by far more deserving than migrants and refugees. Looking at people supporting the disabled and the unemployed, a stronger correlation emerges between the type of solidarity field and the preferred group for donation, even if children are still the most preferred group. Again, these data confirm that groups receiving help need to be perceived as worth being helped. In this regard, foreigners deserve to be helped to the extent that they become part of the national community, at least through work and paying taxes.

Table 6.12 Solidarity actions towards target groups by religiosity (in %)

		Refugees support	Unemployed support	Disabled support	Total
Religiosity	Not religious	30.0	30.4	29.9	*33.4*
	Neutral	12.4	12.9	13.2	*13.0*
	Religious	57.6	56.8	57.0	*53.6*
	Total	*100*	*100*	*100*	*100*
	N	*573*	*739*	*1024*	*2050*

Finally, the profile of solidarity actions towards target groups can vary according to cultural orientations like religiosity[5] (see Table 6.12). Findings show that among Italians involved in solidarity activities, religious people are definitely over-represented compared to the average, being in all fields around 57%.

To sum up, solidarity towards refugees shows some specificities compared to solidarity towards other groups: it is more dependent on personal skills, resources, and social status, selfless, and linked to leftist/libertarian values.

Explanatory Factors of Solidarity Actions Towards the Refugees, the Unemployed, and the Disabled

This section outlines the results of a multivariate logistic regression analysis. Reported solidarity activities in favour of each target group are the dependent variables. In other words, we have three dichotomous dependent variables (for which 0 signifies "no action", 1 "at least one action") for each target group. The goal is to investigate the (different) determinants of solidarity activities among the three target groups. Which factors tend to promote (or inhibit) solidarity at the individual level? Is there variance comparing the target groups?

Four models for each target group have been created to answer our research questions. The results of estimation for the first three models are presented in Table 6.13, which includes odds ratios (with standard errors) as well as goodness-of-fit statistics (AIC and BIC coefficients, pseudo-R-squared values of Nagelkerke). In logistic regression, the odds ratio compares the odds of the outcome event (providing solidarity) one unit apart on the predictor. We have reported the selected independent variables[6] by

Table 6.13 Estimated effects on solidarity actions towards different target groups for some predictors, separated models by blocks of variables

	Refugees		Unemployed		Disabled	
	Odds ratio	SE	Odds ratio	SE	Odds ratio	SE
Model A						
Age	0.613	0.159	0.589*	0.138	2.397***	0.544
Gender (female)	0.979	0.104	0.762**	0.074	0.909	0.085
Intermediate education	0.880	0.108	1.003	0.111	1.054	0.111
High education	1.424*	0.220	1.388*	0.202	1.173	0.170
Middle class	0.432***	0.107	0.785	0.181	0.534**	0.126
Lower middle class	0.530*	0.136	0.955	0.228	0.611*	0.150
Working class	0.316***	0.0899	0.758	0.197	0.413***	0.108
Lower class	0.428**	0.126	0.999	0.268	0.523*	0.141
Other class	1.321	1.078	2.44	1.852	2.059	1.731
Social trust	6.508***	1.438	2.196***	0.429	2.399***	0.439
Frequency of meeting with friends	2.428***	0.444	2.317***	0.390	2.247***	0.378
Constant	0.344***	0.106	0.499*	0.142	0.682	0.194
N	*1982*		*1982*		*1982*	
Pseudo R^2	*0.074*		*0.036*		*0.035*	
AIC	*2197.8*		*2530.4*		*2668.6*	
BIC	*2264.9*		*2597.5*		*2735.7*	
Model B						
Age	0.344***	0.105	0.317***	0.090	1.137	0.305
Gender (female)	1.008	0.126	0.786*	0.093	0.974	0.111
Intermediate education	0.761	0.108	0.892	0.119	0.983	0.124
High education	1.275	0.227	1.194	0.206	0.976	0.156
Middle class	0.428**	0.115	0.894	0.243	0.479**	0.136
Lower middle class	0.483**	0.134	1.063	0.300	0.493*	0.143
Working class	0.327***	0.104	1.119	0.347	0.394**	0.124
Lower class	0.380**	0.128	1.017	0.333	0.486*	0.150
Other class	0.653	0.539	1.833	1.409	1.053	0.837
Political interest	2.290***	0.531	2.924***	0.654	2.489***	0.522
Party attachment	1.793**	0.335	2.043***	0.368	1.288	0.201
Left-right self-placement	0.570*	0.125	0.708	0.150	0.974	0.199
Libertarian-authoritarian index	2.835**	1.058	1.508	0.539	0.934	0.314
Constant	0.478	0.213	0.316**	0.139	1.096	0.458
N	*1369*		*1369*		*1369*	
Pseudo R^2	*0.056*		*0.049*		*0.022*	
AIC	*1616.4*		*1750.8*		*1864.5*	
BIC	*1689.5*		*1823.9*		*1937.6*	

(*continued*)

Table 6.13 (continued)

	Refugees		Unemployed		Disabled	
	Odds ratio	SE	Odds ratio	SE	Odds ratio	SE
Model C						
Age	0.621	0.170	0.448**	0.109	1.840*	0.443
Gender (female)	0.951	0.108	0.741**	0.075	0.851	0.084
Intermediate education	0.921	0.119	1.083	0.125	1.056	0.118
High education	1.387	0.241	1.385*	0.219	1.106	0.173
Middle class	0.451**	0.117	0.836	0.204	0.576*	0.141
Lower middle class	0.486**	0.130	0.939	0.236	0.606*	0.153
Working class	0.316***	0.095	0.848	0.233	0.431**	0.117
Lower class	0.384**	0.120	0.955	0.270	0.563*	0.158
Other class	1.808	1.212	3.147	2.168	2.814	2.200
Religiosity	1.906***	0.364	2.093***	0.359	1.989***	0.328
EU help motive: moral duty	1.339*	0.180	1.229	0.149	1.2	0.147
EU help motive: reciprocity	0.822	0.093	0.87	0.090	1.037	0.103
Conditionality for migrants: after living in Italy for a year	1.720*	0.468	1.668*	0.430	2.345**	0.632
Conditionality for migrants: after having worked and paid taxes for a year	0.489***	0.102	0.693	0.139	1.047	0.207
Conditionality for migrants: once obtaining citizenship	0.322***	0.069	0.579**	0.119	0.767	0.153
Conditionality for migrants: never	0.137***	0.043	0.378***	0.098	0.441***	0.109
Preferred charity group: the unemployed	1.169	0.168	1.825***	0.238	0.927	0.117
Preferred charity group: the disabled	1.114	0.155	1.309*	0.164	1.682***	0.210
Preferred charity group: migrants	5.374***	1.972	3.215***	1.084	2.453*	0.891
Preferred charity group: refugees/asylum seekers	3.284***	1.027	1.618	0.445	1.772*	0.494
Constant	1.535	0.563	0.850	0.292	0.952	0.320
N	1841		1841		1841	
Pseudo R^2	0.118		0.063		0.057	
AIC	1990.5		2327.7		2440.1	
BIC	2106.4		2443.6		2556	

*$p < 0.05$, **$p < 0.01$, ***$p < 0.001$

blocks: first, the socio-demographic variables and social capital measures; secondly, political factors (political interest, party attachment, left-right self-placement, libertarian-authoritarian index) controlled for socio-demographic characteristics (age, gender, education, social class); and thirdly, social beliefs (evaluations of reciprocity, conditionality, deservingness) and religiosity, again controlled for socio-demographic characteristics. Thus, it is possible to assess the contribution given by each group of variables to the model's goodness of fit, compared across target groups. Finally, Table 6.14 presents results for the full model with all independent variables for each target group.

Let us start with the first model. The overall predictive power of model A is quite low, explaining 7% of variance as for support of refugees and 4% as for disabled and unemployed support. It means that socio-demographic variables and social traits do not explain sufficiently the solidarity-based behaviour of the respondents. Looking at the p values of the predictors, clearly social traits prevail over basic socio-demographics. Indeed, for each target group, measures of social capital (social trust and frequency of social connections with friends) are both very significant with p at 0.1%. Furthermore, these variables show the highest odds ratios: higher level of social trust and social connections increase the odds of engaging in solidarity actions.

Regarding subjective social class, some categories are very significant with p at 0.1%: working class as for refugees and the disabled support and middle class as for refugees support (whereas it is significant with p at 1% for disabled support).

Here, a first difference between target groups emerges: social class is not related to solidarity towards the unemployed, whereas it seems to be related to solidarity towards refugees and the disabled. In the latter instance, all the social class dummies (except the residual category of "other class") are significant with respect to the reference category (upper/upper middle class). Looking at the odds ratio, belonging to classes different from the highest class decreases the odds of supporting refugees and the disabled.

Concerning socio-demographic characteristics, a high education level (with respect to the low level) increases the odds of supporting refugees and the unemployed (significant with p at 5%), whereas education does not matter in support for disability. Age is very significant (p at 0.1%) for disabled support and it is significant for unemployed support (p at 5%), but the direction of the effect is the opposite: ageing increases the odds of supporting the

Table 6.14 Estimated effects on solidarity actions towards different target groups for some predictors, full model

	Refugees		Unemployed		Disabled	
	Odds ratio	SE	Odds ratio	SE	Odds ratio	SE
Age	0.645	0.219	0.491*	0.153	2.034*	0.627
Gender (female)	1.242	0.175	0.872	0.112	1.078	0.133
Intermediate education	0.766	0.121	0.928	0.133	1.019	0.139
High education	1.175	0.248	1.079	0.202	0.883	0.167
Middle class	0.447*	0.143	1.049	0.306	0.544*	0.162
Lower middle class	0.589	0.194	1.397	0.423	0.627	0.192
Working class	0.492	0.182	1.763	0.590	0.555	0.184
Lower class	0.6	0.238	1.567	0.548	0.807	0.285
Other class	1.706	1.963	4.058	3.302	2.483	2.241
Social trust	3.567***	1.054	1.543	0.399	1.773*	0.444
Frequency of meeting with friends	2.717***	0.662	2.670***	0.606	2.969***	0.668
Political interest	1.900*	0.500	2.817***	0.685	2.263***	0.515
Party attachment	1.708*	0.377	1.833**	0.361	1.201	0.205
Left-right self-placement	0.854	0.218	0.887	0.206	1.237	0.278
Libertarian-authoritarian index	2.384*	1.039	1.507	0.616	1.023	0.397
Religiosity	2.207**	0.560	2.664***	0.605	2.501***	0.550
EU help motive: moral duty	1.355	0.221	1.32	0.194	1.156	0.168
Conditionality for migrants: after living in Italy for a year	1.518	0.497	1.68	0.521	2.432**	0.816
Conditionality for migrants: after having worked and paid taxes for a year	0.474**	0.118	0.664	0.162	1.054	0.264
Conditionality for migrants: once obtaining citizenship	0.303***	0.079	0.518**	0.131	0.724	0.185
Conditionality for migrants: never	0.126***	0.054	0.315***	0.110	0.449*	0.145
Preferred charity group: the unemployed	1.379	0.241	2.115***	0.342	1.092	0.167
Preferred charity group: the disabled	1.109	0.190	1.399*	0.217	1.843***	0.284
Preferred charity group: migrants	5.070***	2.282	3.936***	1.638	2.742*	1.292
Preferred charity group: refugees/asylum seekers	3.303**	1.214	1.677	0.516	1.745	0.608
Constant	0.134***	0.081	0.0748***	0.042	0.188**	0.102

(continued)

Table 6.14 (continued)

	Refugees		Unemployed		Disabled	
	Odds ratio	SE	Odds ratio	SE	Odds ratio	SE
N	1299		1299		1299	
Pseudo R^2	0.179		0.122		0.09	
AIC	1373.6		1569.5		1668.6	
BIC	1508		1703.9		1803	

*$p < 0.05$, **$p < 0.01$, ***$p < 0.001$

disabled and decreases the odds of supporting the unemployed. Finally, gender is significant (p at 5%) only as for unemployed support: being male increases the odds of supporting the unemployed.

If we move to model B, the contribution of political factors (controlled for socio-demographics) to the model's goodness of fit is low, with a clear difference between solidarity towards the disabled on the one hand and solidarity towards the other groups on the other. In fact, the model explains 6% and 5% of the variance as for refugees and unemployed support, respectively, and only 2% of variance as for the disabled. This confirms our hypothesis: solidarity towards the disabled is not related to political features, with the exception of the level of cognitive political involvement as measured by interest in politics, which is very significant and positively correlated with solidarity actions in favour of all target groups. The other measure of political involvement (party attachment) is very significant (p at 0.1%) for unemployed support and for refugees support (p at 1%). Finally, ideology in terms of left and right (p at 5%) and, above all, political values in terms of libertarian and authoritarian attitudes (p at 1%) are significant only regarding refugees support. The direction of the effect is in line with our expectations: moving to the right of the political space decreases the odds of supporting refugees, whereas the latter is positively associated with libertarian values. This means that solidarity towards refugees is the most characterised in political terms. This confirms that migration is a politically divisive issue.

So far, social traits and political factors (considered as separate blocks) are not sufficient to explain the solidarity-based behaviour of the respondents, and we have to move to Model C including social beliefs and religiosity, again controlled for socio-demographic characteristics. This model has a better predictive power, especially regarding support of refugees: 12%

of the variance is explained, compared to 6% for unemployed and disabled support. Looking at p values and odds ratios of predictors, we can notice similarities and differences between target groups as for explanatory factors of solidarity practices. Concerning similarities, it seems that religiosity is a good predictor of involvement in solidarity actions, regardless of the target group. Indeed, it is always very significant and odds ratios are high.

Regarding the reasons to support fiscal solidarity among EU member states, the dummy variable measuring reciprocity in help is not statistically significant, as well as the variable measuring an unconditioned form of solidarity ("it is our moral duty to help"), except for refugees support. In this latter instance, believing in an unconditioned form of solidarity towards EU countries in need increases the odds of supporting refugees (with p at 5%).

The fact that people supporting refugees have an unconditioned conception of solidarity is confirmed when migrants' entitlements to social benefits are taken into account: with respect to the reference category (granting access to social benefits and services immediately on arrival), both requisites of working/paying taxes and citizenship decrease in a significant way the odds of supporting refugees. Conversely, such dummies are not statistically significant for unemployed and disabled support, except citizenship-related conditionality that decreases the odds of supporting the unemployed with p at 1%. In addition, a tenuous form of conditionality (granting rights after living in Italy for a year) increases the odds of supporting of all target groups, especially the disabled (p at 1%). In this regard, a tenuous form of conditionality is a factor that somehow distinguishes solidarity with different target groups, but in general the absence of conditionality is a factor favouring practices of solidarity, and people against the integration of migrants are very unlikely to be engaged in solidarity actions, regardless of the target group (p at 0.1%).

Considering children as reference category, we notice that citing one of our target groups as the preferred charity group strongly increases the odds of supporting such a group. This occurs especially for the least preferred group by respondents, that is, migrants. Indeed, regardless of the target group, this dummy is always significant, and odds ratios are all very high. This means that a pro-migrants attitude helps solidarity actions in general. Finally, there is a difference between our target groups. Concerning support for refugees, deservingness plays a role only for migrants and refugees dummies (with respect to children). Conversely, as for unemployed support, all dummies are significant (except refugees). As for disabled support, the migrants and refugees dummies are significant in addition to the disabled dummy.

Finally, we have built a full model including all independent variables (except those that were not significant for any of the target groups) in order to see if previous results are confirmed when controlling for different blocks of independent variables (see Table 6.14). This model provides better goodness-of-fit statistics compared to previous models: it explains 18% of the variance for support of refugees, 12% for unemployed support, and 9% for disabled support. Furthermore, AIC and BIC coefficients are definitely lower (and thus better) compared to separated models.

The full model shows also some important differences compared to separated models. First, gender and education are no longer significant for any of the target groups. Therefore, basic socio-demographic characteristics are not explanatory factors of solidarity practices, except for age in the unemployment and disability field. Ageing significantly increases the odds of supporting the disabled, whereas decreases the odds of supporting the unemployed (p at 5%). It has been shown that younger and older citizens are more active in social movements, according to different levels of "biographical availability" in the life course (Beyerlein and Bergstrand 2013).

Secondly, social class in the full model has lost predictive power. Only being middle class is significant (with p at 5%) for refugees and disabled support, with a negative effect compared to the reference category (upper/upper middle class).

Thirdly, the variable that measures the absence of conditionality for fiscal solidarity among EU member states ("moral duty to help") is no longer significant for refugees support.

In general, however, the full model confirms previous results regarding social capital, political interest, religiosity, conditionality, and deservingness.

First of all, for each target group, both measures of social capital (social trust and frequency of social connections with friends) are still significant, except social trust for unemployed support. Significance is always very high with p at 0.1%, except social trust for disabled support with p at 5%. Furthermore, these variables show high odds ratios: higher levels of social trust and social connections increase the odds of engaging in solidarity actions. This occurs in particular as regards social trust with respect to support for refugees and the frequency of social connections for disabled support: one unit increase in trust in others increases 3.6 times the odds of supporting refugees, and one unit increase in frequency of meeting with friends increases around three times the odds of supporting the disabled. Therefore, our first hypothesis is confirmed: the more an individual is socially embedded and trustworthy of others (the more her/his social capital), the more she/he will support people in need (regardless who are these people in need). This is line with previous research that has shown the importance of social capital for solidarity (Putnam et al. 2003; Jenkins 1983; Bourdieu 1986). Indeed, solidarity actions are positively linked to social capital because a high level of interpersonal trust fosters cooperation among individuals and a good frequency of social connections give people access to a wider range of possible support in times of need, producing positive outcomes at a community level (Halpern 2005).

Regarding political factors, the level of cognitive political involvement as measured by interest in politics is a significant variable fostering the odds of being involved in solidarity actions, regardless of the aided group (with high odds ratios between 1.9 and 2.8). The other measure of political involvement (party attachment) is still significant for unemployed support (p at 1%) and for refugees support (p at 5%). This confirms our hypothesis that political factors are more related to solidarity towards the unemployed and refugees than to disabled support. Political involvement in terms of interest in politics and party attachment is often associated with civic engagement (Scrivens and Smith 2013). The latter is another element that can help individuals to develop their skills and social values (such as trust in others), and, consequently, it can foster solidarity (Putnam et al. 1994).

Nevertheless, an important difference emerges when political factors are controlled for other blocks of independent variables. Indeed, as regards refugees support, the libertarian-authoritarian index is still significant, whereas the left-right self-placement is no longer significant compared to previous separated model for political variables (Model B). Ideological orientations in terms of left and right are not important predictors of solidarity practices in Italy for any of our target groups, contrary to our expectations based on previous literature (Likki and Staerklé 2014). Conversely, according to our expectations, political values in terms of authoritarian and libertarian attitudes foster solidarity actions towards a specific target group like refugees. This confirms that migrants-related issues are divisive issues that are strongly politicised by right-wing populist parties like the Northern League in order to gain votes (Mudde 2011). Indeed, voters of these parties are often characterised by both authoritarian values on social issues and leftist orientations on economic issues. This also confirms that the libertarian-authoritarian dimension is something different from the traditional left-right dimension, bringing a new set of culture war issues onto the political agenda (Flanagan and Lee 2003). One of these new cultural issues is precisely the migration issue.

As for traditional cultural orientations, it is conversely confirmed that religiosity is a very good predictor of involvement in solidarity actions, regardless of the target group. Indeed, it is always very significant (with p at 0.1% or at 1%), and odds ratios are high (between 2.2 and 2.7). Definitely, we can say that Italian religious people are more likely to be engaged in solidarity actions. This confirms our expectation based on scholarly writing (Abela 2004; Stegmueller et al. 2012; Lichterman 2015), which has shown the importance of religiosity to explain different levels of solidarity.

With regard to conditionality for migrants' entitlements to social benefits, previous results are generally confirmed: people against the integration of migrants are very unlikely to be engaged in solidarity actions, regardless of the target group, even if this occurs especially for actions in favour of refugees and unemployed people (p at 0.1%). Furthermore, both requisites of working/paying taxes and citizenship decrease in a significant way the odds of supporting refugees. Conversely, such dummies are not statistically significant for support of other target groups, except the requisite of citizenship that also significantly decreases the odds of supporting unemployed people. Furthermore, this time a tenuous form of conditionality (granting rights after living in Italy for a year) increases only the odds of supporting the disabled. In this regard, we can say that in general the absence of conditionality is a factor favouring practices of solidarity, especially those towards refugees, whereas people involved in solidarity practices towards the disabled share a tenuous form of conditionality as regards migrants' entitlements to social benefits. Our hypothesis is therefore confirmed: the more an individual conceive solidarity in universalistic terms without perceptions of reciprocity and conditionality, the more she/he will support refugees.

Regarding deservingness, once again, citing one of our target groups as the preferred charity group strongly increases the odds of supporting such a group. Thus, deservingness is definitely a factor fostering solidarity actions in favour of a specific group considered as worth receiving help (Oorshot 2000, 2006), confirming our expectation. Nevertheless, people engaged in solidarity actions are more likely to have positive dispositions not only towards the group they are supporting. This is true especially for people engaged in solidarity actions towards the unemployed: the odds of supporting the unemployed do not depend on a specific preferred charity group. Indeed, all dummies are significant, as previously seen in Model C. Furthermore, once again, a pro-migrants attitude helps solidarity actions in general (albeit to a lesser extent when support towards the disabled is taken into consideration). In previous section, we showed that for Italian respondents, migrants are definitely the group less deserving of charity donations. Therefore, we can argue that people mentioning migrants as the preferred charity group are those who share universalistic conceptions of solidarity (i.e. solidarity towards the humankind, not towards a specific target group) and consequently are more likely to support needy people in general, regardless of their ethnic, social, or physical characteristics, as confirmed by our data.

Conclusions

This chapter aimed to deepen knowledge on solidarity in Italy by providing fresh empirical analyses on solidarity practices with respect to three target groups (the disabled, the unemployed, and refugees) and to explain such solidarity actions with reference to social traits of the respondents, their beliefs, and their political preferences. This study was needed for substantial and theoretical reasons. As regards the first aspect, solidarity is at the centre of the public debate in European societies, drawing the attention of the media, policy-makers, and ordinary citizens. Enduring conflicts among EU member states about financial solidarity with indebted states and a fair burden-sharing in regard to the high numbers of refugees, as well as the rise of xenophobic and populist parties in most European countries, unveil that solidarity is highly contested not only at interstate level but also among European citizens. In this regard, Italy is a relevant case study to explain factors which can strengthen (or inhibit) solidarity actions, because the country in the last years has faced two different crises: the global financial crisis of 2008 that hit hard on Southern European countries and the refugee crisis that since 2014 particularly affected a country positioned at the centre of several migration routes in the Mediterranean Sea. It is evident that in such a difficult landscape, solidarity is particularly under pressure. Hence, understanding factors that foster (or inhibit) solidarity actions towards vulnerable groups that have been strongly affected by different crises can help to shed new light on the most important triggers of interpersonal solidarity in general (working even in contexts of crisis and welfare state retrenchment).

From a theoretical standpoint, previous research has provided a variety of insights, even though it was marked by a number of limitations. First, previous empirical research has privileged the attitudinal dimension of solidarity, describing and explaining the disposition to help. Less attention has been paid to the explanation of solidarity practices. Second, much research has focused on public support of redistributive policies (Alesina and Giuliano 2011; Amat and Wibbels 2009; Fong 2001; Rehm 2009), but less knowledge was available in regard to interpersonal forms of solidarity. Furthermore, previous studies have not addressed solidarity-related issues in a systematic manner, focusing only on specific explanatory factors: some have focused on social capital (Putnam et al. 2003; Jenkins 1983), others on social beliefs like perceptions of deservingness (Oorschot 2000, 2006), others on religiosity (Abela 2004; Stegmueller et al. 2012; Lichterman 2015), others on political preferences (Likki and Staerklé 2014), and so on. This study has permitted to fill this gap, providing a comprehensive explanation of social, political, and attitudinal triggers of solidarity practices towards specific groups of needy people.

Throughout the chapter, first we have provided a general picture of a variety of solidarity attitudes and practices in Italy in times of crises; secondly, we have investigated the (different) determinants of solidarity activities towards the three target groups.

The picture of the solidarity activities' context shows that Italians are open to solidarity even in times of crises and this entails to some extent other Europeans and non-Europeans. Furthermore, Italian citizens support the typical redistributive policies of the European social model. Nevertheless, this social model remains strictly linked to the traditional nation state. Indeed, solidarity has a strong political element: it requires, in first instance, that the targets of solidarity are part of the (national) community in terms of citizenship. This citizenship, however, is not a purely formal status but requires shared rights and obligations. Indeed, our findings suggest that most citizens are sceptical about a universalistic and humanitarian conception of solidarity (i.e. solidarity towards human being as such) that entails unconditional solidarity. Overall, for most citizens, solidarity is rights based and thus tied to the notion of citizenship, that is, delimited by legal entitlements and mutual obligations (such as receiving social benefits and paying taxes or contributions). Moreover, groups receiving help need to show that they are worth being helped.

Regarding target groups, the disability field is the most "crowded" field in terms of solidarity engagement, involving around half of respondents. If we look at the different types of solidarity practices, political protest-oriented activities are carried out especially in favour of the unemployed, whereas the other two fields seem to be less contentious, especially the disability field.

Indeed, charity behaviour definitely characterises solidarity actions towards the disabled. As regards solidarity towards refugees, after the charity behaviour of donating money, the most frequent activity is a relatively more political one, that is, buying or refusing to buy products in support to the goals in favour of refugees. Furthermore, the descriptive analysis shows that solidarity towards refugees displays some specificities compared to solidarity towards other groups: it is more dependent on personal skills, resources, and social status, selfless, and linked to leftist/libertarian values.

As far as the explanatory analysis of the determinants of solidarity activities towards target groups is concerned, findings show that solidarity is a multifaceted phenomenon and its practices can be fostered by a variety of factors: social, political, attitudinal. Hence, focusing only on one kind of these factors would be quite limiting and not sufficient to understand the complexity of reasons underlying the individual choices to support others in need (or, conversely, to not support others). In addition, our analysis shows that there are not only general triggers of solidarity practices but also explanatory factors that are related to specific target groups. As regards similarities between target groups, the most important factors fostering solidarity practices in Italy are social capital, religiosity, cognitive political involvement, and deservingness. Our main hypotheses based on previous research have been confirmed: Italians are more likely involved in solidarity activities (regardless of the target group) when they trust in others and/or have frequent social connections, are religious, and consider the group they are supporting as worth being helped. Another key lesson can be drawn from our analysis: cognitive political involvement measured by interest in politics is another important factor favouring solidarity activities, regardless of the target group. We can argue that this can be the signal, once again, of the importance of social embeddedness. Indeed, people interested in politics are usually individuals characterised by a high level of social resources and civic engagement (Scrivens and Smith 2013). The latter is another element that can help individuals to develop their social capital, and, consequently, it can foster solidarity (Putnam et al. 1994).

As regards group-specific triggers of solidarity, our hypothesis that political factors play a more important role for refugees and unemployed support compared to disabled support has been confirmed. This finding can be explained by the fact that solidarity towards the disabled is not a contested issue in the Italian context and most of the people engaged in disability organisations are not motivated by ideological-political objectives but by philanthropic or personal reasons (for instance, many disability organisations in Italy are composed by people with disabilities and/or their families).

Furthermore, as expected, libertarian values foster solidarity actions towards refugees. Nevertheless, contrary to our expectations, left-right ideology does not matter when controlled for other variables. This also confirms the specificity of the libertarian-authoritarian dimension compared to the traditional left-right dimension and the importance of new cultural issues (e.g. migration) for contentious politics (Flanagan and Lee 2003). This is particularly important for a country (Italy) that has faced in the last years both economic turmoil and refugee crisis: right-wing populist parties like Northern League (Mudde 2011) have mobilised more on the libertarian-authoritarian dimension than on the economic left-right divide in order to gain votes among the lower classes by using migrants as scapegoating of their fears and economic distress. Therefore, solidarity towards refugees entails political commitment to libertarian values as opposed to authoritarian stances. The fact that solidarity with the unemployed does not separate people with different political orientations in terms of left and right, conversely, can be explained by the over-representation of the Five Star Movement voters among people supporting the unemployed. According to several studies, indeed, the Five Star Movement is a web-populist party (Corbetta and Gualmini 2013) that cross-cuts the traditional left-right dimension (Maggini 2014; Tronconi 2015).

Finally, another key finding emerges from what has been said so far: solidarity towards refugees shows more specific explanatory factors compared to support for other disadvantaged groups. It is more bounded by political orientations, as above mentioned, and at the same time is clearly an unconditioned form of solidarity. Indeed, it is closely tied to social beliefs like absence of conditionality as regards granting migrants the entitlements to social benefits and services. Conversely, people supporting the disabled are more likely to agree with a tenuous form of conditionality as for migrants' access to social benefits. According to our respondents, refugees and migrants, among our target groups, are those less deserving of charity donations, whereas the disabled is the most preferred group. Consequently, we can argue that solidarity towards refugees entails a more selfless and universalistic conception of solidarity compared to solidarity towards disadvantaged groups (e.g. the disabled) that are considered by the majority of society as worth being helped. In other words, support for refugees can be considered as a specific aspect of solidarity with human beings as such. It should be added that, according to our data, people against the integration of migrants are very unlikely to be engaged in solidarity actions, regardless of the field, and people who mention migrants as preferred charity group for donation are more likely to carry out solidarity activities in favour of all target groups.

Appendix

Table 6.15 Variables used for the analysis: original wording, recoding, and distributions within the sample

Variable and item(s)	First recoding	Distribution	Second recoding	Distribution
[age] How old are you?	1 = 18–24 years, 2 = 25–34 years, 3 = 35–44 years, 4 = 55–64 years, 5 = 65 years and older	7.2%, 14.3%, 17.6%, 18.9%, 23.7%, 18.3%	Standardised	M = 0.44
[gender] Are you male or female? 1 = male, 2 = female	0 = male; 1 = female	52.0%		
[education_set] What is the highest level of education that you have completed? (ISCED-list)	0 = lower education; 1 = higher education; 2 = intermediate education	52.5%, 12.3%, 35.2%		
[income_IT] What is your household's *MONTHLY* net income, after tax and compulsory deductions, from all sources? (ten deciles)	1 = 0–1305 euro; 2 = 1306–1920 euro; 3 = 1921–2665 euro; 4 = 2666–3780 euro; 5 = 3781 euro or more	28.1%, 26.2%, 22.9%, 16.6%, 6.2%		
[refsup] Have you ever done any of the following in order to support the rights of refugees/asylum seekers? (six options)	0 = 0; 1 = refugees support	27.6%		
[unemprights] Have you ever done any of the following in order to support the rights of the unemployed? (six options)	0 = 0; 1 = unemployed support	35.5%		
[dissup] Have you ever done any of the following in order to support disability rights? (six options)	0 = 0; 1 = disabled support	49.4%		

(*continued*)

Table 6.15 (continued)

Variable and item(s)	First recoding	Distribution	Second recoding	Distribution
[supotherc] Have you ever done one of the following in order to support the rights of people/groups in your own country? (six options)	0 = 0; 1 = in your country	46.7%		
[supEU] Have you ever done one of the following in order to support the rights of people/groups in other countries within the European Union? (six options)	0 = 0; 1 = in a country in the EU	31.7%		
[supoutsideEU] Have you ever done one of the following in order to support the rights of people/groups in countries outside the European Union? (six options)	0 = 0; 1 = outside the EU	32.8%		
[EUaid] The European Union provides development aid to assist certain countries outside the EU in their fight against poverty and in their development. How important do you think it is to help people in developing countries? (1–5)	–	3.5%, 6.9%, 18.3%, 45.6%, 25.7%		
[socialclass] People often say that they belong to the working class, the middle class, the upper class, and so forth. Which of the following classes do you feel that you belong to? (seven classes)	0 = upper/upper middle class; 1 = middle class; 2 = lower middle class; 3 = working class; 4 = lower class; 5 = other class	4.4%, 40.4%, 27.2%, 15.9%, 11.5%, 0.5%		
[polint] How interested, if at all, would you say you are in politics? (1–4)	Standardised	M = 0.58		
[metfriends] During the past month, how often have you met socially with friends not living in your household? (1–4)	Standardised	M = 0.35		

(continued)

Table 6.15 (continued)

Variable and item(s)	First recoding	Distribution	Second recoding	Distribution
[conditionality] Thinking of people coming to live in Italy from other countries, when do you think they should obtain the same rights to social benefits and services as citizens already living here?	0 = immediately on arrival; 1 = after living in Italy for a year (worked or not); 2 = only after they have worked and paid taxes for at least a year; 3 = once they have become an Italian citizen; 4 = they should never get the same right	7.7%, 6.5%, 38.3%, 35.7%, 11.8%		
[givecharity] There are many reasons why people can't give to charity. If you had to choose to donate money to ONLY ONE charity of the following groups, which one would you choose?	0 = children; 1 = unemployed; 2 = people with disabilities; 3 = migrants; 4 = refugees	49.1%, 20.9%, 23.8%, 2.4%, 3.8%		
[EUhelpmotiv] There are many reasons to state for or against financial help for EU countries in trouble. Which one of the following best reflects how you feel? (four options) 2. It is our moral duty to help other member states that are in need (0–1)	–	20.2%		
3. The European Union member states should help each other, as somewhere along the way every country may require help (0–1)	–	51.8%		
[fairsociety_income] In order to be considered fair, what should a society provide? Please tell me how important or unimportant it is to you eliminating big inequalities in income between citizens (1–5)	–	1.4%, 3.0%, 14.9%, 40.0%, 40.7%		
[EUdebt] The EU is currently pooling funds to help EU countries having difficulties in paying their debts. To what extent do you agree or disagree with this measure? (1–5)	–	5.2%, 11.2%, 17.6%, 47.4%, 18.7%		

(continued)

Table 6.15 (continued)

Variable and item(s)	First recoding	Distribution	Second recoding	Distribution
[socialtrust] Generally speaking, would you say that most people can be trusted or that you can't be too careful in dealing with people? Please state your answer on a scale of 0–10	0 = people cannot be trusted (0–4); 1 = neutral (5); 2 = people can be trusted (6–10)	51.2%, 20.0%, 28.8%	Standardised	M = 0.40
[lrscale] People sometimes talk about the left and the right in politics. Where would you place yourself on the following? (0–10)	1 = centre left (0–4); 2 = centre (5); 3 = centre right (6–10); 4 = not self-placed (999)	33.4%, 15.6%, 33.0%, 18.0%	Standardised	M = 0.50
[libauth] How would you place your opinion on this scale? 0 means you agree completely with the statement on the left; 10 means you agree completely with the statement on the right	Index, recoded: 0 = authoritarian (0–4.4); 1 = neutral (4.6–5.4); 3 = libertarian (5.6–10)	42.1% 22.3% 35.7%	Index, standardised	(alpha = 0.93) M = 0.48
[libauth_career] Children vs. career (0–10)				
[libauth_abortion] No abortion vs. freedom of abortion (0–10)				
[libauth_parenting] Authority vs. independent judgement (0–10)				
[libauth_criminals] Tougher sentences vs. no tougher sentences (0–10)				
[libauth_adoption] No adoption vs. adoption for homosexuals (0–10)				
[partyattach] Which of the following parties do you feel closest to? (ten options)	0 = no party; 1 = close to a party	76.1%		
[votenowparty_IT] If there were a general election in Italy tomorrow, for which party would you vote? (ten options: Sinistra Ecologia e Libertà (SEL)/Sinistra Italiana, Partito Democratico, Movimento 5 Stelle, Area Popolare (Nuovo Centrodestra–UDC), Forza Italia, Lega Nord, Fratelli d'Italia Alleanza Nazionale, Partito della Rifondazione Comunista, other party, do not know)	–	2.3%, 18.0%, 23.9%, 1.3%, 5.9%, 10.6%, 3.2%, 1.5%, 3.2%, 30.2%		
[religiosity] Regardless of whether you belong to a particular religion, how religious would you say you are on a scale from 0 to 10?	0 = not religious (0–4); 1 = neutral (5); 2 = religious (6–10)	33.4%, 13.0%, 53.6%	Standardised	M = 0.53

Notes

1. The initiative was unilaterally launched and financed by the Italian government in October 2013 and ended in December 2014 to rescue migrants in the Mediterranean.
2. Weights have been used for all analyses.
3. In particular, we have run a principal component factor (PCF) analysis including variables measuring respondents' opinions on 0–10 agreement scales linked to several values-related issues: on "women career" versus "children care", on "freedom of abortion" versus "prohibition of abortion", on "child adoption for homosexuals" versus "prohibiting child adoption", on "tougher sentences to fight crime" versus "tougher sentences bring nothing", on "parenting authority" versus "child independent judgement". We detected just one statically significant dimension. Factor loadings were particularly high (between 0.85 and 0.93) for all items and the reliability scale was very high (alpha test 0.93). Hence, relying on the five above-mentioned items, it is possible to build an additive index of libertarian values.
4. The Democratic Party is in government with minor allies since 2013.
5. This variable measures how religious the respondent is on a scale from 0 to 10, where 0 stands for "not at all religious" and 10 for "very religious". This variable has been recoded in order to make cross-tabulations more readable by classifying values between 0 and 4 as "not religious", 5 as "neutral", and values between 6 and 10 as "religious".
6. In order to select independent variables, we have looked at the bivariate Pearson's correlations between variables introduced in the previous section for cross-tabulations. According to the strength of the associations (Cohen 1988), we have excluded some variables (e.g. income level, voting choices) in order to avoid items picking up on the same covariance component. Finally, before running logistic regression models, independent variables have been normalised trough rescaling.

References

Abela, A. M. (2004). Solidarity and Religion in the European Union: A Comparative Sociological Perspective. In P. Xuereb (Ed.), *The Value(s) of a Constitution for Europe* (pp. 71–101). Malta: European Documentation and Research Centre.

Ajzen, I., & Fishbein, M. (2005). The Influence of Attitudes on Behavior. In D. Albarracín, B. T. Johnson, & M. P. Zanna (Eds.), *The Handbook of Attitudes* (pp. 173–221). Mahwah, NJ: Erlbaum.

Alesina, A., & Giuliano, P. (2011). Preferences for Redistribution. In J. Benhabib, A. Bisin, & M. Jackson (Eds.), *Handbook of Social Economics* (pp. 93–131). San Diego, CA: North-Holland.

Amat, F., & Wibbels, E. (2009). *Electoral Incentives, Group Identity and Preferences for Redistribution.* Instituto Juan March de Estudios e Investigaciones, Working Paper 246.

Arendt, H. (1972). *Crises of the Republic.* New York: Harcourt Brace Jovanovich.

Baglioni, S. (2010). The Role of Civil Society Actors in the Contentious Politics of Unemployment. In M. Giugni (Ed.), *The Contentious Politics of Unemployment in Europe* (pp. 127–151). Basingstoke: Palgrave Macmillan.

Beyerlein, K., & Bergstrand, K. (2013). Biographical Availability. In D. A. Snow, D. Della Porta, B. Klandermans, & D. McAdam (Eds.), *The Wiley-Blackwell Encyclopedia of Social and Political Movements* (pp. 137–138). New York: Wiley-Blackwell.

Blekesaune, M., & Quadagno, J. (2003). Public Attitudes Toward Welfare State Policies: A Comparative Analysis of 24 Countries. *European Sociological Review, 19*(5), 415–427.

Blumer, H. (1955). Attitudes and the Social Act. *Social Problems, 3*(2), 59–65.

Bourdieu, P. (1986). The Forms of Capital. In J. Richardson (Ed.), *Handbook of Theory and Research for the Sociology of Education* (pp. 241–258). New York: Greenwood.

Cainzos, M., & Voces, C. (2010). Class Inequalities in Political Participation and the "Death of Class" Debate. *International Sociology, 25*(3), 383–418.

Campbell, A., Converse, P. E., Miller, W. E., & Stokes, D. (1960). *The American Voter.* New York: Wiley.

Chan, J., To, H.-P., & Chan, E. (2006). Reconsidering Social Cohesion: Developing a Definition and Analytical Framework for Empirical Research. *Social Indicators Research, 75,* 273–302.

Cohen, J. (1988). Set Correlation and Contingency Tables. *Applied Psychological Measurement, 12*(4), 425–434.

Corbetta, P., & Gualmini, E. (Eds.). (2013). *Il partito di Grillo.* Bologna: Il Mulino.

Delhey, J. (2007). Do Enlargements Make the European Union Less Cohesive? An Analysis of Trust Between EU Nationalities. *Journal of Common Market Studies, 45*(2), 253–279.

Festinger, L. (1964). Behavioral Support for Opinion Change. *The Public Opinion Quarterly, 28*(3), 404–417.

Flanagan, S. C., & Lee, A.-R. (2003). The New Politics, Culture Wars, and the Authoritarian-Libertarian Value Change in Advanced Industrial Democracies. *Comparative Political Studies, 36*(3), 235–270.

Fong, C. (2001). Social Preferences, Self-Interest, and the Demand for Redistribution. *Journal of Public Economics, 82*(2), 225–246.

García-Albacete, G. (2014). *Young People's Political Participation in Western Europe: Continuity or Generational Change?* Basingstoke: Palgrave Macmillan.

Giugni, M., & Passy, F. (Eds.). (2001). *Political Altruism? Solidarity Movements in International Perspective.* Lanham, MD: Rowman & Littlefield.

Halpern, D. (2005). *Social Capital.* Cambridge: Polity Press.

Hechter, M. (1988). *Principles of Group Solidarity.* Berkeley, CA: University of California Press.

Helliwell, J. F., & Wang, S. (2010). *Trust and Well-being.* NBER Working Paper Series No. 15911.

Jeannotte, M. S. (2000). *Social Cohesion Around the World: An International Comparison of Definitions and Issues.* Paper SRA-390.

Jenkins, J. C. (1983). Resource Mobilization Theory and the Study of Social Movements. *Annual Review of Sociology, 9*, 527–553.

Lelkes, O. (2010). *Social Participation and Social Isolation.* Eurostat Methodologies and Working Papers. Luxembourg: EU Publications.

Lichterman, P. (2015). Religion and Social Solidarity. A Pragmatist Approach. In L. Hustinx, J. von Essen, J. Haers, & S. Mels (Eds.), *Religion and Volunteering. Complex, Contested and Ambiguous Relationships* (pp. 241–261). Cham: Springer.

Likki, T., & Staerklé, C. (2014). A Typology of Ideological Attitudes Towards Social Solidarity and Social Control. *Journal of Community and Applied Social Psychology, 24*, 406–421.

Lochner, K., Kawachi, I., Brennan, R., & Buka, S. (2003). Social Capital and Neighbourhood Mortality Rates in Chicago. *Social Science and Medicine, 56*, 1797–1805.

Maggini, N. (2014). Understanding the Electoral Rise of the Five Star Movement in Italy. *Czech Journal of Political Science, 21*(1), 37–59.

Maggini, N. (2016). *Young People's Voting Behaviour in Europe. A Comparative Perspective.* London: Palgrave Macmillan.

Mudde, C. (2011). Radical Right Parties in Europe: What, Who, Why? *Participation, 34*(3), 12–15.

Neill, B., & Gidengil, E. (Eds.). (2006). *Gender and Social Capital.* New York: Routledge.

van Oorschot, W. (2000). Who Should Get What, and Why? On Deservingness Criteria and the Conditionality of Solidarity among the Public. *Policy & Politics, 28*(1), 33–48.

van Oorschot, W. (2006). Making the Difference in Social Europe: Deservingness Perceptions Among Citizens of European Welfare States. *Journal of European Social Policy, 16*(1), 23–42.

Putnam, R. D., Leonardi, R., & Nanetti, R. Y. (1994). *Making Democracy Work: Civic Traditions in Modern Italy.* Princeton, NJ: Princeton University Press.

Putnam, R. D., Feldstein, L., & Cohen, D. J. (2003). *Better Together: Restoring the American Community.* New York: Simon and Schuster.

Rehm, P. (2009). Risks and Redistribution. An Individual-Level Analysis. *Comparative Political Studies, 42*(7), 885–881.

Rehm, P., Hacker, J. S., & Schlesinger, M. (2012). Insecure Alliances: Risk, Inequality, and Support for the Welfare State. *American Political Science Review, 106*(2), 386–406.

Schianchi, M. (2014). Associations of People with Disabilities in Italy: A Short History. *Modern Italy, 19*(2), 121–133.

Scrivens, K., & Smith, C. (2013). *Four Interpretations of Social Capital: An Agenda for Measurement.* OECD Statistics Working Papers, 2013/06, OECD Publishing.

Stegmueller, D., Scheepers, P., Roßteuscher, S., & de Jong, E. (2012). Support for Redistribution in Western Europe. Assessing the Role of Religion. *European Sociological Review, 28*(4), 482–497.

Stjernø, S. (2012). *Solidarity in Europe. The History of an Idea.* Cambridge: Cambridge University Press.

Svallfors, S. (1997). Worlds of Welfare and Attitudes to Redistribution: A Comparison of Eight Western Nations. *European Journal of Sociology, 13*(3), 283–304.

Thomassen, J. (Ed.). (2005). *The European Voter.* Oxford: Oxford University Press.

Tronconi, F. (Ed.). (2015). *Beppe Grillo's Five Star Movement: Organisation, Communication and Ideology.* Farnham: Ashgate Publishing, Ltd.

Valentova, M. (2016). How Do Traditional Gender Roles Relate to Social Cohesion? Focus on Differences Between Women and Men. *Social Indicators Research, 127*(1), 153–178.

Verba, S., Nie, N., & Kim, J. (1978). *Participation and Political Equality: A Seven Nation Comparison.* London: Cambridge University Press.

Open Access This chapter is licensed under the terms of the Creative Commons Attribution 4.0 International License (http://creativecommons.org/licenses/by/4.0/), which permits use, sharing, adaptation, distribution and reproduction in any medium or format, as long as you give appropriate credit to the original author(s) and the source, provide a link to the Creative Commons license and indicate if changes were made.

The images or other third party material in this chapter are included in the chapter's Creative Commons license, unless indicated otherwise in a credit line to the material. If material is not included in the chapter's Creative Commons license and your intended use is not permitted by statutory regulation or exceeds the permitted use, you will need to obtain permission directly from the copyright holder.

CHAPTER 7

Volunteering for Refugees and Asylum Seekers in Greece

Stefania Kalogeraki

Introduction

Forced displacement hit a record high in 2015 (UNHCR 2016). Worldwide, 65.3 million individuals—including refugees, internally displaced people and asylum seekers—were forcibly displaced[1] due to persecution, conflict, generalized violence and human rights violations. Over four million people have been displaced by the conflict in Syria, while we have seen rapid increase in refugees/asylum seekers from African countries affected by war and violence. Consequently, European countries have struggled to cope with the influx of people and how to deal with resettling them (UNHCR 2016).

According to FRONTEX,[2] the main migratory routes into Europe through the Mediterranean include the Western Mediterranean route to Spain, the Central Mediterranean route to Italy and the Eastern Mediterranean route to Greece. By the beginning of 2015, the main gateway to Europe was through the Central Mediterranean route; however, by the end of 2015, the total number of registered arrivals of

S. Kalogeraki (✉)
Department of Sociology, University of Crete, Rethymno, Greece

refugees/asylum seekers in Greece reached the record figure of 821,000. The bulk of the flow was directed towards the Greek islands bordering Turkey (IOM 2015).[3] The large-scale arrival of refugees/asylum seekers and the resulting transformation of the migrant landscape in the country have challenged Greeks to cope with a dual crisis: the current refugee crisis as well as the economic depression which has severely affected the country over the last six years.

While the European response has been characterized by confusion and lack of universal policy (Tramountanis 2017) and traditional donors delayed funding, thousands of ordinary people have joined efforts to provide services and support to refugees/asylum seekers arriving to Greek shores. The role of volunteers in responding to the refugee crisis has been remarkable. Volunteers have provided a plethora of solidarity activities including food supplies, collecting and sorting clothes, providing medical aid, legal and financial support, rescuing people from the sea, cooking, setting up laundries, building shelters and so on (Evangelinidis 2016; Gkionakis 2016; Latimir 2016). Several media reports emphasize that despite the acute economic crisis, volunteers in Greece have stepped into covering for the gap left by the Greek state and EU leaders to support for refugees' humanitarian needs.[4,5]

Previous research has consistently underpinned the lower levels of volunteering in Greece (e.g. European Commission 2007, 2010, 2011) along with a weaker civil society (Mouzelis 1995; Lyrintzis 2002) compared to other European countries. Despite such arguments, other scholars emphasize that there is a vibrant, informal, non-institutionalized and often non-registered Greek civil society sector which does not fall into the normative definitions (Karamichas 2007; Rozakou 2011). This informal civil society usually tends to be distant from the state and primarily aims to protect vested interests in specific local areas or volunteer to help people in need (Sotiropoulos 2004).

The main rationale of the chapter is to explore volunteering for refugees/asylum seekers which is defined in the present study as active membership in an organization (volunteering in an organization) to support the rights of refugees/asylum seekers in Greece. Greece becomes an interesting case of investigating volunteering for the specific vulnerable group as in the context of the recent refugee crisis the country has experienced an unprecedented influx of refugees/asylum seekers entering its territory en route to wealthier countries. Moreover,

Table 7.1 Volunteering for refugees/asylum seekers, unemployed and disabled in countries participating to TransSOL project

Country	Volunteering for refugees/ asylum seekers f (%)	Volunteering for unemployed f (%)	Volunteering for disabled f (%)
Denmark	93 (4.3)	122 (5.6)	126 (5.8)
France	61 (2.9)	71 (3.4)	107 (5.1)
Germany	129 (6.3)	101 (4.9)	155 (7.5)
Greece	166 (8.1)	192 (9.3)	212 (10.3)
Italy	117 (5.6)	129 (6.2)	173 (8.3)
Poland	58 (2.7)	98 (4.6)	189 (8.9)
Switzerland	105 (4.7)	100 (4.5)	157 (7.1)
United Kingdom	53 (2.5)	53 (2.6)	105 (5.1)

Notes: Data weighted

as shown in Table 7.1, volunteering for refugees/asylum seekers is higher in Greece (8.1%) compared to other countries participating in TransSOL project. However, despite its higher prevalence cross-nationally, in Greece fewer individuals volunteer for refugees/asylum seekers than for other vulnerable groups such as the unemployed (9.3%) and disabled (10.3%).

Although past international research has produced numerous and valuable insights into volunteering, the domain of volunteering specifically for refugees/asylum seekers has been little explored. Exceptions involve Erickson's study (Erickson 2012) in Fargo, North Dakota, during 2007–2008, which investigates how volunteers embrace and contest hegemonic forms of "worthy" citizenship. A study conducted in Hungary shows that the current refugee crisis has a strong mobilizing effect for almost 3% of the Hungarian population; some volunteers have altruistic motivations, whilst others are mainly driven as a response to the political situation (Toth and Kertesz 2016). In Germany, recent empirical evidence underpins that since 2015 volunteering for refugees/asylum seekers has become a widespread phenomenon with thousands of people donating money and distributing food, medicines, clothing and other essentials (Karakayali and Kleist 2015, 2016; Rose 2016).

The recent explosion of refugees/asylum seekers fleeing conflict and persecution and the pivotal role of volunteers to tackle the refugee crisis has led to a drastic increase of scientific interest in the field. Although the other chapters in the book explore different forms of civic engagement, activism or "solidarity" practices to different vulnerable groups,[6] the present chapter focuses on volunteering specifically for refugees/asylum seekers in Greece. Based on a hybrid approach which combines the sociological and political approaches to volunteering, the analysis is guided by the research question of "*Who volunteers for refugees/asylum seekers in Greece?*" The findings shed some light on our research question by portraying the profiles of volunteers helping refugees/asylum seekers arriving in the country.

THEORETICAL BACKGROUND AND HYPOTHESES

Volunteering embraces different functions and explanations in different disciplines (Musick and Wilson 2008; Hustinx et al. 2010). For instance, sociological approaches emphasize different forms of capital or resources, such as human, social and cultural capital in explaining volunteering (Wilson and Musick 1997a; Wilson 2000). Psychologists focus on key traits of personality such as extraversion, agreeableness and resilience that impact on individuals' predisposition to volunteer (Bekkers 2005; Matsuba et al. 2007). For political scientists, volunteering acts as a critical form of civic engagement and an expression of democratic values (Theiss-Morse and Hibbing 2005), underlying the critical impact of citizens' political engagement on volunteering (Bekkers 2005). Economic scientists adopt a rational-based approach, viewing volunteering as a form of unpaid labour where volunteers undertake activity depending on the consuming resources and the rewards they may gain (Wilson 2000; Musick and Wilson 2008; Hustinx et al. 2010; Wilson 2012).

The present paper adopts a hybrid approach. It explores the profiles of individuals volunteering for refugees/asylum seekers in Greece based on their demographic attributes, their human, social and cultural capital developed in sociological approaches and their political conventional and unconventional behaviours developed in political approaches.

Literature has shown that, generally, people with different demographic characteristics vary in their propensities to volunteer (Wilson 2000; Musick and Wilson 2008; Hustinx et al. 2010). With respect to gender, previous research shows different rates and patterns of volunteering

(Wilson 2012). Gaskin and Smith (1997) suggest there is no clear pattern of gender differences in volunteering across European countries. However, other scholars suggest that gender does make a difference in specific domains of volunteering, since women tend to have higher rates in informal volunteering activities associated with more caring tasks and lower rates in political activities (Thompson 1993; Schlozman et al. 1994; Cnaan et al. 1996; Rochester et al. 2010). This pattern appears quite consistent across different age groups and countries (Wuthnow 1995). Gender ideologies, as well as the gendered division of labour, partly explain why women tend to volunteer more in activities associated with caring tasks (Wilson 2000).

Age-related variables are also important in determining volunteering. Some scholars underpin that voluntary participation varies by age or life-cycle stage associated with the different adult roles (e.g. with work, family obligations) taken throughout the life cycle (Wilson 2000; Musick and Wilson 2008; Smith and Wang 2016). The empirical evidence shows that volunteering is generally higher among middle-aged citizens compared to the elderly and youth (Wymer 1998; Curtis et al. 2001; Pho 2008). However, Wilson (2000) argues that high-risk volunteering activities primarily attract younger people compared to older people. Moreover, he suggests that different types of volunteering activities become more or less attractive in different life-cycle stages. For instance, younger citizens mainly volunteer in organizations related to self- and career-oriented activism, middle-aged volunteers primarily engage in community-oriented work, whereas older volunteers participate to "service organizations, recreational clubs and agencies to help the elderly" (Wilson 2000, p. 227).

A plethora of scholars emphasize that, at least in advanced industrial societies, education is often the most consistent predictor of volunteering (Brady et al. 1995; Nie et al. 1996; Wilson 2000, 2012; Musick and Wilson 2008; Huang et al. 2009; Rochester et al. 2010; Van Ingen and Dekker 2011). The critical impact of education on volunteering is associated with the outcomes of educational processes that expose individuals to norms and values favourable to volunteering as well as to civic skills, advanced awareness of problems and stronger feelings of efficacy.

From a sociological perspective, individuals' decision to volunteer is influenced by various types of resources or capital, such as human capital, cultural capital and social capital (Wilson and Musick 1997a; Wilson and Musick 1998; Wilson 2000; Musick and Wilson 2008). Human capital primarily involves income, occupational class and employment status (Wilson and Musick 1997a; Wilson 2000). Most empirical evidence across different countries reports that low-income earners are less likely to volunteer than higher earners (Vaillancourt 1994; Freeman 1997; Hurley et al. 2008). For instance, Pho (2008) explored volunteering in the United States from 2002 to 2005 and found that low- to medium-wage earners are less likely to volunteer than high-wage earners.

Whether or not someone is employed and the nature of their employment can influence volunteering in several ways. Employment is a prime determinant of social status, it provides opportunities to integrate into society and develop those adequate civic skills that increase the likelihood of volunteering. The relation between employment status and volunteering has been explored by various scholars, underlying that part-time employees are more likely to volunteer than either full-time employees or individuals who are not in the labour force (Johnson et al. 2004; Lasby 2004; Low et al. 2007; Hurley et al. 2008; Einolf 2011). Meanwhile, unemployment status is usually associated with lower levels of volunteering (Pho 2008; Wilson 2012).

In Wilson's (2000, p. 221) words: "As occupational status increases so does the likelihood of volunteering." Occupational status has been shown to play a critical role in volunteering (Wilson and Musick 1997b; Hodgkinson 2003; Rotolo and Wilson 2007). For instance, Reed and Selbee (2001) found that individuals in Canada with jobs high in occupational prestige, higher income and higher educational attainment are more likely to volunteer. Similarly, Rotolo and Wilson (2007) show that even after controlling for family traits, women with professional and managerial occupations exhibit greater tendencies to volunteer than women in lower occupational jobs. The association between volunteering and high occupational prestige is related to the fact that top managers or professionals are more likely to be asked to volunteer as well as to be socially active as part of their job role (Wilson 2000; Wilson and Musick 1997b).

For Putnam (2000, p. 19), social capital refers to "social networks and the norms of reciprocity and trustworthiness that arise from them". The key resources that form "social capital" involve social networks or social ties, including friendship networks as well as trust in others, that is, elements which tend to foster collective action (Wilson and Musick

1997a). Much research has been conducted on social capital in recent years, in particular measured as individuals' friendship networks, informal social interactions and social trust, as correlates of volunteering. For instance, Wilson and Musick (1997a) found a positive association between formal volunteering and informal social interactions measured as frequent conversations and meetings with friends and acquaintances. Brown and Ferris (2007) found that individuals' associational networks, their trust in others and in their community are important determinants of giving and volunteering. Cross-national surveys underpin that social trust is positively associated with volunteering regardless of socio-economic differences (Anheier and Kendall 2002). It should be noted that some scholars underline that social trust is associated with specific types of volunteering activities which primarily target to provide services to individuals in need. On the contrary, trusting people are "less likely to volunteer in activities that involve confrontation with authorities or working to change the system" (Musick and Wilson 2008, p. 46). In line with such arguments, Greenberg (2001) supports that politically oriented volunteering associated with government-related activities, among others, is motivated by lack of social trust, whereas service-oriented volunteering including non-governmental activism is motivated by trust in others.

In Wilson and Musick's (1997a) integrated theory of volunteer work, religiosity is an indicator of cultural capital which is positively associated with formal volunteering. A cultural capital perspective posits that religiosity provides an ethic of caring which reinforces the decision to volunteer (Wuthnow 2004). As most religions encourage altruistic values, highly religious individuals are more concerned with the welfare of others (Dillon et al. 2003); therefore their value preferences are more compatible with volunteering. Previous research underpins that more religious individuals are more likely to be involved in volunteering than their secular counterparts (Wilson and Janoski 1995; Becker and Dhingra 2001; Musick and Wilson 2008; McNamara and Gonzales 2011).

The political approach to volunteering highlights its role as a form of civic engagement and expression of democratic values. Putnam argues that "volunteering is part of the syndrome of good citizenship and political involvement" (Putnam 2000, p. 132). Different scholars report that volunteers tend to be more politically active compared to non-volunteers

(Verba et al. 1995; Dekker and Van den Broek 1998; Hodgkinson 2003; Musick and Wilson 2008). The grounds of the association between volunteering and political engagement involve, among others, the opportunity to develop specific civic skills (such as the ability to organize a meeting), sharing information and fostering general trust (Verba et al. 1995; Stolle 1998).

Hodgkinson (2003), in her study using EVS/WVS 1999–2002 data, found that volunteers are more likely to be politically engaged (in terms of discussing politics and signing petitions) than non-volunteers in the vast majority of the countries under study.[7] Dekker and Van den Broek (1996), using data from five countries (the United States, Great Britain, West Germany, Italy and Mexico), found that active volunteers compared to passive volunteers[8] are more likely to be politically engaged in conventional and unconventional political acts (such as contributing time to political organizations, participation to protests/demonstrations, etc.).[9] Bekkers' (2005) study in the Netherlands shows that individuals with a greater interest in politics and post-materialistic value orientations are more likely to be volunteers—also, voting preferences are important since non-voters are less likely to volunteer than voters who prefer leftist or Christian political parties. Similarly, Knoke (1990) found that active volunteering goes along with being active in local politics, including among others, voting in local elections.

Drawing on the theoretical arguments and the empirical evidence discussed, we hypothesize the following:

Hypothesis 1 Individuals with specific demographic attributes, that is, women, middle-aged and higher educated individuals, are more likely to volunteer for refugees/asylum seekers.

Hypothesis 2 Individuals' human capital in terms of higher income and occupational class is positively associated with volunteering for refugees/asylum seekers. Moreover, part-time employees are more likely to volunteer than either full-time employees or individuals who are not in the labour force.

Hypothesis 3 Individuals' social capital, in terms of social trust and informal social interactions with friends, is positively associated with volunteering for refugees/asylum seekers.

Hypothesis 4 Individuals' cultural capital, in terms of religiosity, is positively associated with volunteering for refugees/asylum seekers.

Hypothesis 5 Individuals' political engagement in conventional and unconventional political behaviours is positively associated with volunteering for refugees/asylum seekers.

Data and Methods

The analysis draws on an original dataset of *n* = 2061 respondents (aged 18+) in Greece matched for age, gender, region and education level quotas to national population statistics. To explore the profiles of individuals volunteering for refugees/asylum seekers, specific items from the project's questionnaire are used. The dependent variable, that is, volunteering for refugees/asylum seekers, is measured with one item asking respondents, among others,[10] their active membership in an organization (volunteering in an organization) to support the rights of refugees/asylum seekers. The dichotomous variable is used to capture volunteering and non-volunteering for refugees/asylum seekers in Greece.

The independent variables involve a set of items capturing demographic characteristics, including gender, age and education, measures of human, cultural and social capital as well as individuals' political behaviour.[11] Age is measured with an ordinal scale including three broad age groups, that is, 18–34, 35–54 and over 55 years old. Educational attainment is measured with three responses capturing individuals with higher education (i.e. university and above), intermediate education (i.e. upper secondary and post-secondary non-tertiary education) and lower education (i.e. less than primary and lower secondary education).

Human capital is measured with indicators capturing respondents' income, employment status and occupational class. Income is measured with an item asking respondents for their household monthly net income, after tax and compulsory deductions, from all sources. The recoded variable includes three responses measuring lower (i.e. less than 775 euro), middle (i.e. between 776 and 1425 euro) and higher income earners (i.e. more than 1426 euro). Respondents' occupational class is measured with a recoded variable including three responses:

higher occupational class (professional/managerial workers), middle (clerical/sales or services/foreman or supervisor of other workers) and low (skilled/semi-skilled or unskilled manual workers) occupational class. Respondents' employment status is measured with a recoded variable including four responses: full-time employee, part-time employee, other employment status (such as permanently sick or disabled, retired, community or military service, doing housework, looking after children or other persons) and unemployed.

Social capital is measured with indicators associated with respondents' social trust and informal social interactions. The former is captured with one item measuring on a scale from 0 to 10 respondents' level of trustfulness of people, where higher scores indicate higher levels of social trust. The intensity of informal social interactions is measured with one item asking respondents how often, in the past month, they met socially with friends not living in their household. The recoded variable is a dichotomous measure including "Once or twice this month or less" and "Every week or almost every day". The former captures respondents' low intensity of informal social interactions and the latter high intensity of informal social interactions.

Cultural capital is measured with one item capturing religiosity. Specifically, respondents are asked to report on a scale from 0 to 10 how religious they are, with higher scores indicating stronger religiosity.

Political engagement is measured with items capturing involvement in conventional and unconventional political behaviours. The former is measured with a question asking respondents if they voted or not in the last Greek national election (on 20 September 2015). The recoded dichotomous variable captures respondents' engagement or non-engagement in conventional behaviours. Unconventional political behaviour is measured with an additive score based on responses on five items measuring participation in the past 12 months in (a) signing petitions, (b) boycotting products for political/ethical/environmental reasons, (c) attending a demonstration, march or rally, (d) joining a strike and (e) joining an occupation, sit-in or blockade.[12] In the composite index, higher scores indicate higher levels of respondents' involvement in unconventional political behaviour.

The analysis uses exploratory and explanatory analyses to investigate volunteers' profiles supporting refugees/asylum seekers in Greece. With respect to the former, the *Chi-Square test of Independence* and independent sample *t-test* are used to determine associations and differences between volunteers and non-volunteers in relation to the variables under study. Explanatory analysis involves the application of logistic regression to predict volunteering for refugees/asylum seekers (compared to non-volunteering) based on the variables measuring respondents' demographic traits, human, social and cultural capital as well as political conventional and unconventional behaviours. The variables are entered into five blocks; the first includes items associated with demographics, the second with human capital, the third with social capital, the fourth with cultural capital and the last with political behaviours.

Results

Tables 7.2 and 7.3 present *Chi-Square test of Independence* and independent sample *t-test* results, respectively. As shown in Table 7.2, volunteering is significantly associated with gender, age, occupational class, employment status and respondents' informal interactions with friends. Specifically, more women (10.3%) than men (5.7%) volunteer for refugees/asylum seekers. A higher prevalence of volunteering is found for older age groups (i.e. more than 55 years old) (9.9%) and younger age groups (18–34 years old) (8.3%) compared to middle-aged ones (6.2%). Moreover, individuals with higher education (14.1%) are more likely to volunteer for refugees/asylum seekers compared to individuals with intermediate (6.7%) or lower education (6.6%). With respect to income, middle-income earners (i.e. 776–1425 euro) have the highest prevalence of volunteering (9.2%), whereas low-income earners (i.e. less than 775 euro) the lowest one (5.9%). Volunteering is more popular among individuals of higher occupational class (i.e. in professional or managerial positions) (13.6%) than individuals of middle (7.9%) or lower occupational class (7.2%).

Part-time employees (10.2%) and individuals with other employment status (e.g. retired, housewives) (10.4%) have higher rates of *volunteering* compared to full-time employees (6.2%) or unemployed individuals (6.2%). Additionally, more frequent informal interactions with friends (9.5%) are positively associated with volunteering. Although volunteering is higher among individuals with specific conventional political behaviours such as voting (8.9%), the reported association is non-significant.

As shown in Table 7.3, the *t-test* analysis indicates significant differences in social trust and unconventional political behaviour between volunteers

Table 7.2 Volunteers'/non-volunteers' associations with specific demographic attributes, human capital indicators, informal social interactions and conventional political behaviour

		Volunteers f (%)	Non-volunteers f (%)	Chi-square test	p-value
Gender	Male	57 (5.7)	937 (94.3)	14,464	0.000
	Female	110 (10.3)	957 (89.7)		
Age groups	18–34 years old	40 (8.3)	441 (91.7)	7113	0.029
	35–54 years old	50 (6.2)	752 (93.8)		
	More than 55	77 (9.9)	702 (90.1)		
Education	Higher education	57 (14.1)	346 (85.9)	24,556	0.000
	Intermediate education	49 (6.7)	684 (93.3)		
	Lower education	61 (6.6)	864 (93.4)		
Income	Low (less than 775)	39 (5.9)	617 (94.1)	5179	0.075
	Middle (776–1425)	70 (9.2)	693 (90.8)		
	High (more than 1426)	34 (7.9)	395 (92.1)		
Occupational class	Higher class (professional/managerial)	66 (13.6)	418 (86.4)	14,346	0.001
	Middle class	73 (7.9)	851 (92.1)		
	Lower class (manual workers)	21 (7.2)	272 (92.8)		
Employment status	Full-time	34 (6.2)	516 (93.8)	11,690	0.009
	Part-time	22 (10.2)	194 (89.8)		
	Other	76 (10.4)	657 (89.6)		
	Unemployed	35 (6.2)	527 (93.8)		
Informal social interactions with friends	Once or twice this month or less	58 (6.3)	869 (93.7)	7351	0.007
	Every week or almost everyday	108 (9.5)	1026 (90.5)		
Conventional Political behaviour	No voting	22 (6.4)	323 (93.6)	2376	0.123
	Voting	140 (8.9)	1428 (91.1)		

Notes: Data weighted

and non-volunteers. Specifically, volunteers for refugees/asylum report higher scores in social trust ($M = 4.62$, SD = 2.75) and in unconventional political behaviour ($M = 2.44$, SD = 1.19) than non-volunteers. Moreover, the mean score of religiosity is lower among volunteers ($M = 5.46$, SD = 3.18) than non-volunteers ($M = 5.71$, SD = 3.10), however the reported difference is non-significant.

Table 7.3 Volunteers'/non-volunteers' differences in social trust, religiosity and unconventional political behaviour

	Volunteers		Non-volunteers		t-test	95% confidence interval of the difference	
	M	SD	M	SD			
Social trust	4.62	2.75	3.25	2.64	6.418***	0.956	1.797
Religiosity	5.46	3.18	5.71	3.10	−1.003	−0.746	0.241
Unconventional political behaviour	2.44	1.19	1.84	1.00	4.672***	0.344	0.851

M mean, SD std. deviation

†$p < 0.1$, *$p < 0.05$, **$p < 0.01$, ***$p < 0.001$. Data weighted

Table 7.4 presents the results from binary logistic regression models for predicting volunteering for refugees/asylum seekers in Greece. To test the hypothesis associated with demographic attributes (see Hypothesis 1), the first model includes gender, age and education, all of them significantly contribute on predicting volunteering. Volunteers, in line with our hypothesis, are more likely to be women. Similar results are reported in previous studies exploring volunteering for refugees/asylum seekers. For instance, research conducted in Germany shows that volunteers for refugees are predominantly female (Karakayali and Kleist 2015, 2016). Likewise, in Erickson's study (Erickson 2012), the majority of volunteers for refugees in Fargo are women.

The analysis shows that, that in line with our expectations and previous research (Wilson 2000, 2012; Musick and Wilson 2008; Rochester et al. 2010; Van Ingen and Dekker 2011), educational attainment does play a critical role in volunteering as higher educated individuals in Greece are more likely to engage in volunteering for refugees/asylum seekers. Contradicting our hypothesis, volunteers are more likely to belong to younger age groups (i.e. 18–34-year-olds). Karakayali and Kleist's (2015) study finds that volunteers for refugees are more likely to be either in their 20s or over 60, indicating that past empirical evidence supporting that volunteering is more prevalent among middle-aged citizens (Wymer 1998; Curtis et al. 2001; Pho 2008) might not hold for the specific domain of volunteering.

To examine the hypothesis associated with human capital (see Hypothesis 2) income, occupational class and employment status are

Table 7.4 Binary logistic regression analysis of volunteering for refugees/asylum seekers in Greece

	Model 1	Model 2	Model 3	Model 4	Model 5
Gender (ref.: male)					
Female	725***	0.809**	0.876**	0.874**	1.009***
	(0.277)	(0.294)	(0.300)	(0.300)	(0.314)
Educational attainment (ref.: lower education)					
Higher education	1.305***	1.208**	1.024**	1.020**	0.791*
	(0.342)	(0.381)	(0.396)	(0.396)	(0.418)
Intermediate education	0.515	0.545	0.522	0.504	0.220
	(0.354)	(0.365)	(0.373)	(0.377)	(0.403)
Age groups (ref.: 18–34 years old)					
35–54 years old	−0.900**	−0.820*	−0.840*	−0.826*	−0.930*
	(0.349)	(0.364)	(0.372)	(0.374)	(0.391)
More than 55 years old	−0.677*	−0.404	−0.169	−0.168	−0.145
	(0.312)	(0.374)	(0.390)	(0.390)	(0.398)
Income-groups (ref.: low income—less than 775)					
Middle income (776–1425)		−0.096	−0.326	−0.334	−0.325
		(0.315)	(0.331)	(0.332)	(0.348)
High income (more than 1426)		−0.546	−0.880*	−0.902*	−0.932*
		(0.392)	(0.412)	(0.417)	(0.437)
Employment status (ref.: unemployed)					
Full-time		0.019	0.151	0.167	0.143
		(0.387)	(0.400)	(0.403)	(0.416)
Part-time		0.654	0.877*	0.875*	0.855+
		(0.428)	(0.441)	(0.441)	(0.464)
Other		−0.337	−0.333	−0.304	−0.329
		(0.401)	(0.419)	(0.427)	(0.448)
Occupational class (ref.: lower occupational class/manual workers)					
Higher occupational class (managerial/professional)		0.112	0.005	0.003	0.194
		(0.403)	(0.425)	(0.426)	(0.447)
Middle occupational class		−0.742*	−0.734+	−0.724+	−0.589
		(0.381)	(0.393)	(0.394)	(0.417)

(*continued*)

Table 7.4 (continued)

	Model 1	Model 2	Model 3	Model 4	Model 5
Social trust			0.159**	0.155**	0.141**
			(0.051)	(0.052)	(0.054)
Informal social interactions with friends (ref.: once—twice or less per month)					
Every week or almost everyday			0.552+	0.555+	0.673*
			(0.311)	(0.311)	(0.328)
Religiosity				−0.014	−0.010
				(0.040)	(0.041)
Unconventional political behaviour					0.616***
					(0.120)
Conventional political behaviour (ref.: no vote)					
Vote					0.223
					(0.377)
Constant	−2.824***	−2.517***	−3.442***	−3.363***	−4.893***
	(0.383)	(0.472)	(0.548)	(0.591)	(0.733)
Nagelkerke R^2	0.098	0.145	0.183	0.183	0.251

Notes: The dependent variable is a dichotomous measure indicating the probability of volunteering (ref.: non-volunteering) for refugees/asylum seekers in Greece

Table presents logistic regression coefficients B with standard errors in parentheses

$+p < 0.10$, $*p < 0.05$, $**p < 0.01$, $***p < 0.001$. Data weighted

included in the second model. The analysis shows that controlling for the demographic attributes under study, income and employment status do not significantly contribute on predicting volunteering. Only occupational class is associated with volunteering indicating that middle occupational class individuals are less likely to volunteer compared to those from the lowest occupational class (i.e. manual workers). Such findings contradict our hypothesis as well as previous research underlining that volunteering is more strongly supported among individuals with higher human capital, in terms of higher income and occupational class (Rotolo and Wilson 2007; Hurley et al. 2008; Pho 2008).

To test the hypothesis associated with social capital (see Hypothesis 3), the indicators of social trust and informal social interactions with friends are included in the third model. In agreement with our hypothesis, social capital and specifically social trust plays a critical role in volunteering since individuals' social trust is positively associated with volunteering for refugees/asylum seekers (Wilson and Musick 1997a; Brown and Ferries 2007). Respondents' intense informal social interactions (i.e. every week or almost every day) positively contribute to volunteering; however the reported association is significant at $p < 0.10$.

In the fourth model the indicator of cultural capital, that is, religiosity, is added. Contradicting our expectations (see Hypothesis 4), the analysis shows that religiosity is not associated with volunteering for refugees/asylum seekers in Greece. Whilst non-significant, the negative sign of the religiosity coefficient provides some preliminary evidence of the negative association between religiosity and volunteering.

To examine the hypothesis associated with political behaviours (see Hypothesis 5), unconventional and conventional political behaviours are added in the final model. The former significantly contributes on predicting volunteering, as unconventional political behaviour is associated with volunteering for refugees/asylum seekers (Verba et al. 1995; Dekker and Van den Broek 1998; Hodgkinson 2003; Bekkers 2005). Similar results are reported for the conventional political behaviour of voting; however, the reported association is non-significant.

Conclusions

Since 2015, the influx of refugees to Europe—primarily from North Africa in the aftermath of the Arab Spring and from the Middle East due to the civil war in Syria—has challenged Europe to tackle one of the largest movements of displaced people through European borders since World War II (UNHCR 2016). According to Eurostat (2016), in 2015 a record number of over 1.2 million first-time asylum seekers registered in EU member-states. Almost one out of three first-time asylum seekers originate from Syria, while many are also Afghans and Iraqis.

In the context of the recent refugee crisis, Greece has been marked by a fast-paced transit of high numbers of refugees/asylum seekers entering its territory en route to Northern and Central Europe. The large-scale arrival of refugees/asylum seekers have challenged Greeks to cope with a twofold crisis: the economic crisis as well as the refugee crisis. Concerning the economic crisis, in the last six years Greece has faced the most acute recession in its modern history with devastating socio-economic impacts on individuals' lives echoed in record unemployment and poverty rates (Matsaganis and Leventi 2014; OECD 2014). Since 2015, the country has been strained by both economic depression and the massive migration inflows of hundreds of thousands of refugees/asylum seekers.

Despite economic hardship, volunteers have been instrumental in providing help (such as food supplies, medical aid, legal and financial support, etc.) to refugees/asylum seekers arriving on Greek shores—simultaneously relieving the state of one of its core roles. Therefore, the government has come to partly rely on the contributions of volunteers in order to tackle the refugee crisis. As Evangelinidis (2016, p. 33) argues:

> Where the state apparatus was absent, or its structures were insufficient, civil society organizations in many different forms (e.g. professional NGOs, volunteers, ad hoc groups and collectives) tried to fill the gap. With the central government unable to properly provide for many of its citizens, let alone refugees or migrants, the humanitarian vacuum has often been filled with solidarity initiatives.

Based on a hybrid approach which combines the sociological and political approaches to volunteering, the explorative analysis provides some preliminary evidence of volunteers' traits, most in line with past empirical research into volunteering. The explanatory analysis sheds some light on volunteers' profiles who are primarily women, young, higher educated, individuals engaged in unconventional political acts and with higher level of social capital. However, contradicting our hypotheses and previous research, human and cultural resources are not associated with volunteering for refugees/asylum seekers in Greece.

The lack of association between human capital and volunteering may reflect the peculiarities of volunteering in Greece. Some scholars support that individuals with less human capital are more likely to engage in informal volunteering rather than formal volunteering (Williams 2002; Hustinx et al. 2010). As argued in the introduction of the chapter, whilst the official statistics show the low prevalence of formal volunteering in Greece compared to other European countries, some researchers underpin that there is a vibrant informal volunteering sector that has been triggered in different emergency periods

(Sotiropoulos 2004; Karamichas 2007; Rozakou 2011). We can assume that the main trend of volunteering for refugees/asylum seekers, as it has happened in the past in Greece (Sotiropoulos 2004; Karamichas 2007; Rozakou 2011), has primarily followed the informal path, which is more common among individuals with lower human capital.

With respect to the lack of association between religiosity as an indicator of cultural capital and volunteering, the finding might reflect specific shortcomings of the proxy applied. Scholars reporting strong correlations between religiosity and volunteering usually apply as proxies religious practices such as frequency of church attendance and of religious prayer rather than subjective measures of religiosity and intensity of beliefs (Wilson and Musick 1997a; Musick and Wilson 2008; van Tienen et al. 2011; Paxton et al. 2014). These practices are more likely to proffer values (such as self-sacrifice and compassion), which reinforce the decision to volunteer (Son and Wilson 2011).

In the study's questionnaire, there are no available measures of such religious practices that would allow the refined measurement of religiosity. Additional limitations of the study involve its cross-sectional design where causal imputation is difficult. Hence, we are unable to determine the direction of specific causal relationships examined, for example, between cultural capital, social capital and/or political engagement measures and volunteering. It should be noted that concerns over selection bias have consistently plagued the volunteering empirical research (Wilson 2000).

Nevertheless, the study enriches the scarce empirical research on volunteering specifically for refugees/asylum seekers, by portraying the profiles of volunteers providing solidarity to thousands of refugees/asylum seekers arriving in Greece. Undoubtedly, volunteers have been key actors in welcoming and helping refugees/asylum seekers contributing to the first step towards newcomers' integration into the new host countries. However, volunteers' contribution should not be treated as substitute to core state obligations towards refugees/asylum seekers. Policy interventions at the Greek and EU level are urgently necessary to manage the refugee crisis effectively and allow the resettlement of refugees/asylum seekers in safe countries where they can have the opportunity to rebuild their lives.

Appendix

Original survey question	Recoded	%
[agegroups] How old are you? {1.18–24 years, 2.25–34 years, 3.35–44 years, 4.45–54 years, 5.55–64 years, 6.65 years and older}	1. 18–34 years old (1 through 2) 2. 35–54 years old (3 through 4) 3. More than 55 years old (5 through 6)	23.4 38.9 37.8
[class] Which option best describes the sort of paid work you do? {1. Professional or higher technical work, 2. Manager or senior administrator, 3. Clerical, 4. Sales or services, 5. Foreman or supervisor of other workers, 6. Skilled manual work, 7. Semi-skilled or unskilled manual work, 8. Other (e.g. farming, military), 9. Not in employment}	1. Higher occupational class-professional/managerial (1 through 2) 2. Middle occupational class (3 through 5) 3. Occupational class-manual (6 through 7)	28.5 54.3 17.2
[mainact] What you have been doing for the past seven days? {1. In full-time (30 or more hours per week) paid work, 2. In part-time (8–29 hours a week) paid work, 3. In part-time (less than 8 hours a week) paid work, 4. In education (not paid for by employer) even if on vacation, 5. Unemployed and actively looking for a job, 6. Unemployed but not actively looking for a job, 7. Permanently sick or disabled, 8. Retired, 9. In community or military service, 10. Doing housework, looking after children or other persons}	1. Full-time 2. Part-time (2 through 3) 3. Other (4 and 7 through 10) 4. Unemployed (5 through 6)	26.7 10.5 35.6 27.3
[income_GR] What is your household's MONTHLY net income? {1. Less than 575 Euro, 2. 576–775 Euro, 3. 776–980 Euro, 4. 981–1190 Euro, 5. 1191–1425 Euro, 6. 1426–1700 Euro, 7. 1701–2040 Euro, 8. 2041–2500 Euro, 9. 2501–3230 Euro, 10. 3231 Euro or more, 11. Prefer not to say}	1. Less than 775 *Euro* (1 through 2) 2. 776–1425 *Euro* (3 through 5) 3. More than 1426 *Euro* (6 through 10)	35.5 41.3 23.2
[votenatl_GR] Did you vote in the national election on 20 September 2015? {1. No—but I was eligible to vote, 2. No—because I was not eligible to vote, 3. Yes, 4. Don't know)	1. No—but I was eligible to vote 2. Yes	18.0 82.0
[metfriends] Met socially with friends during the past month {1. Less than once this month, 2. Once or twice this month, 3. Every week, 4. Almost every day}	1. Once or twice this month or less (1 through 2) 2. Every week or almost every day (3 through 4)	45.0 55.0

Notes

1. Displaced individuals include refugees, internally displaced people and asylum seekers. A refugee is someone who has been forced to flee his or her home country and is unable or unwilling to return due to fear of persecution. Internally displaced individuals include those who were forced to flee their home but they did not cross a state border. Asylum seekers include individuals who have made a claim that they are refugees and are in the process of waiting for the acceptance of rejection of their claim.
2. FRONTEX, Migratory routes map. Retrieved from http://frontex.europa.eu/trends-and-routes/migratory-routes-map/.
3. FRONTEX, Eastern Mediterranean route. Retrieved from http://frontex.europa.eu/trends-and-routes/eastern-mediterranean-route/.
4. The Guardian, 12 March 2016. Refugee crisis: How Greeks opened their hearts to strangers. Retrieved from https://www.theguardian.com/world/2016/mar/12/refugee-crisis-greeks-strangers-migrants.
5. The Huffington Post, 6 June 2016. The Hidden Heroes of Greece's Refugee Crisis. Retrieved from http://www.huffingtonpost.com/entry/volunteers-with-greek-refugees_us_574f54b3e4b0eb20fa0cb52c.
6. Such as unemployed and disabled.
7. Exceptions included Hong Kong and Latvia.
8. Active volunteers are individuals who regularly provide services which meet the primary goals of their group/organization. Passive volunteers are individuals who just pay dues/fees to their group/organization.
9. In Mexico active members had no differences with passive ones in any measures of political involvement.
10. It should be noted that additional activities include attending a march, protest or demonstration, donate money, donate time, buy or refuse to buy products in support to the goals and engage as passive member of an organization (pay cheque membership). These solidarity practices are not included in the present chapter, as the main research question is primarily associated with volunteering for refugees/asylum seekers.
11. Variables' recoding are included in Appendix.
12. According to Marsh and Kaase (1979), unconventional political participation includes petitions, demonstrations, boycotts, rent or tax strikes, unofficial industrial strikes, occupations of buildings, blocking of traffic, damage to property and personal violence.

REFERENCES

Anheier, H., & Kendall, J. (2002). Interpersonal Trust and Voluntary Associations. *British Journal of Sociology, 53*(3), 343–362. https://doi.org/10.1080/00071 31022000000545.

Becker, P. E., & Dhingra, P. H. (2001). Religious Involvement and Volunteering: Implications for Civil Society. *Sociology of Religion, 62,* 315–335.

Bekkers, R. (2005). Participation in Voluntary Associations: Relations with Resources, Personality, and Political Values. *Political Psychology, 26*(3), 439–454. https://doi.org/10.1111/j.1467-9221.2005.00425.x.

Brady, H., Verba, S., & Schlozman, K. (1995). Beyond SES: A Resource Model of Political Participation. *The American Political Science Review, 89*(2), 271–294. https://doi.org/10.2307/2082425.

Brown, E., & Ferries, J. M. (2007). Social Capital and Philanthropy: An Analysis of the Impact of Social Capital on Individual Giving and Volunteering. *Nonprofit and Voluntary Sector Quarterly, 36*(1), 85–99. https://doi.org/10.1177/0899764006293178.

Cnaan, R., Handy, F., & Wadsworth, M. (1996). Defining Who Is a Volunteer: Conceptual and Empirical Considerations. *Nonprofit and Voluntary Sector Quarterly, 25*(3), 364–383. https://doi.org/10.1177/089976409625300 6.

Curtis, J. E., Baer, D. E., & Grabb, E. G. (2001). Nations of Joiners: Explaining Voluntary Association Membership in Democratic Societies. *American Sociological Review, 66*(6), 783–805. https://doi.org/10.2307/3088873.

Dekker, P., & Van den Broek, A. (1996). Volunteering and Politics: Involvement in Voluntary Associations from a 'Civic Culture' Perspective. In L. Halman & N. Nevitte (Eds.), *Political Value Change in Western Democracies* (pp. 125–152). Tilburg: Tilburg University Press.

Dekker, P., & Van den Broek, A. (1998). Civil Society in Comparative Perspective: Involvement in Voluntary Associations in North America and Western Europe. *Voluntas: International Journal of Voluntary and Nonprofit Organizations, 9*(1), 11–38. https://doi.org/10.1023/A:1021450828183.

Dillon, M., Wink, P., & Fay, K. (2003). Is Spirituality Detrimental to Generativity? *Journal for the Scientific Study of Religion, 42,* 427–442. https://doi.org/10.2307/3088873.

Einolf, C. J. (2011). Gender Differences in the Correlates of Volunteering and Charitable Giving. *Nonprofit and Voluntary Sector Quarterly, 40*(6), 1092–1112. https://doi.org/10.1177/0899764010385949.

Erickson, J. (2012). Volunteering with Refugees: Neoliberalism, Hegemony, and (Senior) Citizenship. *Human Organization, 71*(2), 167–175. https://doi.org/10.17730/humo.71.2.152h5843163031pr.

European Commission. (2007). *Special Eurobarometer 273/Wave 66.3. European Social Reality*. Brussels: European Commission. Retrieved from http://ec.europa.eu/commfrontoffice/publicopinion/archives/ebs/ebs_273_en.pdf.

European Commission. (2010). *Volunteering in the European Union*. Brussels: European Commission. Retrieved from http://ec.europa.eu/citizenship/pdf/doc1018_en.pdf.

European Commission. (2011). *Special Eurobarometer Wave 75.2. Volunteering and Intergenerational Solidarity*. Brussels: European Commission. Retrieved from http://www.europarl.europa.eu/pdf/eurobarometre/2011/juillet/04_07/rapport_%20eb75_2_%20benevolat_en.pdf.

Eurostat. (2016). Record Number of Over 1.2 Million First Time Asylum Seekers Registered in 2015. *Eurostat Newsrelease* (44/2016 – 4 March 2016). Retrieved from http://ec.europa.eu/eurostat/documents/2995521/7203832/3-04032016-AP-EN.pdf/.

Evangelinidis, A. (2016). The Greek State's Response to the Refugee Crisis and the Solidarity Movement. *Contemporary Southeastern Europe, 3*(1), 32–36.

Freeman, R. (1997). Working for Nothing: The Supply of Volunteer Labor. *Journal of Labor Economics, 15*(1), S140–S166.

Gaskin, K., & Smith, J. (1997). *A New Civic Europe? A Study of the Extent and Role of Volunteering*. London: National Center for Volunteering.

Gkionakis, N. (2016). The Refugee Crisis in Greece: Training Border Security, Police, Volunteers and Aid Workers in Psychological First Aid. *Intervention: Journal of Mental Health and Psychosocial Support in Conflict Affected Areas, 14*(1), 73–79.

Greenberg, M. (2001). Elements and Test of a Theory of Neighborhood Civic Participation. *Human Ecology Review, 8*(2), 40–51.

Hodgkinson, V. (2003). Volunteering in Global Perspective. In P. Dekker & L. Halman (Eds.), *The Values of Volunteering: Cross-Cultural Perspectives* (pp. 35–53). New York: Kluwer Academic.

Huang, J., van den Brink, H., & Groot, W. (2009). A Meta-analysis of the Effect of Education on Social Capital. *Economics of Education Review, 28*(4), 454–464. https://doi.org/10.1016/j.econedurev.2008.03.004/.

Hurley, N., Wilson, L., & Christie, I. (2008). *Scottish Household Survey Analytical Report: Volunteering*. Edinburgh: Scottish Government Social Research.

Hustinx, L., Cnaan, A., & Handy, F. (2010). Navigating Theories of Volunteering: A Hybrid Map for a Complex Phenomenon. *Journal for the Theory of Social Behaviour, 40*(4), 410–434. https://doi.org/10.1111/j.1468-5914.2010.00439.x.

International Organization for Migration-IOM. (2015). *Irregular Migrant, Refugee Arrivals in Europe Top One Million in 2015: IOM*. Technical Report. Retrieved from https://www.iom.int/news/irregular-migrant-refugee-arrivals-europe-top-one-million-2015-iom.

Johnson, M. K., Foley, K. L., & Elder, G. H. (2004). Women's Community Service, 1940–1960: Insights from a Cohort of Gifted American Women. *The Sociological Quarterly, 45*(1), 45–66.

Karakayali, S., & Kleist, O. (2015). *EFA-Studie: Strukturen und motive der ehrenamtlichen Flüchtlingsarbeit in Deutschland, 1. Forschungsbericht: Ergebnisse einer explorativen Umfrage vom November/Dezember 2014*. Berlin: BIM, Humboldt–Universität, Berlin.

Karakayali, S., & Kleist, O. (2016). *Strukturen und motive der ehrenamtlichen Flóchtlingsarbeit (EFA) in Deutschland. 2. Forschungsbericht. Ergebnisse einer explorativen Umfrage vom November/Dezember 2015*. Berlin: BIM, Humboldt–Universität, Berlin.

Karamichas, J. (2007). The Impact of the Summer (2007) Forest Fires in Greece: Recent Environmental Mobilizations, Cyber-activism and Electoral Performance. *South European Society and Politics, 12*(4), 521–533. https://doi.org/10.1080/13608740701731473.

Knoke, D. (1990). Networks of Political Action: Toward Theory Construction. *Social Forces, 68*(4), 1041–1063. https://doi.org/10.2307/2579133.

Lasby, D. (2004). *The Volunteer Spirit in Canada: Motivations and Barriers*. Toronto: Canadian Center for Philanthropy. Retrieved from http://www.imaginecanada.ca/sites/default/files/www/en/giving/reports/volunteer_spirit.pdf.

Latimir, K. (2016). National Volunteers in an International Crisis: The View from the Inside. In Humanitarian Practice Network (Ed.), *Humanitarian Exchange* (Number 67) *Refugees and Vulnerable Migrants in Europe* (pp. 29–33). Retrieved from http://odihpn.org/wp-content/uploads/2016/09/HE-67-FINAL.pdf.

Low, N., Butt, S., Ellis, P., & Davis Smith, J. (2007). *Helping Out: A National Survey of Volunteering and Charitable Giving*. London: Cabinet Office. Retrievedfromhttp://www.ivr.org.uk/images/stories/Institute-of-Volunteering-Research/Migrated-Resources/Documents/H/OTS_Helping_Out.pdf.

Lyrintzis, C. (2002). Greek Civil Society in the 21st Century. In P. C. Ioakimidis (Ed.), *Greece in the European Union: The New Role and the New Agenda* (pp. 90–99). Athens: Ministry of Press and Mass Media.

Marsh, A., & Kaase, M. (1979). Measuring Political Action. In S. H. Barnes & M. Kaase (Eds.), *Political Action: Mass Participation in Five Western Democracies* (pp. 57–97). Beverly Hills: Sage.

Matsaganis, M., & Leventi, C. (2014). Poverty and Inequality During the Great Recession in Greece. *Political Studies Review, 12*(2), 209–223. https://doi.org/10.1111/1478-9302.12050.

Matsuba, M., Hart, D., & Atkins, R. (2007). Psychological and Social–Structural Influences on Commitment to Volunteering. *Journal of Research in Personality, 41*(4), 889–907. https://doi.org/10.1016/j.jrp.2006.11.001.

McNamara, T. K., & Gonzales, E. (2011). Volunteer Transitions Among Older Adults: The Role of Human, Social, and Cultural Capital in Later Life. *The Journals of Gerontology, 66B*(4), 490–501. https://doi.org/10.1093/geronb/gbr055.

Mouzelis, N. (1995). Modernity, Late Development and Civil Society. In J. A. Hall (Ed.), *Civil Society: Theory, History, Comparison* (pp. 224–249). Cambridge: Polity Press.

Musick, M., & Wilson, J. (2008). *Volunteers: A Social Profile*. Bloomington: Indiana University Press.

Nie, N., Junn, J., & Stehlik-Barry, K. (1996). *Education and Democratic Citizenship in America*. Chicago: University of Chicago Press.

OECD. (2014). *Society at a Glance 2014, Highlights: Greece, the Crisis and Its Aftermath*. Paris: OECD Publishing. Retrieved from https://www.oecd.org/greece/OECD-SocietyAtaGlance2014-Highlights-Greece.pdf.

Paxton, P., Reith, N., & Glanville, J. L. (2014). Volunteering and the Dimensions of Religiosity: A Cross-national Analysis. *Review of Religious Research, 56*(4), 597–625. https://doi.org/10.1007/s13644-014-0169-y.

Pho, Y. (2008). The Value of Volunteer Labor and the Factors Influencing Participation: Evidence for the United States from 2002 Through 2005. *Review of Income and Wealth, 54*(2), 220–236. https://doi.org/10.1111/j.1475-4991.2008.00271.x.

Putnam, R. (2000). *Bowling Alone: The Collapse and Revival of American Community*. New York: Simon and Schuster.

Reed, P. B., & Selbee, L. K. (2001). The Civic Core in Canada: Disproportionality in Charitable Giving, Volunteering, and Civic Participation. *Nonprofit and Voluntary Sector Quarterly, 30*(4), 761–780. https://doi.org/10.1177/0899764001304008.

Rochester, C., Paine, A. E., Howlett, S., & Zimmeck, M. (2010). *Volunteering and Society in the 21st Century*. Hampshire: Palgrave Macmillan.

Rose, A. M. (2016). *The Roles, Functions, and Motivations of Volunteers in Helping to Ameliorate Reception Conditions for Asylum Seekers and Refugees – A Case Study of Voluntary Engagement at Temporary Asylum Accommodation Centres in Germany*. MSc. Thesis, University of Twente, European Studies. Retrieved from http://essay.utwente.nl/69366/1/ROSE_MA_BMS.pdf.

Rotolo, T., & Wilson, J. (2007). Sex Segregation in Volunteer Work. *The Sociological Quarterly, 48*(3), 559–585.

Rozakou, K. (2011). The Pitfalls of Volunteerism: The Production of the New, European Citizen in Greece. European Institute for Progressive Cultural Policies. Retrieved from http://eipcp.net/policies/rozakou/en.

Schlozman, K., Burns, N., & Verba, S. (1994). Gender and the Pathways to Participation: The Role of Resources. *The Journal of Politics, 56*(4), 963–990.

Smith, D. H., & Wang, L. (2016). Conducive Social Roles and Demographics Influencing Volunteering. In D. H. Smith, R. A. Stebbins, & J. Grotz (Eds.), *The Palgrave Handbook of Volunteering, Civic Participation, and Nonprofit Associations* (pp. 632–681). Basingstoke: Palgrave Macmillan.

Son, J., & Wilson, J. (2011). Generativity and Volunteering. *Sociological Forum, 26*(3), 644–667.

Sotiropoulos, D. (2004). *Formal Weakness and Informal Strength: Civil Society in Contemporary Greece*. Discussion Paper No. 16, The Hellenic Observatory, The European Institute, The London School of Economics and Political Science, London. Retrieved from http://www.lse.ac.uk/europeanInstitute/research/hellenicObservatory/pdf/DiscussionPapers/sotiropoulos.pdf.

Stolle, D. (1998). Bowling Together, Bowling Alone: The Development of Generalized Trust in Voluntary Associations. *Political Psychology, 19*(3), 497–525.

Theiss-Morse, E., & Hibbing, J. (2005). Citizenship and Civic Engagement. *Annual Review of Political Science, 8*(1), 227–249. https://doi.org/10.1146/annurev.polisci.8.082103.104829.

Thompson, A. M. (1993). Volunteers and Their Communities: A Comparative Analysis of Fire Fighters. *Nonprofit and Voluntary Sector Quarterly, 22*(2), 155–166. https://doi.org/10.1177/089976409302200205.

van Tienen, M., Scheepers, P., Reitsman, J., & Schilderman, H. (2011). The Role of Religiosity for Formal and Informal Volunteering in the Netherlands. *Voluntas: International Journal of Voluntary and Nonprofit Organizations, 22*(3), 365–389. https://doi.org/10.1007/s11266-010-9160-6.

Toth, F. M., & Kertesz, A. (2016). Beyond the Humanitarian Miracle. Volunteers' Role During the Refugee Crisis. In B. Simonovits & A. Bernát (Eds.), *The Social Aspects of the 2015 Migration Crisis in Hungary* (pp. 101–119). Budapest: TÁRKI Social Research Institute. Retrieved from http://www.tarki.hu/hu/news/2016/kitekint/20160330_refugees.pdf.

Tramountanis, A. (2017). The Refugee Crisis in Greece and the EU: Political and Social Dimensions. In N. Demertzis, H. Kikilias, D. Balourdos, N. Spiropoulou, & M. Chrisakis (Eds.), *The Social Portrait of Greece, 2016–2017 (under press)*. Athens: National Centre for Social Research. (in Greek).

UNHCR. (2016). *Global Trends: Forced Displacement in 2015*. Geneva: UN High Commissioner for Refugees. Retrieved from http://www.unhcr.org/576408cd7.pdf.

Vaillancourt, F. (1994). To Volunteer or Not: Canada, 1987. *The Canadian Journal of Economics, 27*(4), 813–826. https://doi.org/10.2307/136185.

Van Ingen, E., & Dekker, D. (2011). Changes in the Determinants of Volunteering: Participation and Time Investment Between 1975 and 2005 in the Netherlands. *Nonprofit and Voluntary Sector Quarterly, 40*(4), 682–702. https://doi.org/10.1177/0899764010363324.

Verba, S., Schlozman, K. L., & Brady, H. E. (1995). *Voice and Equality: Civic Voluntarism in American Politics.* Cambridge, MA: Harvard University Press.

Williams, C. (2002). Harnessing Voluntary Work: A Fourth Sector Approach. *Policy Studies, 23*(3), 247–260. https://doi.org/10.1080/0144287022000046019.

Wilson, J. (2000). Volunteering. *Annual Review of Sociology, 26,* 215–240. https://doi.org/10.1146/annurev.soc.26.1.215.

Wilson, J. (2012). Volunteerism Research: A Review Essay. *Nonprofit and Voluntary Sector Quarterly, 41*(2), 176–212. https://doi.org/10.1177/0899764011434558.

Wilson, J., & Janoski, T. (1995). The Contribution of Religion to Volunteer Work. *Sociology of Religion, 56,* 137–152.

Wilson, J., & Musick, M. (1997a). Who Cares? Toward an Integrated Theory of Volunteer Work. *American Sociological Review, 62*(5), 694–713.

Wilson, J., & Musick, M. (1997b). Work and Volunteering: The Long Arm of the Job. *Social Forces, 76*(1), 251–272. https://doi.org/10.2307/2580325.

Wilson, J., & Musick, M. (1998). The Contribution of Social Resources to Volunteering. *Social Science Quarterly, 79*(4), 799–814.

Wuthnow, R. (1995). *Learning to Care.* New York: Oxford University Press.

Wuthnow, R. (2004). *Saving America? Faith-based Services and the Future of Civil Society.* Princeton, NJ: Princeton University Press.

Wymer, W. W. (1998). Youth Development Volunteers: Their Motives, How They Differ from Other Volunteers and Correlates of Involvement Intensity. *Journal of Nonprofit and Voluntary Sector Marketing, 3*(4), 321–336. https://doi.org/10.1002/nvsm.6090030406.

Open Access This chapter is licensed under the terms of the Creative Commons Attribution 4.0 International License (http://creativecommons.org/licenses/by/4.0/), which permits use, sharing, adaptation, distribution and reproduction in any medium or format, as long as you give appropriate credit to the original author(s) and the source, provide a link to the Creative Commons license and indicate if changes were made.

The images or other third party material in this chapter are included in the chapter's Creative Commons license, unless indicated otherwise in a credit line to the material. If material is not included in the chapter's Creative Commons license and your intended use is not permitted by statutory regulation or exceeds the permitted use, you will need to obtain permission directly from the copyright holder.

CHAPTER 8

Civic and Political Solidarity Practices in Switzerland

Eva Fernández G. G.

INTRODUCTION

The study of civic and political engagement has often been addressed in the social sciences within altruistic perspectives encompassing prosocial behaviour beyond the narrowed approach of self-interested individualism (Giugni and Passy 2001). Altruism refers to actions and attitudes on social issues revolving around another persons' well-being. These can be aligned with solidarity beyond one's own group membership (interpersonal relationships), as individuals or collective acts in defence of the interests, rights and identities of others. Altruism is a freely chosen behaviour that benefits others, a group or a cause. It is typically proactive, requiring resources—time, effort or money—from individuals (Brady et al. 1995; Butcher 2010). Nowadays, this kind of behaviour accounts for a fair share of goods and services provided in modern societies, in form of volunteering or engagement in communities and associations and through the participation in community service programmes. Solidarity practices relate to altruism by underscoring individuals' willingness to help others in need but also through the contribution to

---

Eva Fernández G. G. (✉)
Department of Political Science and International Relations, University of Geneva, Geneva, Switzerland

© The Author(s) 2018
C. Lahusen, M. Grasso (eds.), *Solidarity in Europe*,
Palgrave Studies in European Political Sociology,
https://doi.org/10.1007/978-3-319-73335-7_8

collective endeavours. In addition, the range of solidarity practices include various forms of actions (e.g. donated money, donated time, engage as passive or active member of an organisation, engage in lobbying and advocacy). These actions might be explicitly political when directed to social and political change or civic when directed to social goods and involvement. Societies rely heavily on these forms of solidarity, but how can we account for differences between the solidarity practices (civic and political)? Which types of factors (e.g. socio-economic characteristics, attitudes, networks and resources) promote and trigger these forms of civic and political engagement?

Scholarship has frequently examined volunteering as a form of solidarity-based behaviour. Individuals enact in solidarity towards each other, as a form of prosocial behaviour based on norms of reciprocity and altruism (Manatschal and Freitag 2014). Building upon the analysis of the individual factors that promote this kind of behaviour, researchers have examined: education level, gender, age, race, income, free time and citizenship as "human capital" determinants of volunteering (Wilson 2012; Wilson and Musick 1997). In addition, social capital and cultural factors have been also considered as explanatory resources for volunteering. In the social capital perspective, this is often seen as deriving from embeddedness in social networks, trust and social identification (Stadelmann-Steffen and Freitag 2010; van Deth et al. 2007; Wilson 2000; Putnam 2000). The 2014 Swiss Volunteering Survey showed that at least 33% of the resident population in Switzerland aged 15 and older was involved in at least one form of formal or informal voluntary work. Volunteering has been defined as "any activity in which time is given freely to benefit another person, group or organisation" (Gundelach et al. 2010; Wilson 2000, p. 215). Recent research on the interaction between micro and macro factors has examined cross-country variations or in the case of Switzerland to the expected variance between volunteering cultures and interactions between cantons' welfare regimes effects—crowding-in and crowding-out (Manatschal and Freitag 2014; Gundelach et al. 2010). Likewise, in Switzerland, the analysis of regional and cantonal associational cultures has been examined through manifestations of direct democracy that are expected to impact the type of organisations within the civil society (Baglioni 2004). It has also confirmed that the propensity to volunteer is highest in the German-speaking part of Switzerland, followed by the French-speaking and Italian-speaking regions (Manatschal and Freitag 2014). Volunteering as a civic form of solidarity practice produces sustained social and community involvement enhancing social networks based on relationships of trust and reciprocity (Putnam 2000; van Deth 1997). Interestingly, in Switzerland, the densities of these networks differ substantially through linguistic and cultural regions.

Besides, people engage socially in a number of ways within and outside of the political domain. A substantial body of research examines citizenship behaviours and emphasises the importance of solidarity practices to respond individually or collectively to social problems and to common goods dilemma. Particularly interesting for our present purposes are the sociological and psychological perspectives on prosocial behaviour. These studies have centred the attention on the individual interpersonal orientations, traits and motivation explaining why and when individuals act prosocially as well as which social mechanisms, as norms, induce towards reciprocal and altruistic behaviour (Fetchenhauer et al. 2006; Simpson and Willer 2015). The analysis on the interpersonal orientations and emotions underscores the importance of empathic concerns when proving assistance to others (Batson 1998; Batson et al. 1983; Flam and King 2005; Flam 1990). In addition, individual traits as general dispositions of personality are presumably fundamental to engage in collective endeavours showing that extrovert people tend to involve more in collective forms of social participation (Omoto et al. 2010). Much of research on prosocial behaviour motivations conclude that actions as volunteering enhance psychological well-being which is associated with a sense of effectiveness and the expression of personal values (Piliavin and Siegl 2007). Motivation refers to the process that determines the initiation, intensity, direction and persistence of a behaviour (Vallerand and Thill 1993). In the following analysis of solidarity practices, individual factors (socio-economic characteristics and attitudes) and social capital factors are coupled with motivations. We inspire on the Volunteer Function Inventory (VFI) by Clary et al. (1998) to assess the function and the orientation of the motivations of the solidarity practices, as self-regarding or other-regarding and to stress the distinction between altruistic and egoistic behaviour. This motivational orientation investigation might shed some light on the "why" and "how" of the solidarity-based behaviour.

As mentioned before the venues for citizens' participation in collective endeavours are multiple. Given the objectives of this chapter, we will use a simple binary typology to characterise citizens' solidarity-based engagements as civic or political. Under our study and following Brady's (1999) definition of political participation, political solidarity practices are actions carried by ordinary citizens to influence some political outcomes that could benefit others, a group or a common cause. On the other hand, civic solidarity practices refer to a wide variety of activities ranging from informal and formal voluntary work to organisational involvement. This definition of civic engagement underscores citizens' participation collectively or individually to help or to improve the conditions for others or of a community (Ekman and Amna 2012; Adler and Goggin 2005). Obviously, several aspects of this typology are controversial and non-exhaustive. For instance, associational involvement could be characterised as political when referring to activism, however it is characterised as civic when referring to active engagement in charity organisations. We will use this twofold typology for an empirical analysis of citizens' solidarity practices, focusing on behaviours directed by an intention to influence and assert political demands, to validate the distinction between the two types (Teorell et al. 2007).

Broadly, this chapter analyses the motivational orientations of the solidarity practices and seeks to unveil if these are primarily motivated by other-regarding orientations. Conceptually, it links solidarity practices to civic and political forms of participation following previous research on volunteerism and activism (Omoto et al. 2010; Fraser et al. 2009; Caputo 2009; Caputo 1997). More precisely, it aims to analyse solidarity practices in Switzerland beyond volunteering behaviour. We first identify the forms of solidarity and examine the socio-demographic characteristics, attitudes, social capital and motives of the people engaged in these forms of action. Secondly, we examine whether solidarity is based on interpersonal relationships and social proximity, differing from altruistic concerns. For this purpose, we seek to unveil whether political and civic forms of solidarity-based behaviour are similar across three vulnerable groups, migrants, unemployed and people with disability, or whether we observe differences between forms of solidaristic engagement when targeting one group or another. That is, which factors tend to promote or inhibit generalised forms of solidarity across groups at the individual level? Finally, we investigate regional variations in solidarity practices by comparing the major linguistic regions of the country, namely, the German-speaking, French-speaking and Italian-speaking regions. We therefore also take into account the country's cultural diversity. We control if belonging to a particular language community impacts civic and political forms of solidarity practices as for volunteering behaviour (Gundelach et al. 2010). We contribute to the literature by inspiring in the Volunteer Function Inventory (VFI) model to understand variations on forms of solidaristic individual engagement when targeting three different beneficiary groups in Switzerland.

Measuring Solidarity Practices: Between Voluntarism and Activism

The conceptual link between solidarity and civic and political engagement has been mainly developed through the lenses of political activism or the study of acts of compassion. Still, these analyses depict solidarity-based behaviour as a connection with others, enhanced by the membership to a group that presupposes some specific duties (Rochon 1998; Wilson 2012). This presupposition of belonging is expected to impact the relationship between the actor and the recipient. As a result, the degree of social proximity and attachment also affects individual motivations and consequently the form of individual or collective engagement (van der Zee 2006). In addition to these factors, social tolerance also plays a fundamental role. Tolerance (social and political) is not limited to the acceptance of diversity but also to the acceptance on equal terms of certain unpopular and target groups (Leite Viegas 2007). Thus, social tolerance as a covariate for explaining solidarity practices (civic and political) relates to individuals' distance to social groups which is then to be peered to social identification as attachment.

The experimental design of the dictator game implemented by Fowler and Kam (2007) showed that social identification and altruism both trigger political participation. However social identification enhances particularised forms of solidarity, as the norms of reciprocity are stronger within groups than between groups. Still, generosity and unilateral giving behaviours have been shown from other experimental research to cascade individual contributions to public goods (Simpson and Willer 2015; Fehr and Schmidt 2006; Fehr and Fischbacher 2003). The perspective of solidarity as prosocial behaviour based on a sole membership/connection (social identification) suggests that additional acts of support or compassion that target the well-being of others are mainly driven by an altruistic concern. In line with these two perspectives, we use social identification and social tolerance to better understand in-bond (within-group) and out-bond (outer-group) solidarity. We assume that solidarity practices are related to both particularised concerns (within-group) and to more general altruistic concerns (outer-group).

Hypothesis 1a
Individuals reporting higher levels of social group identification are more likely to engage in activities aimed at enhancing within-group well-being.

Hypothesis 1b
Individuals reporting higher levels of social tolerance are more likely to engage in unilateral giving activities enhancing out-group well-being.

Besides, we argue that social dispositions and attitudes are key to understand prosocial behaviour. The analysis of individual social dispositions allows us to explain how solidarity practices are conditioned to interpersonal relationships of proximity and common experiences or to target-oriented projects beyond interpersonal ties to the immediate community (Rippe 1998). Prior research showed that cosmopolitanism and altruism are associated with redistributional attitudes and political participation beyond interpersonal solidaristic ties (Bechtel et al. 2014). Cosmopolitanism and altruism, as covariates to solidarity practices, are means to other forms of belongings at the margins of the groups, communities and nation-states' boundaries. Cosmopolitanism refers to an interest towards groups or individuals that are distant culturally or geographically in opposition to localised and interpersonal interest, while altruism refers to the willingness to incur in personal loss to support distant others' welfare (Elster 2006). We complement the analysis of the in-bond and out-bond solidarity practices by examining how social dispositions explain the possible variance between forms of solidarity-based behaviour across three vulnerable groups (migrants, unemployed and people with disability).

Hypothesis 2a
Individuals reporting higher levels of cosmopolitanism are more likely to engage in activities foreseeing the well-being of undistinguished vulnerable groups.

Hypothesis 2b
Strong communitarian attachment and cultural proximity decrease target-oriented solidarity towards migrants and refugees.

Since we are also interested in the underlying motivations of the solidarity practices, we build upon the behavioural psychological perspective on prosocial behaviour to examine the "why" and "how" of the solidarity-based behaviour (for review, see Fetchenhauer et al. 2006). We follow the argument that the motivational and functional assessment of the action are key to understand how diverse motivations converge into the same form of behaviour. In this sense, the Volunteer Function Inventory (VFI) developed by Clary et al. (1998) showed that individual behaviour embodies various types of motivations and that the distinction between motivational orientations (self- or other-regarding) is associated with the psychological function of the action. For instance, two persons could do the same volunteering work for an association; however, for one individual, the motivation orienting his/her behaviour is mainly the enhancement of his/her professional skills. While for the other individual, the motivation orienting his/her behaviour is primarily the interest in his/her community. As a result, one same action fulfils two contrasting functions related to two distinct motivational orientations at the individual level. In addition, we use the analysis of the solidarity practices' motivational orientations to examine the distinction between forms of solidarity practices: civic and political. First, in line with Rippe (1998) definition of non-interpersonal solidaristic ties, we argue that solidarity as "acts carried out in order to support others, or at the very least to describe a disposition to help and assist" (Bayertz 1996, p. 308; Bayertz 1999) relates to interpersonal and non-interpersonal relationships. This definition captures a solidaristic behaviour based on generalised and particularised concerns, capturing both communitarian loyalties and altruism. However, it is mainly related to civic engagement as it responds to societal problems, and it does not assert political demands. On the other hand, solidarity as a political practice refers to "a moral relation formed when individuals or groups unite around some mutually recognized political need or goal in order to bring about social change" (Scholz 2015, p. 732). Consequently, the grounded commitment to enhance social change is key to differentiating between solidarity forms, which primarily tend to provide help, services and relief to others or to upraise political voicing—advocacy, products' boycotting and activism (Stjernø 2012; Scholz 2008). As a result, when assessing the motivational orientations of the solidaristic engagements, we first identify the form, as political or civic, and then we analyse its motivational orientation. The motivational orientations of the solidaristic practices in this chapter are defined within three categories: self-regarding, based on individualistic concerns; community-regarding, based on interpersonal and community concerns; and other-regarding—based on generalised concerns. Previous literature on the motivational orientations assessment has served to distinguish civic forms of volunteerism from political forms of volunteerism as activism. Omoto et al. (2010) showed that other-regarding orientations are a strong covariate to civic and political engagement but that community-regarding orientations are more correlated to civic volunteerism than to activism. In addition, various studies have shown that self-regarding orientations are still important to understand prosocial behaviour because individual motivations are multifaceted. "It appears that many volunteers' motivations cannot be neatly classified as either altruistic or egoistic, both because some specific motives combine other-interested and self-interested considerations and because many people indicate that they have both kinds of reasons for volunteering" (Clary and Snyder 1999, p. 157). In this chapter, we expect to explain the maximum amount of variance between civic and political solidarity practices based on the distinction between community-regarding and other-regarding orientations while loosely associating both to individual concerns. Additionally, we examine how the motivational orientations account for the variation between the forms of solidaristic individual engagement when targeting three different vulnerable groups. We underscore the importance of the motivational orientations to unveil the support or lack of support to migrants and refugees' populations confronted to unemployed and disabled populations.

Hypothesis 3a
Individual solidarity practices, civic and political, are partly associated with self-regarding orientations and strongly related to other-regarding and community-regarding concerns independently of the beneficiaries' populations.

Hypothesis 3b
Differences on solidarity actions across groups are likely to be more associated with community-regarding orientations than with other-regarding orientations.

Also as part of our analysis of solidarity practices, we will control for human and social capital factors. Scholars have tended to confirm the importance of socio-demographic factors and social traits (e.g. age, gender, education, religion, social class) as covariates to assess the conditions for civic and political engagement. Previous research on political participation has identified factors such as income and education as important socio-economic predictors of political attitudes and actions (Dalton 2008). In addition to these, the research on volunteering behaviour have underscored the importance of gender when assessing woman's role in caring activities; thus we will control for the cultural allocation of women's role as more emphatic and mainly deploying higher solidaristic behaviour than men (Wilson and Musick 1997; Gallagher 1994). Since Almond and Verba (1963; Verba et al. 1995), survey evidence has generally confirmed that education is linked to civic and political engagement. Likewise, we will control for the covariations related to the impact of people's social embeddedness and religiosity on solidaristic practices. In this sense, social capital approaches are also of crucial importance, as it is understood to enhance social trust and tolerance (Putnam 2000; van Deth et al. 2007). A large part of the literature has measured social capital through the proxy of trust closely related to social cohesion and solidarity. Social capital has been also related to the establishment of bonds and norms for cooperative endeavours, as shown in studies of the impact of the social capital of migrants on their political participation (Eggert and Giugni 2010; Morales and Giugni 2011; Smith 1999). In this perspective, solidarity practices are mainly seen as norms of reciprocity which link citizens together (Stolle and Rochon 1998).

DATA AND METHODS

Our analysis draws upon a comprehensive eight-country dataset, collected in 2016, within the EU project "European paths to transnational solidarity at times of crisis: Conditions, forms, role models and policy responses" (TransSOL) which aims to measure individual forms and conditioning factors enhancing transnational solidarity in Europe. The dataset sample contains 2221 observations for Switzerland, with its corresponding weights. It matches national quotas on age, gender, region and education. Appendix 1 to this chapter contains all the variables recordings, used in our models. The statistical procedures applied first give a descriptive overview of the dependent variables—civic and political solidarity practices. Secondly, we propose a logistic regression model to assess the effects of the covariates on solidarity practices by target group: unemployed, migrants/refugees and people with disability.

The study examines six binary dependent variables, one for each kind of solidarity behaviour (civic and political) and per target group (unemployed, migrants/refuges and people with disability). We used three questions to measure civic and political solidarity practices (see Table 8.1):

> —*Have you ever done any of the following in order to support migrant or refugees' rights?*—*Have you ever done any of the following in order to support disable people rights?*—*Have you ever done any of the following in order to support unemployed people rights? (each of the questions had the same seven possible options: "Attended a march, protest or demonstration" and/or "Bought or refused to buy products in support to the goals" and/or "Donated money" and/ or "Donated time" and/or "Engaged as passive member of an organisation" and/or "Engaged as active member of an organisation" or "None of the above").*

Table 8.1 Proportions of solidarity practices towards vulnerable groups in Switzerland (in %)

Activities: Support refugees and migrant		Activities: Support people with disability		Activities: Support unemployed people	
Attended a march, protest or demonstration	4.1	Attended a march, protest or demonstration	3.5	Attended a march, protest or demonstration	3.7
Donated money	17.5	Donated money	41.6	Donated money	11.4
Donated time	11.3	Donated time	24.9	Donated time	11.6
Bought or refused to buy products in support to the goals	11.2	Bought or refused to buy products in support to the goals	23.2	Bought or refused to buy products in support to the goals	13.7
Engaged as passive member of an organisation	3.7	Engaged as passive member of an organisation	11.5	Engaged as passive member of an organisation	4.5
Engaged as active member of an organisation	4.9	Engaged as active member of an organisation	7.0	Engaged as active member of an organisation	4.5
None of the above	66.9	None of the above	33.2	None of the above	67.5
Civic solidarity practices	27.3	Civic solidarity practices	59.3	Civic solidarity practices	24.2
Political solidarity practices	13.6	Political solidarity practices	25.3	Political solidarity practices	16.0
N	2221	N	2221	N	2221

Civic solidarity practices variables (one per group): respondents have stated to engage in at least one of the following actions: "Donated money" and/or "Donated time" and/or "Engaged as passive member of an organisation" and/or "Engaged as active member of an organisation"

Political solidarity practices variables (one per group): respondents have stated to engage in at least one of the following actions: "Attended a march, protest or demonstration" and/or "Bought or refused to buy products in support to the goals"

From these questions, we operationalised three binary civic solidarity practices variables (one per group), in which respondents have stated to engage in at least one of the following actions: "Donated money" and/or "Donated time" and/or "Engaged as passive member of an organisation" and/or "Engaged as active member of an organisation" or "None of the above", and three binary political solidarity variables (one per group), in which respondents have stated to engage in at least one of the following actions: "Attended a march, protest or demonstration" and/or "Bought or refused to buy products in support to the goals" or "None of the above." Political solidarity practices clearly refer to unconventional and consumerism political behaviour as defined in the literature (for a review, see Teorell et al. 2007) while civic solidarity practices refer to passive and active forms of social involvement (Morales and Geurts 2007). As mentioned previously in the introduction of the chapter, several aspects of this typology are controversial and non-exhaustive as some forms of social involvement could be considered to have different weights with respect to the extent of the civic involvement. Still, the key distinction for the typology is the intention to influence and assert political demands through the engaged action. These actions might be explicitly political when directed to social and political change or civic when directed to social goods and involvement.

In addition, two key blocks of independent covariates were used to examine civic and political solidarity practices: motivational orientations covariates (self-regarding, other-regarding and community-regarding orientations) and social dispositions covariates (social distance and cosmopolitanism). With respect to the motivational covariates, we used the following question:

> *People do unpaid work or give help to all kinds of groups for all kinds of reasons. Thinking about all the groups, clubs or organisations you have helped over the last 12 months, did you start helping them for any of the reasons on this list? Choose up to 5 reasons that were most important to you. Please select at least 1 and a maximum of 5 answers (seventeen possible options).*

Then we performed factormat, a factor analysis of a correlation matrix, using a tetrachoric matrix of correlation of the 17 items, to group the items within three categories: self-regarding, other-regarding and community-regarding concerns. As a result, self-regarding motivational orientations refer to: "I wanted to meet people/make friends"; "I thought it would give me a chance to learn new skills"; "I thought it would give me a chance to use my existing skills"; "It helps me get on in my career"; "I had spare time to do it"; "It gave me a chance to get a recognised qualification". Other-regarding motivational orientations refer to: "I felt that it was a moral duty to help others in need"; "I felt that it was important to help because I might be in a similar situation sometime"; "It's part of my philosophy of life to help people"; "It's part of my religious belief to help people"; "It's part of my philosophy of life to help people"; "I wanted to improve things/help people"; "The cause was really important to me". Community-regarding motivational orientations refer to: "I felt there was no one else to do it"; "My friends/family did it"; "It was connected with the needs of my family/friends"; "I felt there was a need in my community".

With respect to the social disposition covariates block, we focused in two key measures. First is social distance, an 18-item additive scale, measured with the following question:

Please say whether you would mind or not having each of the following as neighbours? (items correspond to 18 target groups, e.g. migrants, people suffering from AIDS, left wing extremist, right wing extremist etc. in which the higher score corresponds to large social distance and low social tolerance)

Secondly, we used two questions to capture two dimensions of cosmopolitanism, cultural openness and attachment to humanity. We operationalised cosmopolitanism as cultural openness referring to multicultural appraisal:

To what extent do you agree or disagree with the following statement: It is a good thing to live in a multicultural society. (5—item answer: 1—Strongly disagree, 2—Disagree, 3—Neither, 4—Agree and 5—Strongly agree)

And we operationalised cosmopolitanism as attachment to humanity using the following question:

Please tell me how attached you feel to the world/humanity? (5-item answer: 1—Not at all attached, 2—Not very attached, 3—Neither, 4—Quite attached, 5—Very attached).

Besides, we used several other measures to capture the factors that may predict the probability of engaging in solidarity practices. These predictors include a battery of socio-demographic covariates and attitudinal covariates defined in the Appendices (1 and 2) and discussed in the regression model session. Finally a descriptive overview of the proportion and distribution of civic and political solidarity practices (see Table 8.1) shows that two thirds of the individuals have engaged to support the rights of people with disability, while only a third have engaged to support migrant or unemployed people's rights. The disability field is the most 'crowded' field in terms of solidarity engagement. It has the largest share of social capital (as membership to organisation) doubling the other fields. Also within the disability field, we observe that the most frequent form of engagement is donating money (42%). Conversely, this field seem to be the least contentious; protest-oriented practices are the lowest for disability. Still political solidarity practices are higher than in the other two fields. With regards to solidarity practices, donating money and political consumerism are the most relevant practices. These results are in line with previous analysis on volunteering and associational involvement. Pay-check involvement seems to be very strong in Switzerland where people tend to donated money to more than two associations on average (Morales and Geurts 2007).

Civic Versus Political Solidarity Practices: Explanatory Logistic Model

In this section, we propose six logistic regression models to assess the effects of human, social, motivational and contextual covariates on civic and political solidarity practices by target group. We regress six binary dependent variables, one for each kind of solidaristic form per target group: unemployed people, migrants and refugees' groups and people with disability. Custom to all models are a block to control for socio-demographic covariates effects, which include (age, education, gender, income and living with children); a block of social and political covariates (discuss politics and meet with friends) to account for the effects of interpersonal ties on the solidarity practices; a block of motivational orientations covariates (self-regarding, other-regarding and community-regarding motivations) to investigate the process that facilitates the initiation and orientation of the solidarity behaviour; a block of attitudinal and social dispositions covariates (social distance, social trust, fairness, attachment to country and to humanity, religiosity, multicultural appraisal and xenophobic attitudes) to account for the variation in social dispositions of the individuals engaging in solidarity practices; and lastly we also included a block of contextual covariates for the three main linguistic regions of the country to control for the linguistic cultures effect in the solidarity behaviour.

In general terms, the three civic dependent variables refer to 1 when in engaging in at least one form of civic action per target group—for example, "Donated money" and/or "Donated time" and/or "Engaged as passive member of an organisation" and/or "Engaged as active member of an organisation." Equally the three political dependent variables refer to 1 when engaging in at least one form of political action per each target group—for example, "Attended a march, protest or demonstration" and/or "Bought or refused to buy products in support to the goals." For interpretative purposes, the six logistic models are presented as odds ratios instead of log odds, which express the odds variation of the dependent variable for each unit of change in the covariates. With respect to the overall explained variance, the civic models of solidarity have the highest explanatory power, more specifically the model explaining the civic support to migrants and refugees counts for 15% of the overall variance, while the other two are limited to 9% (see *Pseudo-R²* in Tables 8.2 and 8.3). Similarly,

Table 8.2 Logistic regression models on civic solidarity engagement strength (odds ratios)

	Support to refugees and migrant		Support to people with disability		Support to unemployed people	
		SE		SE		SE
Age	0.95*	(0.02)	1.04*	(0.02)	1.03	(0.02)
Age2	1.00*	(0.00)	1.00	(0.00)	1.00	(0.00)
Gender (ref. woman)	1.02	(0.11)	1.01	(0.10)	0.61***	(0.07)
Income (ref. low-income groups)						
Middle income	1.13	(0.15)	1.14	(0.13)	1.13	(0.15)
High income	1.49*	(0.26)	1.19	(0.19)	1.05	(0.19)
Education (ref. secondary school or lower)						
BA or equivalent	0.96	(0.13)	1.04	(0.12)	0.95	(0.13)
MA or higher degree	1.07	(0.15)	1.10	(0.14)	1.22	(0.18)
Live with child	1.15	(0.16)	1.03	(0.13)	0.92	(0.13)
Discuss politics	1.04	(0.02)	1.04*	(0.02)	1.05*	(0.02)
Meet with friends	0.94	(0.06)	1.09	(0.06)	0.91	(0.06)
Self-regarding motivation	1.35**	(0.15)	1.30*	(0.15)	1.63***	(0.19)
Other-regarding motivation	2.16***	(0.27)	2.08***	(0.22)	2.22***	(0.29)
Community-regarding motivation	1.33*	(0.15)	1.45***	(0.16)	1.53***	(0.18)
Social distance	0.94***	(0.02)	0.97*	(0.01)	0.97	(0.02)
Social trust	1.11	(0.13)	1.01	(0.11)	0.98	(0.11)
Fairness	0.87	(0.10)	1.01	(0.10)	1.24	(0.14)
Attachment to country	0.55***	(0.10)	1.11	(0.18)	0.63**	(0.11)
Attachment to humanity	1.84***	(0.28)	1.36**	(0.16)	1.20	(0.17)
Religiosity	1.11***	(0.02)	1.04**	(0.02)	1.03	(0.02)
Multicultural appraisal	1.22**	(0.09)	1.02	(0.06)	0.95	(0.07)
Xenophobic attitudes towards other cultures	0.89***	(0.03)	1.02	(0.02)	1.00	(0.03)
Swiss regions (ref. Swiss-German)						
Swiss-French	0.59***	(0.07)	1.06	(0.11)	1.00	(0.12)
Swiss-Italian	0.46**	(0.12)	0.88	(0.18)	1.36	(0.32)
Constant	0.38	(0.25)	0.07***	(0.04)	0.09***	(0.06)
Pseudo R^2	0.151		0.089		0.090	
N	2221		2221		2221	

Note: Logistic regressions odds ratios shown with standard errors in parentheses (***$p < 0.01$, **$p < 0.05$, *$p < 0.1$). Regressions also include dummy and indicators variables for income, region, education and gender (see references categories for interpretation) the political model concerning migrants and refugees' support counts for 12% of the overall variance, while the political unemployment support model counts for almost the 9% and the political support model towards people with disability explains 5% of the overall variance.

The models concerning the civic practices of solidarity per target group show that the socio-demographic covariates have mainly a positive effect on the dependent variables, but the odds are scarcely relevant (see Table 8.2). However, being a woman has a significant and negative effect on civic support practices towards unemployed people. Also individuals with high income tend to engage 1.5 times more than low-income individuals when supporting migrant and refugees' groups. The social and political covariates are positive and fairly significant when explaining civic support towards unemployed people and people with disability, but still their odds coefficients are less revealing. With respect to the motivational covariates as presupposed in our Hypothesis 3a, self-regarding and other-regarding motivations are relevant to explain civic forms of engagement through all the groups, nevertheless the other-regarding motivations have a stronger explanatory power and positive statistical significance. Likewise as assumed in Hypothesis 3b, community-regarding motivations are positive and statistically significant when explaining civic support towards unemployed people and people with disability, but against our expectations these are still somehow relevant to explain civic support towards migrants. Within the block of attitudinal and social dispositions covariates, we have two types of significant effects: negative effects concerning strong communitarian attachment and xenophobic attitudes towards other cultures and positive effects related to cosmopolitanism and religiosity. More in detail, in line with our Hypothesis 2b, communitarian attachment and xenophobic attitudes negatively impact solidaristic behaviour to support migrant and refugees. Likewise, as partly presupposed in Hypothesis 2a, cosmopolitanism (as multicultural appraisal and attachment to humanity) is positively associated with civic forms of solidarity. Still this is only relevant to explain civic solidaristic behaviour towards migrants/refugees and people with disability. The cosmopolitanism variables were unable to capture the well-being of vulnerable groups as undistinguishable, as they did not have a significant effect across all three groups. Also religiosity, as expected and tested in other research, is positively related to civic practices. In addition, we can confirm Hypothesis 1b when describing civic solidarity practices across the three beneficiary groups, social distance does have a negative and significant impact on civic forms of engagement towards migrants. Finally, with regard to the contextual covariates, these are significant and negatively associated with civic support towards migrant and refugees. On an average, people in Swiss-French regions tend to engage 0.6 times less than in Swiss-German region when supporting migrants; within the same field, people in the Swiss-Italian region tend to engage 0.5 times less than in the Swiss-German region. These contextual results are particularly interesting as they show that the linguistic cultures in Switzerland impact solidarity practices negatively when target oriented to migrants as solidarity recipients.

As for the civic models, the socio-demographic covariates have significant effect in predicting political solidarity practices, but these are scarcely relevant (see Table 8.3). Only gender and income have a significant and relevant effect to explain political solidarity practices. Being a woman has a significant and positive effect when supporting migrants and refugees—women engage 1.3 times more than men in this kind of actions. In comparison to civic models, the high-income covariate has a reverse effect; individuals with high income tend to engage less when politically supporting migrant and refugees' groups. This suggests that income has undistinguishable positive effect across groups when examining civic solidarity practices. However, income affects negatively the particularised political solidarity support toward migrants. Previous literature results on political consumerism underscored income as a key variable to explain forms of consumerism (Stolle and Micheletti 2013) and some approaches on protesting behaviour considered income to be no longer a preoccupation because of post-materialist values (Inglehart and Welzel 2005). Yet, with these results we could advance that unconventional and political consumerism practices are negatively dependent on income when describing internal variations between generalised and particularised forms of political solidarity.

The political covariates are positive and statistically significant when explaining political support towards migrant, and social covariates are only relevant to explain political support towards people with disability. With respect to the motivational covariates, Hypothesis 3a is confirmed; other-regarding motivations are the most relevant to explain political forms of engagement through all the groups. The other-regarding motivations have a stronger explanatory power and statistical significance. Additionally as presupposed in Hypothesis 3b, community-regarding motivations are positive and statistically significant when explaining political support toward unemployed people and people with disability, but

Table 8.3 Logistic regression models on political solidarity engagement strength (odds ratios)

	Support to refugees and migrant		Support to people with disability		Support to unemployed people	
		SE		SE		SE
Age	0.95*	(0.02)	1.01	(0.02)	1.09**	(0.03)
Age2	1.00*	(0.00)	1.00	(0.00)	1.00**	(0.00)
Gender	1.29*	(0.17)	1.14	(0.12)	0.87	(0.11)
Income (ref. low-income groups)						
Middle income	0.76	(0.12)	0.96	(0.12)	0.87	(0.12)
High income	0.56**	(0.12)	1.02	(0.17)	0.82	(0.17)
Education (ref. secondary school or lower)						
BA or equivalent	0.89	(0.15)	1.19	(0.16)	1.26	(0.21)
MA or higher degree	0.99	(0.18)	1.17	(0.17)	1.26	(0.22)
Live with child	1.12	(0.20)	0.99	(0.13)	0.82	(0.13)
Discuss politics	1.12***	(0.03)	1.02	(0.02)	1.05	(0.03)
Meet with friends	1.00	(0.08)	1.15*	(0.07)	1.09	(0.08)
Self-regarding motivation	1.52**	(0.22)	1.13	(0.13)	1.37*	(0.18)
Other-regarding motivation	1.91***	(0.32)	1.71***	(0.21)	1.88***	(0.29)
Community-regarding motivation	1.23	(0.18)	1.35**	(0.15)	1.65***	(0.22)
Social distance	0.94**	(0.02)	1.00	(0.02)	0.98	(0.02)
Social trust	1.11	(0.16)	1.21	(0.14)	1.29	(0.17)
Fairness	1.05	(0.15)	1.17	(0.13)	1.06	(0.14)
Attachment to country	0.48***	(0.10)	1.14	(0.21)	0.65*	(0.13)
Attachment to humanity	0.87	(0.16)	1.01	(0.13)	0.96	(0.16)
Religiosity	1.04*	(0.02)	1.01	(0.02)	1.04*	(0.02)
Multicultural appraisal	0.96	(0.09)	0.94	(0.06)	0.96	(0.08)
Xenophobic attitudes towards other cultures	.85***	(0.03)	1.01	(0.03)	0.96	(0.03)
Swiss regions (ref. Swiss-German)						
Swiss-French	1.23	(0.18)	0.98	(0.11)	0.93	(0.13)
Swiss-Italian	1.13	(0.35)	1.12	(0.26)	1.50	(0.40)
Constant	0.69	(0.10)	0.05***	(0.04)	0.01***	(0.01)
Pseudo R^2	0.116		0.045		0.087	
N	2221		2221		2221	

Note: Logistic regressions odds ratios shown with standard errors in parentheses (***$p < 0.01$, **$p < 0.05$, *$p < 0.1$). Regressions also include dummy and indicators variables for income, region, education and gender (see references categories for interpretation) these are not relevant to explain political support towards migrants. Within the block of attitudinal and social dispositions covariates, we continue to have two types of significant effects, negative effects concerning strong communitarian attachment and positive effects related to social trust and religiosity. Also as presupposed in Hypothesis 2b, attachment to the country negatively impacts solidaristic behaviour to support migrants and refugees. Yet, country attachment is still negatively associated with political support to unemployed people. On the other hand, religiosity continues to have a positive effect when supporting politically vulnerable people. For both types of actions civic and political, religiosity patterns are clearly consistent with the volunteering literature. Lastly, Hypothesis 1a and 1b are confirmed, as social distance has a significant negative impact when explaining political forms of solidarity towards migrants and refugees and not across all three beneficiary groups. Finally, with regard to the contextual covariates, in contrast to the civic engagement models, contextual covariates have no significant impact on political solidarity practices.

Findings

Differentiating Civic and Political Solidarity Practices

The results reported in Tables 8.2 and 8.3 show that motivational orientations account for the variation between civic and political solidarity practices. The psychological perspectives on prosocial behaviour have allowed us to evaluate the function and orientation of the solidarity behaviours. We have showed that solidarity practices are primarily motivated by other-regarding orientations even though individual motivations are multifaceted (Clary and Snyder 1999). Hypothesis 3a suggested that civic and political solidarity practices are associated with other-regarding and with community-regarding concerns independently of the beneficiaries' populations. However, our analysis shows that this is the case only for civic solidarity practices. Political solidarity practices with respect to motivational orientations are more complex. First, all political solidarity practices presuppose a strong dependence on other-regarding concerns, while the other two motivational orientations are dependent on the target group (beneficiaries). Second, we were expecting to confront political solidarity practices against civic solidarity practices through the analysis on community-regarding orientations. To our surprise the models showed that community-regarding concerns do not explain the variation between political and civic solidarity-based behaviours as for volunteerism and activisms (Kleres 2017; Omoto et al. 2010; Miller and Krosnick 2004; Caputo 1997) but the variation of political solidarity engagements between the groups as partially suggested in Hypothesis 3b. Thus, we underscore the importance of the motivational orientations to unveil the support or lack of support to migrants and refugees' populations confronted to unemployed people and to people with disability. In our particular case, we could suggest that the differences on political solidarity actions across these three groups are associated with interpersonal ties to the community. More precisely, the marginal effects on the civic and political forms of solidarity (see Figs. 8.1 and 8.2) corroborate that the motivational orientations effects are relevant to both kinds of practices independently of the

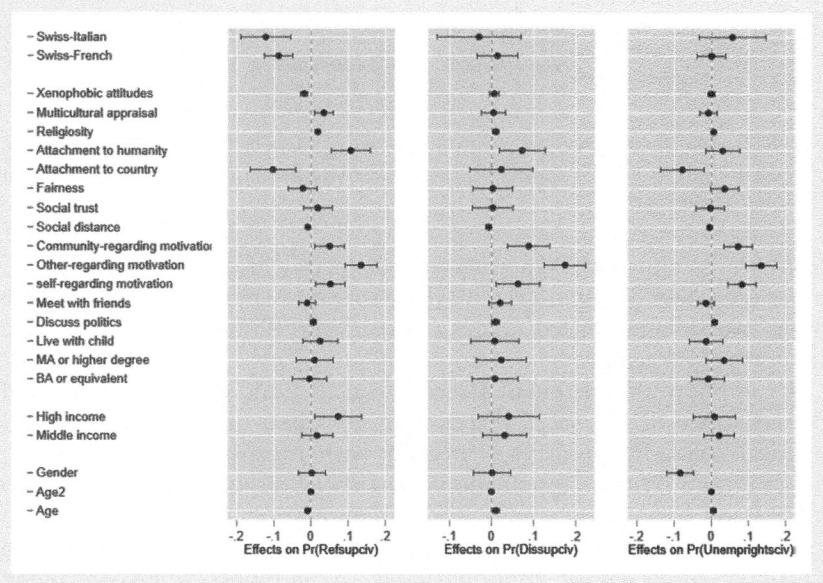

Fig. 8.1 Marginal effects on civic solidarity practices by target group. Note: Marginal effects for each model in Table 8.2. The horizontal lines indicate 0 95 confidence intervals

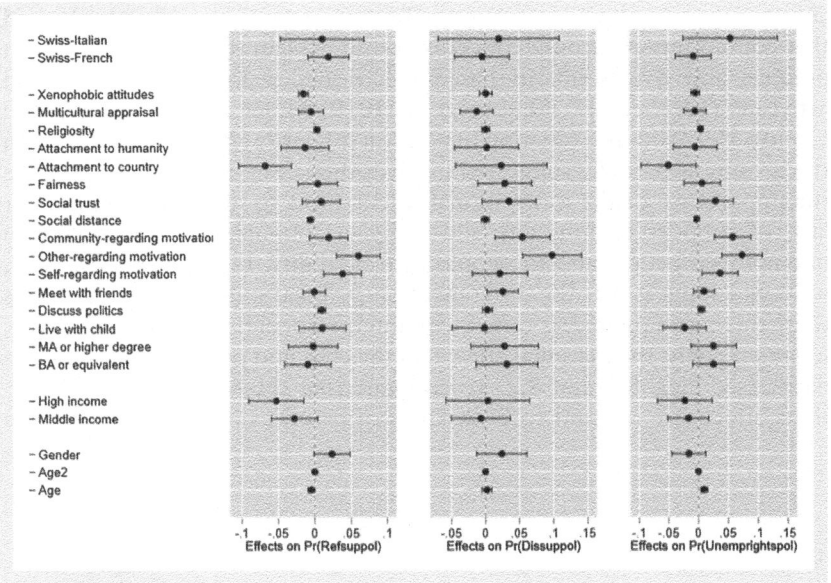

Fig. 8.2 Marginal effects on political solidarity practices by target group. Note: Marginal effects for each model in Table 8.3. The horizontal lines indicate 0.95 confidence intervals

reference group. However, with respect to this block of covariates, the other-regarding orientations have the strongest marginal effect, while the other two orientations covariates translate into differentiated solidaristic support across groups.

In addition, the marginal effects in Figs. 8.1 and 8.2 also highlighted the relevance of the social dispositions covariates to examine civic and political solidarity practices, especially with regard to the support to migrants and refugees' populations. The social dispositions were used to understand how the degree of social identification and attachment to a group affect forms of individual engagement, because the membership to a group presupposes some specific duties. In our models when controlling for social distance, attachment to country and cosmopolitanism, we confirmed Hypothesis 1b and showed that social distance relates negatively to civic and political solidarity practices almost independently of the beneficiary group. Still, the model also confirmed that social identification is strongly significant only to solidarity-based behaviours towards migrants and refugees' groups. As a result, civic and political forms of solidarity unveiled that high levels of social identification enhance within-group well-being concerns, while decreasing out-bond solidarity towards other vulnerable groups specially migrants.

Finally, our analysis showed that general altruistic concerns are negatively correlated to social identification and attachment to a group. Yet, cosmopolitanism as covariate to solidarity practices in opposition to localised and interpersonal ties showed that other forms of belonging at the margins of groups, communities and nation-states boundaries are only relevant to understand civic solidarity practices towards migrants (Hypothesis 2b). Against Hypothesis 2a cosmopolitanism captured important variation across the support to the well-being of our three target groups. So how should one interpret the strong association between cosmopolitanism and solidarity-based behaviour only towards migrants and refugees? One possibility is to argue that communitarians forms of belonging are robust in the other two cases, so the civic or political mobilisation to support unemployed or people with disability is rooted in strong interpersonal ties of reciprocity within the community which give little place to cosmopolitan forms of belonging.

Concluding Remarks

People engage socially in numerous ways within and outside of the political domain. Solidarity practices are ways to respond individually or collectively to social problems. Substantial body of research have examined citizenship behaviours and emphasised the importance of prosocial behaviour to contribute to collective endeavours. Through the chapter, we have argued that these actions might be explicitly political when directed to social and political change or civic when directed to social goods and involvement. The study of civic and political solidarity practices in Switzerland has allowed us to analyse solidaristic behaviour in a twofold process within and at the margins of group membership perspectives. Our analysis refers to the impact of social dispositions and motivations to understand prosocial behaviour, beyond the narrow scope of self-interest. We have confirmed that socio-demographic factors as well as socio-political attitudes are relevant to explain various forms of prosocial behaviour but that social dispositions and motivational orientations seem to be the key triggers for civic and political solidarity practices. More precisely, following the motivational and functional assessment proposed by the VFI model, we have corroborated that the motivational orientation effects are multifaceted. In this sense, we have shown that solidarity practices are not only motivated by other-regarding concerns but strongly driven by these. And we have shown that in contrast to one of the major distinctions between volunteerism and activism, political solidarity practices are also driven by community-regarding orientations. Precisely, the community-regarding orientations seem only to account for the variations in political solidarity-based engagements across groups.

In addition and pertinent to our analysis was the differentiation between civic and political forms of solidaristic behaviour. They have shed some light on the covariation between other-regarding and community-regarding orientations to explain target-oriented support to groups which embodied spatial referencing (migrants). Variations between civic and political solidarity actions across the three vulnerable groups, unemployed people, people with disability and migrant and refugees' groups, have been associated with interpersonal ties to the community, which increase social identification and decrease out-bond solidarity towards other vulnerable groups specially migrants. Finally, the chapter results also point toward complementary research venues. We could investigate the role of interpersonal ties, altruistic and emphatic concerns on solidarity practices. This particular analysis will robust the community-regarding orientations taking into account interpersonal measurements of community ties. Secondly, we might need to complement our analysis of cosmopolitanism by analysing other forms of social identification and belonging—for example, ethnic- or gender-driven identities, regional identities and/or European identities—to show how these could enhance solidarity practices beyond the prescribed duties to a specific national community.

APPENDICES

Appendix 1: Variables recoding

Variable	Item(s)	Recoding	Distribution
Gender	1 = woman; 0 = man		53.08, 46.92
Age	How old are you?		M: 44.8 years
Education	What is the highest level of education that you have completed? (ISCED-list)	Education, highest completed level of education, three categories: 1 "Education Group 1 (low educational achievement)" 2 "Education Group 2 (intermediate educational achievement)" 3 "Education Group 3 (high educational achievement)"	26.6, 42.77, 30.44
Income	What is your *household's monthly* net income, after tax and compulsory deductions, from all sources? (ten deciles)	1—low income 2—middle income 3—high income	25.39, 58.98, 15.62
Live with child	I currently live with... (please choose all that apply) my or my partner's child/children	1 = "child/children in the household" and 0 = "no children in the household"	21.52, 78.48
Discuss politics	Discuss political matters with friends and/or family? (1–10)	1—never 10—frequently	M: 5.1
Meet with friends	During the past month, how often have you met socially with friends not living in your household? (1-4)	1—less than once this month 4—almost every day	M: 2.61

Variable	Item(s)	Recoding	Distribution
Self-regarding motivation	People do unpaid work or give help to all kinds of groups for all kinds of reasons. Thinking about all the groups, clubs or organisations you have helped over the last 12 months, did you start helping them for any of the reasons on this list? Choose up to 5 reasons that were most important to you	0 "none"; 1 "for all the battery of career and individual enhancement motivations (I wanted to meet people/make friends; I thought it would give me a chance to learn new skills; I thought it would give me a chance to use my existing skills; it helps me get on in my career; I had spare time to do it; it gave me a chance to get a recognised qualification)"	70.46, 29.64
Other-regarding motivation	People do unpaid work or give help to all kinds of groups for all kinds of reasons. Thinking about all the groups, clubs or organisations you have helped over the last 12 months, did you start helping them for any of the reasons on this list? Choose up to 5 reasons that were most important to you	0 "none"; 1 "for all the battery of values and other understanding motivations (I felt that it was a moral duty to help others in need; I felt that it was important to help because I might be in a similar situation sometime; it's part of my philosophy of life to help people; it's part of my religious belief to help people; it's part of my philosophy of life to help people; I wanted to improve things/help people; the cause was really important to me)"	42.1, 57.9
Community-regard motivation	People do unpaid work or give help to all kinds of groups for all kinds of reasons. Thinking about all the groups, clubs or organisations you have helped over the last 12 months, did you start helping them for any of the reasons on this list? Choose up to 5 reasons that were most important to you	0 "none"; 1 "for all the battery of social and community motivations (I felt there was no one else to do it; my friends/family did it; it was connected with the needs of my family/friends; I felt there was a need in my community)"	59.66, 40.34

Variable	Item(s)	Recoding	Distribution
Social distance (tolerance towards)	Please say whether you would mind or not having each of the following as neighbours? (18-item additive scale)	The higher score corresponds to higher number of groups towards which the individual is socially intolerant	M: 5.76
Social trust	Generally speaking, would you say that most people can be trusted or that you can't be too careful in dealing with people? (0–10)	0—you can't be too careful 10—most people can be trusted	M: 4.65
Fairness	In order to be considered fair, what should a society provide? Please tell me for each statement how important or unimportant it is to you: (income) eliminating big inequalities in income between citizens (1–5)	1—not at all important 2—not very important 3—neither 4—fairly important 5—very important	M: 3.78
Attachment to country	Please tell me how attached you feel to your country? (1–5)	1–3:0; 4–5:1 1—not at all attached 2—not very attached 3—neither 4—quite attached 5—very attached	9.41, 90.5
Attachment to humanity	Please tell me how attached you feel to the world/humanity? (1–5)	1–3:0; 4–5:1 1—not at all attached 2—not very attached 3—neither 4—quite attached 5—very attached	22.65, 77.35
Religiosity	How religious would you say you are? (1–10)	1—not at all religious 10—extremely religious	M: 3.84

Variable	Item(s)	Recoding	Distribution
Multicultural appraisal	To what extent do you agree or disagree with the following statement: it is a good thing to live in a multicultural society? (1–5)	1—strongly disagree, 2—disagree, 3—neither, 4—agree and 5—strongly agree	M: 3.55
Xenophobic attitudes towards other cultures	Would you say that cultural life is generally undermined or enriched by people coming to live here from other countries? (0–10)	0: "undermined"; 10: "enriched"	M: 6.78
Intolerance to migrants and refugees' groups	Please say whether you would mind or not having each of the following as neighbours? Refugees and asylum seekers and/or migrants/foreign workers	0 no; 1 yes (if at least one of the two groups is chosen)	52.86, 47.14
Swiss regions	Swiss-German (all the rest), Swiss-French (Vaud, Valais, Neuchatel, Geneva, Jura, Fribourg), Swiss-Italian (Ticino)	1: Swiss-German; 2: Swiss-French; 3: Swiss-Italian	62.85, 32.01, 5.13
Political forms of solidarity towards migrants and refugees	Have you ever done any of the following in order to support migrant or refugees' rights?	0 "none"; 1 "attended a march, protest or demonstration" and/or "bought or refused to buy products in support to the goals"	Table 8.1
Political forms of solidarity towards people with disability	Have you ever done any of the following in order to support disable people rights?	0 "none"; 1 "attended a march, protest or demonstration and/orbought or refused to buy products in support to the goals"	Table 8.1
Political forms of solidarity towards unemployed people	Have you ever done any of the following in order to support unemployed people rights?	0 "none"; 1 "attended a march, protest or demonstration and/orbought or refused to buy products in support to the goals"	Table 8.1

Variable	Item(s)	Recoding	Distribution
Political forms of solidarity towards vulnerable groups	Have you ever done one of the following in order to support the rights of people/groups in your own country?	0 "none"; 1 "attended a march, protest or demonstration and/orbought or refused to buy products in support to the goals"	Appendix B
Civic forms of solidarity towards migrant and refugees	Have you ever done any of the following in order to support migrant or refugees' rights?	0 "none"; 1 "donated money" and/or "donated time" and/or "engaged as passive member of an organisation" and/or "engaged as active member of an organisation"	Table 8.1
Civic forms of solidarity towards people with disability	Have you ever done any of the following in order to support disable people rights?	0 "none"; 1 "donated money" and/or "donated time" and/or "engaged as passive member of an organisation" and/or "engaged as active member of an organisation"	Table 8.1
Civic forms of solidarity towards unemployed people	Have you ever done any of the following in order to support unemployed people rights?	0 "none"; 1 "donated money" and/or "donated time" and/or "engaged as passive member of an organisation" and/or "engaged as active member of an organisation"	Table 8.1
Civic forms of solidarity towards vulnerable groups	Have you ever done one of the following in order to support the rights of people/groups in your own country?	0 "none"; 1 "donated money" and/or "donated time" and/or "engaged as passive member of an organisation" and/or "engaged as active member of an organisation"	Appendix B

Appendix 2: Generalised and particularised solidarity practices by geographical regions and by gender in Switzerland (in %)

	Support refugees and migrants		Support people with disability		Support unemployed people		Support others (in general)		Total
	No	Yes	No	Yes	No	Yes	No	Yes	
Political solidarity practices									
Swiss regions									
	87.4	12.6	75.0	25.0	84.3	15.7	70.1	29.9	62.9
Swiss-German									
	84.5	15.5	74.1	25.9	83.7	16.3	65.5	34.5	32.0
Swiss-French									
	86.8	13.2	75.4	24.6	81.6	18.4	69.3	30.7	5.1
Swiss-Italian									
Total	86.4	13.6	74.7	25.3	84.0	16.0	68.6	31.4	100
Gender									
Man	88.0	12.0	75.2	24.8	82.8	17.2	70.1	29.9	53.1
Woman	84.7	15.3	74.2	25.8	85.3	14.7	67.0	33.0	46.9
Total	86.4	13.6	74.7	25.3	84.0	16.0	68.6	31.4	100
N		301		561		356		697	2221
Civic solidarity practices									
Swiss regions									
	70.6	29.4	41.8	58.2	76.5	23.5	52.1	47.9	62.9
Swiss-German									
	75.4	24.6	37.7	62.3	74.8	25.2	45.6	54.4	32.0
Swiss-French									
	81.6	18.4	47.4	52.6	72.8	27.2	59.6	40.4	5.1
Swiss-Italian									
Total	72.7	27.3	40.7	59.3	75.8	24.2	50.4	49.6	100
Gender									
Man	73.5	26.5	39.9	60.1	71.7	28.3	49.4	50.6	53.1
Woman	71.7	28.3	41.7	58.3	80.4	19.6	51.5	48.5	46.9
Total	72.7	27.3	40.7	59.3	75.8	24.2	50.4	49.6	100
N		607		1316		538		1102	2221

(*continued*)

Appendix 2: (continued)

Note: The Support others (in general) was measured using the following question: Have you ever done one of the following in order to support the rights of people/groups in your own country? (multiple choice); seven possible options: "Attended a march, protest or demonstration" and/or "Bought or refused to buy products in support to the goals" and/or "Donated money" and/or "Donated time" and/or "Engaged as passive member of an organisation" and/or "Engaged as active member of an organisation" or "None of the above." Also for the general support question, we operationalised (1) civic solidarity practices variables (one per group)— respondents have stated to engage in at least one of the following actions: "Donated money" and/or "Donated time" and/or "Engaged as passive member of an organisation" and/or "Engaged as active member of an organisation" and (2) political solidarity practices variables (one per group)— respondents have stated to engage in at least one of the following actions: "Attended a march, protest or demonstration" and/or "Bought or refused to buy products in support to the goals." The regions variable was measured by grouping the Swiss cantons by linguistic regions, taking as main criterion the largest linguistic population of the canton

REFERENCES

Adler, R. P., & Goggin, J. (2005). What Do We Mean By 'Civic Engagement'? *Journal of Transformative Education, 3*(3), 236–253.

Almond, G., & Verba, S. (1963). *The Civic Culture: Political Attitudes and Democracy in Five Nations.* Princeton University Press.

Baglioni, S. (2004). *Société civile et capital social en Suisse. Une enquête sur la participation et l'engagement associatif.* Paris: L'Harmattan.

Batson, C. D., O'Quin, K., Fultz, J., Vanderplas, M., & Isen, A. M.(1983). Influence of self-reported distress and empathy on egoistic versus altruistic motivation to help. *Journal of Personality and Social Psychology, 45*(3), 706-718.

Batson, C. D. (1998). Altruism and Prosocial Behavior. In D. T. Gilbert, S. T. Fiske, & G. Lindzey (Eds.), *The Handbook of Social Psychology* (Vol. 2, 4th ed., pp. 282–316). New York: McGraw-Hill.

Bayertz, K. (1996).Staat und Solidarität. In Bayertz, K. (ed.), *Politik und Ethik (pp. 305–330). Stuttgart: Reclam.*

Bayertz, K. (1999). Four Uses of Solidarity. In *Solidarity – Philosophical Studies in Contemporary Culture* (Vol. 5, pp. 3–28). London: Kluwer.

Bechtel, M., Hainmueller, J., & Margalit, Y. (2014). Preferences for International Redistribution: The Divide Over the Eurozone Bailouts. *American Journal of Political Science, 58*(4), 835–856.

Brady, H. (1999). Political Participation. In J. P. Robinson, P. R. Shaver, & L. S. Wrightsman (Eds.), *Measures of Political Attitudes* (pp. 737–801). San Diego: Academic Press.

Brady, H. E., Verba, S., & Schlozman, K. L. (1995). Beyond SES: A Resource Model of Political Participation. *The America Political Science Review, 89*(2), 271–294.

Butcher, J. (2010). Conceptual Framework for Volunteer Action and Acts of Solidarity. In J. Butcher (Ed.), *Mexican Solidarity: Citizen Participation and Volunteering* (pp. 1–32). New York: Springer.

Caputo, R. (1997). Woman as Volunteers and Activists. *Nonprofit and Voluntary Sector Quarterly, 26,* 156–174.

Caputo, R. (2009). Religious Capital and Intergenerational Transmission of Volunteering as Correlates of Civic Engagement. *Nonprofit and Voluntary Sector Quarterly, 38,* 983–1002.

Clary, E. G., & Snyder, M. (1999). The Motivations to Volunteer: Theoretical and Practical Considerations. *American Psychological Society (Blackwell Publishers), 8*(5), 156–160.

Clary, E. G., Snyder, M., Ridge, R. D., Copeland, J., Stukas, A. A., Haugen, J., & Miene, P. (1998). Understanding and Assessing the Motivations of Volunteers: A Functional Approach. *Journal of Personality and Social Psychology, 74*(6), 15–16.

Dalton, R. (2008). *Citizen Politics: Public Opinion and Political Parties in Advanced Industrial Democracies.* Washington, DC: CQ Press.

Eggert, N., & Giugni, M. (2010). Does Associational Involvement Spur Political Integration? Political Interest and Participation of Three Immigrant Groups in Zurich. *Swiss Political Science Review, 16,* 175–210.

Ekman, J., & Amna, E. (2012). Political Participation and Civic Engagement: Towards a New Typology. *Human Affairs, 22*(3), 283–300.

Elster, J. (2006). Altruistic Behavior and Altruistic Motivations. In S. Kolm & J. Mercier Ythier (Eds.), *Handbook of the Economics of Giving, Altruism and Reciprocity* (pp. 183–206). Amsterdam: North Holland.

Fehr, E., & Fischbacher, U. (2003). The Nature of Human Altruism. *Nature, 425,* 785–791.

Fehr, E., & Schmidt K. M. (2006). The Economics of Fairness, Reciprocity and Altruism: Experimental Evidence and New Theories. In S. Kolm & J. Mercier Ythier (Eds.), *Handbook of the Economics of Giving, Altruism and Reciprocity* (pp. 615–691). Amsterdam: North Holland.

Fetchenhauer, D., Flache, A., Buunk, A., & Lindenberg, S. (Eds.). (2006). *Solidarity and Prosocial Behavior. An Integration of Sociological and Psychological Perspectives.* New York: Springer.

Flam, H. (1990). The Emotional Man and the Problem of Collective Action. *International Sociology, 5,* 39–56.

Flam, H., & King, D. (2005). *Emotions and Social Movement.* London: Routledge.

Fowler, J. H., & Kam, C. (2007). Beyond the Self: Social Identity, Altruism, and Political Participation. *Journal of Politics, 69*(3), 811–825.

Fraser, J., Clayton, S., Sickler, J., & Taylor, A. (2009). Belonging to the Zoo: Retired Volunteers, Conservation Activism and Collective Identity. *Ageing and Society, 29,* 351–368.

Gallagher, S. (1994). Doing Their Share: Comparing Patterns of Help Given by Older and Younger Adults. *Journal of Marriage and the Family, 56*, 567–578.
Giugni, M., & Passy, F. (2001). *Political Altruism? Solidarity Movements in International Perspective.* Lanham, MD: Rowman & Littlefield.
Gundelach, B., Freitag, M., & Stadelmann-Steffen, I. (2010). Making or Breaking Informal Volunteering. Welfare Statism and Social Capital in a Subnational Comparative Perspective. *European Societies, 12*, 627–652.
Inglehart, R., & Welzel, C. (2005). *Modernization, Cultural Change, and Democracy: The Human Development Sequence.* New York: Cambridge University Press.
Kleres, J. (2017). *The Social Organization of Disease: Emotions and Civic Action.* London: Routledge.
Leite Viegas, J. M. (2007). Political and Social Tolerance. In J. W. van Deth, J. R. Montero, & A. Westholm (Eds.), *Citizenship and Involvement in European Democracies: A Comparative Analysis.* London: Routledge.
Manatschal, A., & Freitag, M. (2014). Reciprocity and Volunteering. *Rationality and Society, 26*(2), 208–235.
Miller, J., & Krosnick, J. (2004). Threat as a Motivator of Political Activism: A Field Experiment. *Political Psychology, 25*(4), 507–524.
Morales, L., & Geurts, P. (2007). Associational Involvement. In J. W. van Deth, J. R. Montero, & A. Westholm (Eds.), *Citizenship and Involvement in European Democracies: A Comparative Analysis.* London: Routledge.
Morales, L., & Giugni, M. (2011). *Social Capital, Political Participation and Migration in Europe: Making Multicultural Democracy Work?* (Vol. 1). Basingstoke: Palgrave Macmillan.
Omoto, A., Snyder, M., & Hackett, J. (2010). Personality and Motivational Antecedents of Activism and Social Engagement. *Journal of Personality, 78*, 1703–1734.
Piliavin, J. A., & Siegl, E. (2007). Health Benefits of Volunteering in the Wisconsin Longitudinal Study. *Journal of Health and Social Behavior, 48*(4), 450–464.
Putnam, R. D. (2000). *Bowling Alone: The Collapse and Revival of American Community.* New York: Simon & Schuster.
Rippe, K. P. (1998). Diminishing Solidarity. *Ethical Theory and Moral Practice, 1*(3), 355–373.
Rochon, T. (1998). *Culture Moves Ideas Activism and Changing Values.* Princeton, NJ: Princeton University.
Scholz, S. (2008). *Political Solidarity.* State College: Pennsylvania State Press.
Scholz, S. (2015). Seeking Solidarity. *Philosophy Compass, 10*(10), 725–735.
Simpson, B., & Willer, R. (2015). Beyond Altruism: Sociological Foundations of Cooperation and Prosocial Behavior. *Annual Review of Sociology, 41*, 43–63.
Smith, E. (1999). The Effects of Investments in the Social Capital of Youth on Political and Civic Behavior in Young Adulthood: A Longitudinal Analysis. *Political Psychology, 20*(3), 553–580.

Stadelmann-Steffen, I., & Freitag, M. (2010). Making Civil Society Work: Models of Democracy and Their Impact on Civic Engagement. *Nonprofit and Voluntary Sector Quarterly, 40,* 526–551.

Stjernø, S. (2012). *Solidarity in Europe. The History of an Idea.* Cambridge: Cambridge University Press.

Stolle, D., & Micheletti, M. (2013). *Political Consumerism: Global Responsibility in Action.* Cambridge: Cambridge University Press.

Stolle, D., & Rochon, R. T. (1998). Are All Associations Alike? Member Diversity, Associational Type, and the Creation of Social Capital. *American Behavioral Scientist, 42,* 47–65.

Teorell, J., Torcal, M., & Montero, J. R. (2007). Political Participation: Mapping the Terrain. In J. W. van Deth, J. R. Montero, & A. Westholm (Eds.), *Citizenship and Involvement in European Democracies: A Comparative Analysis.* London: Routledge.

Vallerand, R. J., & Thill, E. E. (1993). *Introduction à la psychologie de la motivation.* Éditions Études Vivantes: Laval.

van Deth, J. (1997). *Private Groups and Public Life.* London: Routledge.

van Deth, J. W., Montero, J. R., & Westholm, A. (Eds.). (2007). *Citizenship and Involvement in European Democracies. A Comparative Analysis.* London: Routledge.

Verba, S., Schlozman, K., & Brady, H. (1995). *Voice and Equality: Civic Voluntarism in American Politics.* Cambridge: Harvard University Press.

Wilson, J. (2000). Volunteering. *Annual Reviews in Sociology, 26,* 215–240.

Wilson, J. (2012). Volunteerism Research: A Review Essay. *Nonprofit and Voluntary Sector Quarterly, 41*(2), 176–212.

Wilson, J., & Musick, M. (1997). Who Cares? Towards an Integrated Theory of Volunteer Work. *American Sociological Review, 62,* 694–713.

van der Zee, K. (2006). Ethnic Identity and Solidarity with Functional Groups. In D. Fetchenhauer, A. Flache, A. Buunk, & S. Lindenberg (Eds.), *Solidarity and Prosocial Behavior. An Integration of Sociological and Psychological Perspectives* (pp. 175–190). New York: Springer.

Open Access This chapter is licensed under the terms of the Creative Commons Attribution 4.0 International License (http://creativecommons.org/licenses/by/4.0/), which permits use, sharing, adaptation, distribution and reproduction in any medium or format, as long as you give appropriate credit to the original author(s) and the source, provide a link to the Creative Commons license and indicate if changes were made.

The images or other third party material in this chapter are included in the chapter's Creative Commons license, unless indicated otherwise in a credit line to the material. If material is not included in the chapter's Creative Commons license and your intended use is not permitted by statutory regulation or exceeds the permitted use, you will need to obtain permission directly from the copyright holder.

CHAPTER 9

Trajectories of Solidarities in France Across Fields of Vulnerability

Manlio Cinalli and Maria Jimena Sanhueza

INTRODUCTION

Solidarity has come under heavy strain in Europe over the last decade, at the same time as the economic, social, and political crisis of 2008 has had a tremendous impact on the attitudes and behaviours of European citizens (Giugni and Grasso 2015). In the media, the crisis has often been discussed using footage depicting human despair. These images have included pictures of destitute unemployed people queuing outside soup kitchens or sleeping rough (Department for Communities and Local Government 2015), in the face of general indifference on the part of bystanders (Andersson and Sundin 2016; Darley and Latané 1968) or of refugees and their babies drowning in European waters due to the negligence of rescue officers, without altering the broad indifference of the general public.[1] In Europe, appeals to human solidarity have also gone unheard at difficult moments like when Europe faced the threat of Grexit, or in the aftermath of the UK referendum on European membership (Berend 2016; Calhoune 2017). This widespread "desensitisation" (Arendt 1982; Wilde 2013) went so far that some commentators chose to refer to a handful of countries with very little direct responsibility for the global economic crisis as PIGS

M. Cinalli (✉) • M. J. Sanhueza
Centre de Recherches Politiques de Sciences Po, Paris, France

© The Author(s) 2018
C. Lahusen, M. Grasso (eds.), *Solidarity in Europe*,
Palgrave Studies in European Political Sociology,
https://doi.org/10.1007/978-3-319-73335-7_9

(Portugal, Ireland, Greece, and Spain), in a tendentious attempt to single out culprits (de la Dehesa 2006). Ultimately, the idea that solidarity—a notion which has had an essential influence on the emergence of a sense of European *citizenship*—may well have lost its importance has given rise to systematic criticisms of the European project (Dainotto 2007).

The possibility that Europe may have entered a new *homo homini lupus* era calls for further research on the topic of solidarity, in order to assess whether Europeans can still rely on solidarity as a community resource (Bourgeois 1896; Hanagan 1980; Hyman 1986), or whether they have fractured into different and dispersed archipelagos of special interests. Nowhere is an analysis of solidarity more crucial than in France, which in this respect seems to stand at a crossroads. Solidarity is one of the major pillars of the French constitutional ethos, an essential component of "Fraternity" (*Fraternité*), a notion symbolically portrayed in the revolutionary tricolour, and that plays a prominent part in the national anthem. In recent years, however, many public policies based on solidarity have been scrutinised, heavily criticised, and eventually restricted so as to shrink the country's welfare expenditure (Cinalli and De Nuzzo 2017).

This chapter approaches the study of solidarity in France by comparing three important vulnerable groups, namely, the disabled, the unemployed, and refugees. If we begin with the disabled, one notes that protection for the disabled has worsened in France, particularly if we consider the impact of public expenditure cuts and the reduction in the overall scope of government action. While public authorities do oversee a generous healthcare system, they only dedicate a minor fraction of its resources to disability policies, prompting increasing outcries from disability groups. In terms of the erosion of welfare entitlements, another group that has been massively affected are the unemployed, who have faced a significant decline in the amount of financial support made available to them and in their chances of being reinserted into the labour market (Chabanet 2014, 2017). Refugees, meanwhile, have been the target of many restrictive measures. This underscores how negative the agenda of successive French governments has been, both on the left and on the right, and this has deterred new arrivals and has made it difficult for citizens to show their solidarity with refugees while staying within the boundaries of the law (Müller 2009, 2014).

The way we approach solidarity in this chapter is quite comprehensive and hinges on an important distinction between two different meanings of solidarity: solidarity understood as an input and solidarity understood as an output. On the one hand, we focus on areas where solidarity expresses itself as a process, whether at the individual level of empathy with the vulnerable or at the political level through partaking within the republican community. On the other hand, we also consider the instances where solidarity expresses itself through one-off actions carried out by individuals at a specific time and place. In particular, we are attentive to the very varied nature of the *repertoire* of actions carried out by different individuals (Teorell et al. 2007), including when they act as part of a group (Tilly 1978). Our dual focus on solidarity as an input and as an output thus enables us to distinguish between various "trajectories of solidarity" and thereby to better understand the way certain individual variables (such as self-identification and proximity) combine with political variables (like voting, an interest in politics, or the reading of newspapers) in very different ways, to produce different configurations of solidarity actions in each of the three fields of vulnerability considered here.

Our first major goal in this chapter is to provide a detailed analysis of the way solidarity actions vary within and across the three fields of vulnerability analysed here. The second, more ambitious, goal of the present chapter is to search for the broad causes that could help to explain these variations in the nature of the solidarity actions carried out. In this specific instance, the distinction we establish between individually based and politically based solidarity trajectories makes it possible for us to determine whether solidarity actions are propelled more by self-identification and by a great degree of proximity between individuals in the private sphere, or whether they are the outcome of the republican process of transforming the "general will" into specific policies and laws through the mediation of public institutions. The chapter starts by presenting the three fields of vulnerability that are the focus of our analysis, and it outlines the theoretical foundations for choosing these groups in particular. We also focus on the difference between various solidarity actions (and thus on solidarity as an output) and on the two main trajectories that lead to this type of actions, one centred on the individual and one on communal republican processes (here solidarity is understood as an input). The following step consists in focussing on different degrees of solidarity and on the various forms solidarity takes across all three fields of vulnerability (section "The Different *Repertoires* of Solidarity Actions"), before moving on to examine the two main trajectories that inform solidarity actions (section "Explaining the Dynamics of Solidarity: Individual Closeness Versus Republican Citizenship"). Finally, we sum up our most important findings and identify some important challenges that need be tackled by future research on vulnerability and solidarity (section "Conclusion").

Solidarity and Vulnerability: A Cross-Field Theoretical Framework

Any study of solidarity in France must take a critical distance to the idealised picture of "Fraternity" (*Fraternité*) that is typically presented as an essential pillar of French *republicanism*. Undeniably France is a country where health standards and the provision state protection in cases of illness remain relatively high compared to other developed countries, where dismissed workers have often united with other vulnerable groups under the same banner, and where some children of refugees (and of migrants more generally) have achieved leading positions in the business world and also at the head of the state itself.[2] Beyond this evidence however, we also know that the decreased protection offered by the state to various vulnerable groups and welfare retrenchment in general have been going on for a long while, an evolution which is bound to have had an impact on the meaning and practice of solidarity. Fraternity has increasingly become a fundamental value in words only, unable to prevent vulnerable groups from being marginalised. Fraternity has also become a somewhat fuzzy term with respect to its ontological content; and progressively, political references to solidarity as a "public" fundamental, an essential aspect of republican *citizenship*, have become few and far between, replaced by a more individual notion of solidarity understood as a private virtue.

In the case of the disabled, for instance, there has been a change for the worse both in terms of health policies and in terms of the protection offered to sick people, particularly when one takes into account policies designed to reduce public spending. Throughout the 2000s and the 2010s, disability aid has suffered regular cuts in spite of the outcries of major French disability groups.[3] As regards the unemployed, contentious issues such as work activation, long-term unemployment, and social dumping have all featured prominently in the public debate throughout the 2000s and the 2010s, with huge protests having been organised to denounce an overly contractualist approach to welfare as well as the broader, supply-focused trend governing many EU policies. The conditions governing unemployment benefits have become more restrictive, the use of sanctions has increased, while the latest reform of the French labour market in 2016, the *Loi Travail*, has outlined a range of cases where employers are now entitled to resort to economic redundancy. Lastly, political developments throughout the 2000s and 2010s have also resulted in an increasingly restrictive stance, on the part of the French state, towards refugees. This restrictive response has led to many evictions as well as to the final closure of the "jungle", a refugee camp close to Calais; it has also resulted in the tough border controls implemented at the time of the "Arab Spring" and of the Syrian war, which effectively expressed a lack of solidarity with the large number of Tunisians and Syrians who were fleeing from slaughters and inhuman conditions. This hardline position has even led to coercive measures being enforced to punish "solidarity crimes" committed by individual activists, on the basis of article L622-1 of the CESEDA, the Code regulating the Arrival and Residence of Foreigners and the Right of Asylum (Müller 2009, 2014).

These developments across various fields of vulnerability in France call for a more systematic evaluation of the trajectories that lead to solidarity actions, solidarity being understood both as an input and as an output. As an output, we analyse solidarity by considering the various forms of solidarity action that French citizens carry out across the fields of disability, unemployment, and support for refugees. In so doing, we draw on some of the seminal literature that appeared between the end of the 1990s and the early 2000s, and that focused on "altruism" and on the concrete instances of mobilisation carried out by *pro-beneficiaries* on behalf of weak groups (Cinalli 2004; Giugni and Passy 2001; Simeant 1998), but which has not so far resulted in many empirical studies of a systematically comparative nature (see however Lahusen 2013; Baglioni and Giugni 2014). While social research on solidarity has developed over the last decade, it has tended to focus on attitudes, commitments, and norms, for example, in terms of social *citizenship* (Bellamy et al. 2006), readiness to share one's own resources with others (Stjerno 2012: 2), support for fiscal policies of redistribution (Rehm 2009), resilient cleavages within Europe (Delhey 2007), and the weakening of bonds between member states. What our specific focus on solidarity as an output should allow us to do is to shed light on solidarity actions that either reinforce or weaken the position of vulnerable groups.

While the following section focuses mostly on the importance of distinguishing between the various forms that the solidarity *repertoire* can take, the main point we wish to make here is that by looking at these configurations, we also want to trace them back to solidarity understood as an input. In so doing, we approach solidarity as an active force, which itself tends to change according to the context in which it expresses itself. More specifically, our ambition is to determine whether solidarity actions follow from (1) trajectories that originate in the private sphere and that are triggered by emphatic feelings of self-identification and real proximity between *pro-beneficiaries* and vulnerable beneficiaries or (2) trajectories that originate within the French body politic that are triggered by a feeling of Fraternity as understood under *republicanism*. In the latter case, this type of trajectory must be related to a series of variables that are almost ubiquitous in the scholarly works that look at the interpenetration between citizens and their broader *political community* (Nie et al. 1996; Parry et al. 1992). In addition to another variable that considers information-seeking through the medium of newspapers, we examine voting and having a general interest in politics: these variables have often been used by scholars, for example, to establish a positive relationship between political interest and voting (Verba et al. 1995) or, on the contrary, to question this relationship (Lassen 2005).

By taking into account the complex relationship between solidarity as an input and as an output, our ultimate aim is to distinguish between on the one hand a "private-individual" (henceforth, individual) solidarity trajectory and on the other hand a "public-republican" (henceforth, political) trajectory. This dual approach to solidarity is also valuable since it allows us to understand the interplay between different *citizenship* traditions that have developed either through mutual acknowledgement and shared purposes or through access to the policy domain of rule-making (Cinalli 2017). More specifically, the distinction we establish between an individual solidarity trajectory and a political one works as follows. On the one hand, we expect individual variables including self-identification and closeness to vulnerable groups to be especially relevant in the field of disability, owing to the universal sense of responsibility that people for whom solidarity is important can appeal to when they act in support of fellow citizens who often suffer from a disability that neither they nor power holders can be held responsible for. On the other hand, political variables including the internalisation of republican norms are expected to be especially relevant in the field of unemployment, owing to the politically based sense of responsibility that French people can appeal to in support of fellow citizens who are vulnerable as a result of politics, and specifically of unemployment policies and of specific decisions taken by power holders.

Lastly, the field of refugee assistance provides us with a further opportunity to disentangle the individual and political determinants of solidarity actions. In this case, the main expectation going into the study is that individual variables will prove to be more effective in terms of leading to solidarity actions. Since refugees are not part of the republican community of citizens, the solidarity trajectory leading French nationals to help them should logically be determined by individual rather than by political variables. France often considers itself to be a "civilising power" (Burrow 1986), a country where refugees (and migrants in general) are the objects (rather than the subjects) of politics, at least until they become fully integrated into the republican community of citizens (Schnapper 2003).

Given that both solidarity trajectories are relevant when it comes to support for the disabled, we expect to find a much higher level of solidarity actions in the field of disability than in the other two fields. We expect the individual trajectory to be rather ineffective in the field of unemployment and the political trajectory to be likewise ineffective as a means of triggering support to refugees. This also means that we expect the general level of solidarity actions to be at its lowest in the field of refugee assistance, since self-identification and a feeling of proximity are determinants that are likely to work less well when we have a high number of national respondents being polled about their solidarity with non-national refugees, who represent a much more distant community of equals, compared for instance to the disabled. Furthermore, we also anticipate some important variations in the pattern of solidarity actions in each of the fields considered. We expect individual types of action to prevail in the field of disability and in the field of refugee assistance owing to the greater importance of the individual trajectory in these fields. Conversely, collective forms of solidarity mobilisation are expected to prevail in the unemployment field, since this issue appears at lot more straightforwardly political in its nature.

The Different *Repertoires* of Solidarity Actions

As we said earlier, our cross-field comparison of solidarity follows two main steps. We start by analysing the *repertoire* of solidarity actions carried out by French citizens, in order to examine whether different fields of vulnerability are characterised by different configurations of solidarity actions. We then continue by focusing on intra-field variations in solidarity, in order to examine whether specific forms of action are prevalent in each of the fields considered here. This is grounded on scholarly work that has emphasised the necessity to distinguish between the various facets of a varied *repertoire* of individual action (Teorell et al. 2007); in our study this analysis of individual actions must also include instances where individuals participate in larger, collective forms of mobilisation (Tilly 1978). In particular, we analyse "donating money" and "donating time" as types of solidarity actions that are individually based and less direct while also taking into account actions such as "protesting" and "buying or refusing to buy specific products", which are collective and more direct forms of mobilisation.

The figures in Table 9.1 reflect the relative importance of these four types of solidarity action across the three fields. The large cross-field variations (cf. the totals in first column) clearly show that solidarity actions vary substantially depending on the specific vulnerable groups that they target. Our first important finding is that a large majority of the people in our sample (54.7% out of 2098 respondents) engage in multiple forms of solidarity action at the same time (as suggested by the fact that the percentages add up to more than 100%). The individuals who take part in these actions are particularly mobilised by disability issues, while their level of participation decreases steeply when the focus is on unemployment, and even more so when actions are meant to help refugees. More specifically, Table 9.1 shows that when all variables are combined, 47% of the individuals in the sample are willing to support the disabled: in this case the most common types of solidarity actions carried out are "donating money" and "donating time", which account for respectively 27% and 17% of the actions carried out by the surveyed population. "Buying or refusing to buy specific products" only concerns 12.9% of the sample, while protest actions

Table 9.1 Overall support and specific forms of solidarity actions per field (in %[4])

	%	Protests	Donating money	Donating time	Buying or refusing to buy specific products
Disability	47.6	6.6	27.4	17	12.9
Unemployment	21.8	5.2	6.6	9.4	7.4
Refugees	17.7	3.8	8.3	6.1	5.6
Total	54.7 (2098)				

such as demonstrations or strikes concern a much tinier proportion of 6.6%.

In the unemployment field, the proportion of people engaging in solidarity actions decreases to 22% of the total sample. The percentages of people ready to donate time and money reflect the patterns in the disability field, since they also indicate that the participants' *repertoire* consists primarily of actions that are individual and less direct. Perhaps not surprisingly, it is more common to contribute time rather than money in the field of unemployment, while the opposite is true in the field of disability. This must no doubt be related to the more financially precarious position of the unemployed, who are systematically excluded from the labour market. However, the percentages indicating people's participation in collective and direct forms of solidarity—by means of product boycotts or protests— show that there is no direct analogy between solidarity for the unemployed and solidarity for the disabled. In particular, contributions of time and money do not clearly prevail over more direct and collective forms of solidarity actions, which together represent nearly 13%. Lastly, we find the smallest percentages of participation in solidarity actions in the field of refugee assistance: fewer than 18% of respondents stated that they would actively participate in support actions for refugees. 8.3% of the individuals in the sample said they had donated money, and a smaller proportion (6.1%) had donated time to help refugees through volunteering. Compared to the fields of disability and unemployment, participation in protest actions represents no more than 3.8%, and buying or refusing to buy specific products concerns 5.6% of the total sample.

The evaluation of field-specific actions further enhances our understanding of internal, field-related dynamics. In the second phase of our comparative analysis, we have therefore indicated percentages only as a ratio of the total number of people engaging in solidarity actions ($n = 1149$) and no longer as a ratio of the entire sample of interviewed people. In this way, intra-field differences can be tracked more precisely, and it is easier to see the difference between the types of actions that are individually based and less direct (like donating money or time) and those that are collective and that entail direct mobilisation (such as participating in protests or in product boycotts). Overall, the general patterns characterising each of the three fields of vulnerability are confirmed, and we can once more see that solidarity increases as we move from support for refugees to support for the unemployed, and then to support for the disabled.

These figures also confirm that individuals engage in several types of solidarity actions at the same time.

However, a closer look at field-specific percentages also shows that in the field of disability, individual and indirect forms of action clearly predominate over other forms of action. The latter are practised by almost the entire sample of people who engage in solidarity actions (over 93%). Individual forms of action also prevail in the field of unemployment, but with a much lower margin. In this case, findings show that a majority of the people in the sample also engage in collective forms of direct mobilisation (57.5%). This is more or less in line with the general perception that France is a country where social movements are a pillar of republican *citizenship* (Sirot 2014). Lastly, as regards refugees, our findings show that this field has the smallest group of people engaged in solidarity actions ($n = 372$, just over a third of those active within the field of disability). Just as in the field of disability, people who help refugees overwhelmingly choose solidarity actions that are individually based and less direct. In fact, this is where we note a significant gap between the individually based and the collectively based *repertoire*, given that the latter represents two thirds of the former (53.2% vs. 81.1%; larger than the same gap in the field of unemployment).

To sum things up, Tables 9.1 and 9.2 confirm that a majority of people in France engage in solidarity actions, with more than 54% of individuals participating in one or more forms of solidarity to support the disabled, the unemployed, or refugees. The main result to emerge from this analysis consists in the much greater level of participation in solidarity actions in the field of disability than in the other two fields: findings show that support for the disabled is the most frequent expression of solidarity in France, followed by support for the unemployed. Support for refugees stands out by its low level; refugees receive help from fewer than one-fifth of the people in our sample. However, findings also show that each field is

Table 9.2 Individual versus collective *repertoire* (in %)

	N	Collective mobilisation	Individual participation
Disability	999	40.9	93.1
Unemployment	458	57.5	73.1
Refugees	372	53.2	81.1
Total	1149		

characterised by its own, typical *repertoire* of solidarity. Individual forms of action prevail in the field of disability and, in relative terms, also in the field of refugees (in the latter case, in an overall context of much lower solidarity). By contrast, collective forms of action prevail in the field of unemployment. These first results concerning the amount of solidarity expressed and its *repertoire* certainly go some way to confirm our expectations. Solidarity expresses itself most strongly in the field of disability, since it brings together both of the trajectories that connect French citizens to the disabled. On the one hand, emphatic feelings of self-identification and proximity—which express themselves most strongly in the case of people who do not enjoy the same good health as the majority of the population—go hand in hand with a high prevalence of individual forms of solidarity actions. On the other hand, since the disabled are themselves citizens, it is logical that their problems should also be seen as issues that concern the whole republican community, hence the high amount of collective forms of solidarity action. Solidarity actions are less common in the field of unemployment. This is also in line with our theoretical framework, since our expectation was that feelings of empathy would not play the same role as in the case of the disabled. Just as expected, the high prevalence of collective types of solidarity actions indicates that unemployment in France tends to be seen as a political matter rather than as an individual one and that the whole republican community is held accountable for the problem. Lastly, solidarity is at its weakest in the case of refugees, which further serves to reinforce our argument. Since their status means that they stand outside the republican community, refugees only benefit from the type of solidarity that springs from a general empathy with human suffering and an ability to see all people as fellow human beings (yet, as said, a much more distant community of equals than fellow citizens).

We can now move on to consider the respective impacts of the individual trajectory and of the political one. Indeed, the results in this section suggest that the links between these trajectories and solidarity actions deserve additional scrutiny. We must therefore pay closer attention to the specific assumptions underpinning these expectations, namely, that each of these two trajectories represents significant predictors of solidarity action in the field of disability, while only one of the two functions as a significant predictor in the other two fields (the political trajectory in the case of the unemployed and the individual trajectory for the disabled).

Explaining the Dynamics of Solidarity: Individual Closeness Versus Republican *Citizenship*

This section is designed to assess and explain some of the important arguments that have driven our analyses throughout this chapter, namely, that solidarity actions are more likely to result from an individual trajectory or from a political trajectory depending on the specific field of vulnerability under consideration. For example, we have argued that the political trajectory is most likely to have a strong impact in the field of unemployment, which would go a long way towards explaining why we did indeed note the large amount of collective forms of solidarity action in the field of unemployment. And we have argued that the individual trajectory would be a stronger trigger for solidarity actions in the fields of disability and refugees, which would go a long way towards explaining why we did indeed note the extensive prevalence of individual forms over collective forms.

Regression data does show that in all three fields, the individual trajectory proves relevant when the respondent is empathetically concerned by one of vulnerabilities respectively. Two variables have been included in the first regressions: (1) whether or not the respondent belongs to a vulnerable group (the disabled, the unemployed, or foreigners)[5] and (2) whether the respondent has relatives or friends who are either disabled, or unemployed, or of foreigner origins. The assumption here is that if individuals are themselves affected by these processes, or if they have a close relationship to other people being affected by same processes, then they are also more likely to be actively engaged in solidarity actions in the relevant field. The second trajectory proves to be more relevant when the respondent's mobilisation follows the political prescriptions of the French Republic. In this case, the crucial variables include being interested in politics, being politically active by voting, and following the political debate by regularly reading newspapers. The objective is to understand whether a political trajectory, informed by political participation and interest in public issues, can help to explain cross-field variations in terms of solidarity actions.

Tables 9.3, 9.4, and 9.5 examine in some detail to what extent solidarity actions in each field follow from the individual trajectory. On the basis of the arguments and of the data that have been laid out in the previous sections, we expected this first trajectory to prove much more important when it comes to solidarity with the disabled and with refugees than for

Table 9.3 Solidarity towards the disabled individual factors

	Coefficient	Standard error	95% Confidence interval
Considers him-/herself as having a disability	0.0289	0.0346	−0.0390, 0.0969
Has family or friends who are disabled	0.184***	0.0262	0.1330, 0.2360
_Cons	0.431***	0.0125	0.4069, 0.4561

***$p < 0.01$, **$p < 0.05$, *$p < 0.1$

Table 9.4 Solidarity towards the unemployed individual factors

	Coefficient	Standard error	95% Confidence interval
Declared that he/she was unemployed	−0.052	0.0377	−0.1269, 0.0212
Has unemployed family or friends	0.033*	0.0190	−0.0036, 0.0709
_Cons	0.209***	0.0115	0.1866, 0.2318

***$p < 0.01$, **$p < 0.05$, *$p < 0.1$

Table 9.5 Solidarity towards refugees individual factors

	Coefficient	Standard error	95% Confidence interval
Born in France	0.045	0.0407	−0.0346, 0.1253
Has family, friends, or acquaintances coming from a different country	0.033*	0.0174	−0.0011, 0.0673
_Cons	0.122***	0.0412	0.0412, 0.2032

***$p < 0.01$, **$p < 0.05$, *$p < 0.1$

solidarity with the unemployed. Conversely, the second, political trajectory will presumably play a more important role in the field of unemployment. Tables 9.6, 9.7, and 9.8 therefore combine individual and political variables, in order to show to what extent solidarity can be explained by empathy or by a practice of republican *citizenship*. Finally, the model also relies on control filters, namely, gender, level of education, and age.

Findings show that individuals who are personally affected by disability or who self-identify with the disabled are not more likely to participate in activities to support the disabled than any other individual. However, the

Table 9.6 Solidarity towards the disabled individual and political factors

	Coefficient	Standard error	95% Confidence interval
Considers him-/herself as having a disability	0.0353	0.0341	−0.0315, 0.1022
Has family or friends who are disabled	0.170***	0.0258	0.1200, 0.2216
Voted in the most recent 2012 elections	0.0743***	0.0246	0.0259, 0.1227
Reads the newspaper +3 days a week	0.125***	0.0218	0.0831, 0.1687
Considers him-/herself to be moderately or very interested in politics	0.076***	0.0226	0.0319, 0.1205
_Cons	0.274***	0.0236	0.2284, 0.3210

***$p < 0.01$, **$p < 0.05$, *$p < 0.1$

Table 9.7 Solidarity towards the unemployed: individual and political factors

	Coefficient	Standard error	95% Confidence interval
Declared that he/she was unemployed	−0.041	0.0371	−0.1147, 0.0311
Has unemployed family or friends	0.036**	0.0186	0.0003, 0.0735
Voted in the most recent 2012 elections	−0.008	0.0206	−0.0488, 0.0322
Reads the newspaper +3 days a week	0.118***	0.0182	0.0830, 0.1543
Considers him-/herself to be moderately or very interested in politics	0.097***	0.0188	0.0604, 0.1344
_Cons	0.099***	0.0205	0.0592, 0.1398

***$p < 0.01$, **$p < 0.05$, *$p < 0.1$

Table 9.8 Solidarity towards refugees individual and political factors

	Coefficient	Standard error	95% Confidence interval
Born in France	0.054	0.0401	−0.0246, 0.1327
Has family, friends, or acquaintances coming from a different country	0.022	0.0171	−0.0108, 0.0565
Voted in the most recent 2012 elections	−0.071***	0.0191	−0.1090, −0.0340
Reads the newspaper +3 days a week	0.114***	0.0168	0.0811, 0.1470
Considers him-/herself to be moderately or very interested in politics	0.091***	0.0174	0.0576, 0.1262
_Cons	0.061	0.0422	−0.0214, 0.1444

***$p < 0.01$, **$p < 0.05$, *$p < 0.1$

second variable of empathy, namely, proximity, does indeed appear to be correlated with solidarity as an output, thus confirming our hypothesis: the individual trajectory is highly relevant when it comes to explaining solidarity actions in support for the disabled.

The integration of political indicators into the survey improves the model's accuracy. In particular, we observe that both an interest in politics and voting have some impact on solidarity actions in the field of disability, while reading the newspaper has a strong impact. The introduction of political variables does not, however, bring into question our expectations. The individual and the political trajectory both stand out as relevant when it comes to explaining variations in terms of solidarity actions within the field of disability. We can conclude that it is when the individual trajectory and the political trajectory combine that we see the highest levels of solidarity actions across the three fields (cf. section "The Different *Repertoires* of Solidarity Actions").

The incorporation of a number of sociodemographic controls has a limited effect on the results obtained in Tables 9.3 and 9.6. The model proves to be slightly more effective than the earlier ones at explaining solidarity actions in support of the disabled. Table 9.9 shows that age is not a relevant factor when it comes to explaining solidarity as an output. The same is true of the respondents' level of education. The distribution of individuals with university-level education who do not engage in solidarity actions is equivalent that of less educated people who are likewise not active. Similarly, of all those with secondary-level education, 53% do not participate in disability-related solidarity actions, compared to 46% who can be qualified as active or engaged in such actions. A similar conclusion can be drawn in terms of gender. The proportion of women who are active and not active is very similar to the proportion of men who fall in both of these categories.

Data for the field of unemployment proves to be quite different from what we have observed for the field of disability. First of all, Table 9.4 establishes a weak negative relationship between self-identification and the decision to engage in solidarity actions. Even though the validity of this interaction may be limited by the small number of unemployed people featured in the sample, it is nevertheless somewhat surprising to observe that four-fifths of the unemployed are not active, with only one-fifth of them actively engaged in actions designed to combat unemployment. The low ratio of participation suggests that other external factors are likely to be relevant, such as social processes of stigmatisation and defeatism, all of

Table 9.9 Solidarity towards the disabled individual and political factors (controlled)

	Coefficient	Standard error	95% Confidence interval
Considers him-/herself as having a disability	0.036	0.0343	−0.0310, 0.1035
Has family or friends who are disabled	0.171***	0.0259	0.1204, 0.2224
Voted in the most recent 2012 elections	0.055**	0.0267	0.0032, 0.1081
Reads the newspaper +3 days a week	0.127***	0.0218	0.0845, 0.1701
Considers him-/herself to be moderately or very interested in politics	0.074***	0.0231	0.0292, 0.1199
Gender	0.011	0.0218	−0.0317, 0.0540
Age	0.001*	0.0007	−2.07e−07, 0.0029
Level of education	0.033	0.0232	−0.0115, 0.0794
_Cons	0.178***	0.0575	0.0660, 0.2917

***p < 0.01, **p < 0.05, *p < 0.1

which have been discussed in the literature (Jahoda et al. 1971; Schnapper 1981; Demazière and Pignoni 1998). When it comes to having a relationship of empathy with unemployed people, figures reveal that the individual trajectory only has a weak impact on solidarity actions, indeed far less influential than in the field of disability. This confirms that individual variables are inadequate in order to explain the variations in solidarity actions in the field of unemployment.

The political variables provide us with further material to explain solidarity actions in the field of unemployment. We observe that the importance of proximity becomes less relevant than before if we add a number of political variables. In particular, both an interest in politics and (especially) reading newspapers have a positive correlation to the choice of engaging solidarity actions. However participating in elections does not appear to increase solidarity towards the unemployed, which reinforces the argument, outlined in several scholarly works, that there is a great distance between traditional politics and the politics of unemployment (Piven and Cloward 1977; Bagguley 1991, 1992).

The use of controlled regressions suggests once more that sociodemographic variables have a low impact. As far as age is concerned, findings show that being young or old makes no difference when it comes to being actively engaged in support actions—as we had already seen in the case of disability. The same conclusion can be drawn for educational level. Given that out of the total number of respondents who support the unemployed ($N = 458$) one-third has finished their secondary education, and two-thirds have undertaken higher studies, education appears to have a more important influence than age but nevertheless not a determinant one. The same pattern repeats itself in the case of gender-related indicators, since a similar proportion of men and women engage in solidarity in the field.[6]

To sum things up, Table 9.10 depicts the main drivers behind solidarity towards the unemployed. The most salient indicators in the field refer to the political trajectory. We conclude—in line with our expectations—that solidarity vis-à-vis the unemployed is not best explained by the individual trajectory, but rather by the political trajectory that is rooted within French *republicanism*.

As regards solidarity, the first individual variable taken into account is the individual's place of birth, which is used here to deduce whether he or she is a refugee or more broadly a migrant. Our findings reveal that French nationals are more likely to engage in solidarity actions to support refugees, compared to both non-nationals and individuals born abroad. However, the relationship between place of birth and solidarity actions only has a limited significance. Following the same logic, an individual who has relatives or friends that are refugees or

Table 9.10 Solidarity towards the unemployed individual and political factors (controlled)

	Coefficient	Standard error	95% Confidence interval
Declared that he/she was unemployed	−0.061*	0.0372	−0.1345, 0.0117
Has unemployed family or friends	0.035*	0.0186	−0.0005, 0.0724
Voted in the most recent 2012 elections	0.023	0.0223	−0.0206, 0.0668
Reads the newspaper +3 days a week	0.115***	0.0181	0.0801, 0.1512
Considers him-/herself to be moderately or very interested in politics	0.085***	0.0192	0.0480, 0.1235
Gender	−0.050***	0.0181	−0.0857, −0.0145
Age	−0.002***	0.0006	−0.0037, −0.0012
Level of education	0.005	0.0191	−0.0320, 0.0432
_Cons	0.277***	0.0488	0.1817, 0.3735

***$p < 0.01$, **$p < 0.05$, *$p < 0.1$

migrants will be slightly more inclined to become active in this field. In this case, we find that self-identification seems to play a major role and proximity a minor one for refugee-related solidarity (contrary to what we had observed for disability).

The inclusion of political indicators provides a clearer picture of the mechanisms accounting for solidarity towards refugees (Table 9.11). While voting has a weak relationship to participation in solidarity actions, interest in politics and reading the newspaper come across as relevant explanatory variables. Therefore, we can conclude so far that the political trajectory appears to account more effectively for the choice to engage in solidarity actions. Undeniably, this is the most surprisingly finding of all, which deserves full consideration in our last section, where we deal with the main results of this chapter.

As regards our control variables, they appear to confirm the patterns that emerged from our study of the two previous fields, since educational level, age, and gender do not appear to be essential factors in explaining solidarity towards refugees. Even though younger people have a slightly stronger tendency to become activists, the correlation with age is nevertheless not very significant. In the same way, but with a clearer discrepancy, men appear to be slightly more active than women. In particular, we see that in the sub-samples of men and women, 19% of the former and 16% of

Table 9.11 Solidarity towards refugees individual and political factors (controlled)

	Coefficient	*Standard error*	*95% Confidence interval*
Born in France	0.045	0.0402	−0.0335, 0.1241
Has family, friends, or acquaintances coming from a different country	0.021	0.0171	−0.0122, 0.0548
Voted in the most recent 2012 elections	−0.037*	0.0207	−0.0784, 0.0028
Reads the newspaper +3 days a week	0.111***	0.0167	0.0787, 0.1443
Considers him-/herself to be moderately or very interested in politics	0.082***	0.0178	0.0472, 0.1171
Gender	−0.026	0.0167	−0.0596, 0.006
Age	−0.002***	0.0005	−0.0035, −0.0012
Education level	0.021	0.0177	−0.0132, 0.0565
_Cons	0.193***	0.0601	0.0758, 0.3118

***$p < 0.01$, **$p < 0.05$, *$p < 0.1$

the latter are activists. Lastly, educational level has a more limited impact here than in the case of unemployment, but a more important influence than in the field of disability.[7]

Conclusion

This chapter has analysed variations in the pattern of solidarity actions designed to support the disabled, the unemployed, and refugees. These three groups have become increasingly vulnerable in France during the last few years as a result of decreasing social protection and of welfare cuts: the notion that one ought to feel an unconditional solidarity towards the vulnerable has lost its hold, paving the way for a new state approach to "conditional" forms of welfare and protection. As a result, state-run solidarity systems now require the vulnerable themselves to assume ever more responsibility for their problems (Cinalli and De Nuzzo 2017). Against this background of increasing policy restrictions, the present chapter has analysed the bottom-up dynamics of solidarity linking French people to some of most vulnerable groups. The main aim has been to understand which factors are more likely to lead to solidarity actions (this is what we mean by solidarity as an output). In particular, we have focused on two major solidarity trajectories—an individual trajectory and a political trajectory (that is what we mean by solidarity as an input)—with the expectation that both of them would prove important in accounting for variations in the amount and the type of solidarity actions in each of the fields of vulnerability considered here.

What characterises the individual trajectory is that the solidarity actions in which a person chooses to engage (the output) must be understood as a direct consequence of individual variables of empathy, in this case self-identification and proximity (the input). Conversely, in the political trajectory, solidarity actions (the output) are determined by political variables like voting, having an interest in politics, and keeping abreast of the public debate (the input). We did not, however, expect that both trajectories would always combine in the same way. For example, if one considers the usual argument of social capital scholarship that associations are extremely important since they enable individuals to form human bonds (the individual variables, in our theoretical framework) while also engaging in purposeful political action (the political variables, in our theoretical framework) (Rosenstone and Mark Hansen 1993; Lichterman 2005; Putnam 1993, 2000), this could have prompted us to simplistically assume that both trajectories would have worked in synergy for all vulnerable groups. On the contrary, we suspected that for some vulnerable groups, individual bonding could in fact reinforce their self-exclusion from politics (cf. the notion of "polarisation" in Sunstein 2002). In the case of the unemployed, for instance, self-identification can be hampered by the increasing stigmatisation they face in society at large.

The only field where we expected both trajectories to neatly combine was the field of disability, given that solidarity with the disabled can be triggered by both individual and political variables. We expected that the political trajectory would prevail in the field of unemployment, given that solidarity, in this case, is directed towards fellow citizens penalised by specific policies, but with whom it might not be easy to form bonds (especially in terms of self-identification). Lastly, we expected the individual trajectory to prevail as a driver of solidarity actions for refugees, since the latter can be seen as fellow human beings, but not as fellow citizens since their status places them outside the *political community*.

Our results did indeed prove that the individual trajectory and the political trajectory combine in various ways and that they can help to account for variations in the amount and forms of solidarity actions across different fields of vulnerability, even when controlling for important sociodemographic factors like age, education, and gender. Among the expectations that were confirmed by our data was the suspicion that the political trajectory was the only possible driver of solidarity actions in the unemployment field. As expected, French citizens who engage with politics and follow the public debate are also more likely to see unemployment as the consequence of certain political choices and of specific policies, which makes it a problem to be solved by calling for collective action and for public solutions. Solidarity actions will therefore be carried out (mainly in a public and collective way) in spite of the processes of stigmatisation that are at work and that weaken the effectiveness of the individual trajectory. By contrast, the individual trajectory plays an important role in the field of disability, where it combines with political variables in a way to lead to the highest level of solidarity actions across all three fields.

However, the main point to emphasise is that results did fall short of our expectations when it came to solidarity towards refugees. While we were initially unsurprised to see that solidarity actions were at their lowest level in this field, and that they were mainly the result of an individual and private *repertoire*, we were quite surprised to discover that solidarity actions were especially tied to political variables. This means that the political trajectory proved to be the one with a relevant impact even in the case of a vulnerable group that falls outside the *political community* of republican citizens. This result stands out as an important discovery, insofar as it undermines two of the assumptions on which we based our research. One of these was that republican *citizenship* can only account for solidarity that is acted through a collective, public understanding of political intervention. But manifestly this is not the case given that the political trajectory proves relevant to explain the dynamics of solidarity across all fields of vulnerability, including in fields where the individual and private *repertoire* prevails significantly over the public and collective *repertoire*. Secondly, and most importantly, our findings show that in spite of the prevailing culture of disenchantment towards public institutions, people in France remain interested in politics, and, one could say, very republican. The *political community* cannot be in such bad health in France as pundits and commentators repeatedly claim it is, if republican *citizenship* appears to be a key mechanism to mobilise people when dealing with vulnerability.

This chapter has focused on the French case, but it has a much broader relevance since it shows that the notion of solidarity is neither simple nor monolithic, and that one should ideally talk not of one, but of several "types of solidarities" to account for the complex articulations of the different trajectories that link solidarity as an input and solidarity as an output. The same can be said for the notion of vulnerability, since we have shown that trajectories of solidarity do indeed change, and quite significantly so, depending on the specific vulnerable group that they target. While our scholarly pride may have been piqued by the discovery that our theoretical framework was not adequate to account for our unexpected results in the field of refugees, as citizens, these results provide us with much to rejoice over. In particular, we have discovered that the political trajectory of solidarity can have a remarkable potential even when it comes to helping vulnerable people outside the boundaries of the *political community* in France. Or put more simply, *republicanism* appears, at least this once, to fully live up to its universalist ideals. This may be due to the resilience of French *republicanism* but also, more broadly, to the fact that the strength of a community of nationals, either in France or elsewhere, can exceed the strict definition of its borders, both in human and in geographic terms.

The resilience of the French citizenry does not, therefore, necessarily play into the hands of those who increasingly seek to use it as an instrument to further extremist views that preach the rejection of refugees and of non-national "aliens" in general.

Notes

1. See, for example, the article entitled "11 October 2013 migrant tragedy: Italians navy officers placed under investigation", *The Independent*, 23 October 2016, or the article "Stiamo morendo, per favore: le telefonate del naufragio dei bambini", *L'Espresso*, 9 May 2017.
2. Cf. the article "How Nicolas Sarkozy's father once lived rough in Paris", *The Telegraph*, 11 April 2009.
3. http://www.connexionfrance.com/social-benefits-student-housing-disability-home-help-cut-income-support-rsa-11820-view-article.html.
4. N sample is 2098. All variables in the tables were weighted.
5. Self-identification with refugees was assessed through a broader reference to foreigners in general. The assumption was that self-identification and proximity to foreigners and people of foreigner origins provide some strong bases for empathy with refugees.
6. Yet, the effect of sociodemographic variables in the model appears to be relevant, since the impact of self-identification increases, while the importance of voting changes to a positive and slightly more significant one.
7. Once again, the impact of sociodemographic controls on the model proves to be crucial, since they improve the model's accuracy. In particular, including these controls illustrates the impact of all the respective variables. It reduces the negative impact of voting. Since the reading of newspapers and having an interest in politics remain important factors, we are drawn to conclude that the political trajectory stands out as the most important path accounting for support towards refugees.

References

Andersson, L., & Sundin, E. (2016). *Disaster Tourists, Smartphone Bystanders, Mediated Witnesses or Citizen Journalists? Bystander Theories and Mobile Media Practices at Accident Sites* (1st ed.). Prague: ECREA.

Arendt, H. (1982). *Les Origines du totalitarisme*. Paris: Seuil.

Bagguley, P. (1991). *From Protest to Acquiescence? Political Movements of the Unemployed*. London: Macmillan.

Bagguley, P. (1992). Protest, Acquiescence and the Unemployed: A Comparative Analysis of the 1930s and 1980s. *British Journal of Sociology, 43*, 443–461.

Baglioni, S., & Giugni, M. (2014). *Civil Society Organizations, Unemployment, and Precarity in Europe*. Basingstoke: Palgrave Macmillan.
Bellamy, R., Castiglione, D., & Shaw, J. (Eds.). (2006). *Making European Citizens: Civic Inclusion in a Transnational Context*. Basingstoke: Palgrave Macmillan.
Berend, T. I. (2016). *The Contemporary Crisis of the European Union*. London: Routledge.
Bourgeois, L. (1896). *Solidarité*. Paris: A. Colin.
Burrow, M. (1986). Mission Civilisatrice. *The Historical Journal, 29*(1), 109–135.
Calhoune, C. (2017). *Brexit: Sociological Responses, in William Outhwaite*. London: Anthem.
Chabanet, D. (2014). Between Youth Policy and Employment Policy: The Rise, Limits and Ambiguities of a Corporatist System of Youth Representation within the EU. *Journal of Common Market Studies, 52*(3), 479–494.
Chabanet, D. (2017). The Social Economy Sector and the Welfare State in France: Toward a Takeover of the Market? *Voluntas, 28*(6), 2360–2382.
Cinalli, M. (2004). Horizontal Networks vs. Vertical Networks in Multi-Organisational Alliances: A Comparative Study of the Unemployment and Asylum Issue-Fields in Britain. *EurPolCom, 8*(4), 1–31.
Cinalli, M. (2017). *Citizenship and the Political Integration of Muslims*. Basingstoke: Palgrave Macmillan.
Cinalli, M. and C. De Nuzzo (2017). *Disability, Unemployment, Immigration: Does Solidarity Matter in Times of Crisis? (French Case)*. WP1 Report for the TransSOL Project, Unpublished Manuscript.
Dainotto, R. (2007). *Europe (in Theory)*. Durham: Duke University Press.
Darley, J., & Latané, B. (1968). Bystander Intervention in Emergencies: Diffusion of Responsibility. *Journal of Personality and Social Psychology, 8*, 377–383.
de la Dehesa, G. (2006). *Winners and Losers in Globalization*. Oxford: Blackwell.
Delhey, J. (2007). Do Enlargements Make the European Union Less Cohesive? An Analysis of Trust Between EU Nationalities. *Journal of Common Market Studies, 45*(2), 253–279.
Demazière, D., & Pignoni, M. T. (1998). *Chômeurs: du silence à la révolte*. Paris: Hachette.
Department of Communities and Local Government. (2015). Statistics. Retrieved May 24, 2017, from https://www.gov.uk/government/organisations/department-for-communities-and-local-government.
Giugni, M., & Grasso, M. (2015). *Austerity and Protest: Popular Contention in Times of Economic Crisis*. Farnham: Ashgate.
Giugni, M., & Passy, F. (2001). *Political Altruism? Solidarity Movements in International Perspective*. Lanham, MD: Rowman & Littlefield Publishers.
Hanagan, M. P. (1980). *The Logic of Solidarity: Artisans and Industrial Workers in Three French Towns 1871–1914*. Urbana, IL: University of Illinois press.

Hyman, R. (1986). Reflections on the Mining Strike. *Socialist Register*, 22, 330–354.

Jahoda, M., Lazarsfeld, P. F., & Zeisel, H. (1971 [1933]). *Marienthal. The Sociography of an Unemployed Community* (trans.: Reginall, J., & Elsaesser, T.). New York: Aldine-Atherton.

Lahusen, C. (2013). The Protests of the Unemployed in France, Germany and Sweden (1994–2004): Protest Dynamics and Political Contexts. *Social Movement Studies. Journal of Social, Cultural and Political Protest*, 12(1), 1–22.

Lassen, D. D. (2005). The Effect of Information on Voter Turnout: Evidence from a Natural Experiment. *American Journal of Political Science*, 49(1), 103–118.

Lichterman, P. (2005). *Elusive Togetherness: Church Groups Trying to Bridge America's Divisions*. Princeton, NJ: Princeton University Press.

Müller, O. (2009). *Analyse critique de la pénalisation du phénomène migratoire en France et en Italie*. PhD thesis, Université de Nantes.

Müller, O. (2014). *La pénalisation de l'aide au séjour irrégulier: De la volonté politique à la réalité judiciaire*. Master's thesis, IEP, 2009. Retrieved May 29, 2017, from http://www.gisti.org/IMG/pdf/Memoire__IEP_olivia_-muller__2009.pdf.

Nie, N., Junn, J., & Stehlik-Barry, K. (1996). *Education and Citizenship in America*. Chicago: Cambridge University Press.

Parry, G., Moyser, G., & Day, N. (1992). *Political Participation and Democracy in Britain*. Cambridge: Cambridge University Press.

Piven, F. F., & Cloward, R. A. (1977). *Poor People's Movements: Why They Succeed, How They Fail*. New York: Pantheon Books.

Putnam, R. D. (1993). *Making Democracy Work. Civic Traditions in Modern Italy*. Princeton, NJ: Princeton University Press.

Putnam, R. D. (2000). *Bowling Alone. The Collapse and Revival of American Community*. New York: Simon and Schuster.

Rehm, P. (2009). Risks and Redistribution: An Individual-Level Analysis. *Comparative Political Studies*, 42(7), 855–881.

Rosenstone, S., & Mark Hansen, J. (1993). *Mobilization, Participation, and Democracy in America*. New York: Macmillan.

Schnapper, D. (1981). *L'épreuve du chômage*. Paris: Gallimard.

Schnapper, D. (2003). *La communauté des citoyens*. Paris: Gallimard.

Siméant, J. (1998). *La Cause des Sans-Papiers*. Paris: Presses de Science Po.

Sirot, S. (2014). *1884, des syndicats pour la République*. Lormont: Le Bord de l'eau.

Stjerno, S. (2012). *Solidarity in Europe. The History of an Idea*. Cambridge: Cambridge University Press.

Sunstein, C. (2002). The Law of Group Polarization. *The Journal of Political Philosophy*, 10(2), 175–195.

Teorell, J., Torcal, M., & Montero, J. R. (2007). *Political Participation: Mapping the Terrain*. In J. W. van Deth, J. R. Montero, & A. Westholm (Eds.), *Citizenship and Involvement in European Democracies: A Comparative Analysis*. London: Routledge.

Tilly, C. (1978). *From Mobilization to Revolution*. Reading, MA: Addison-Wesley.

Verba, S., Lehman Schlozman, K., & Brady, H. (1995). *Voice and Equality: Civic Voluntarism in American Politics*. London: Harvard University Press.

Wilde, L. (2013). *Global Solidarity*. Edinburgh: Edinburgh University Press.

Open Access This chapter is licensed under the terms of the Creative Commons Attribution 4.0 International License (http://creativecommons.org/licenses/by/4.0/), which permits use, sharing, adaptation, distribution and reproduction in any medium or format, as long as you give appropriate credit to the original author(s) and the source, provide a link to the Creative Commons license and indicate if changes were made.

The images or other third party material in this chapter are included in the chapter's Creative Commons license, unless indicated otherwise in a credit line to the material. If material is not included in the chapter's Creative Commons license and your intended use is not permitted by statutory regulation or exceeds the permitted use, you will need to obtain permission directly from the copyright holder.

CHAPTER 10

Solidarity in Europe: A Comparative Assessment and Discussion

Christian Lahusen and Maria Grasso

INTRODUCTION

Citizens across Europe are committed to solidarity in its various manifestations. As we know from previous studies, almost two-thirds of the population support redistributive policies aimed at reducing income inequalities (Burgoon 2014). Asked about their own commitment in practical terms, every fifth European citizen reports to have donated time or money to non-profit organizations (Bauer et al. 2013), and every third says to have joined an unconventional protest such as signing petitions or boycotting products (Hafner Fink 2012). Overall, the European citizenry cherishes solidarity as a private and public virtue. However, differences between the European people are considerable, particularly when comparing the high levels of voluntary engagement and political participation in Northern Europe with the lower rates in the Mediterranean and Eastern European countries (Anheier and Salamon 1999; Oorschot et al. 2005). Moreover, people tend to differentiate between groups in deciding whom

---

C. Lahusen (✉)
Department of Social Sciences, University of Siegen, Siegen, Germany

M. Grasso
Department of Politics, University of Sheffield, Sheffield, UK

© The Author(s) 2018
C. Lahusen, M. Grasso (eds.), *Solidarity in Europe*,
Palgrave Studies in European Political Sociology,
https://doi.org/10.1007/978-3-319-73335-7_10

to support. In this respect, they see the elderly and the sick as more deserving than the jobless and the latter as more deserving than immigrants (Oorschot 2000, 2006). Solidarity is thus a complex and multidimensional phenomenon.

The chapters of this book validate these general findings by making use of survey data gathered in the winter of 2016 by a EU-funded project (TransSOL). A significant proportion of the European population supports redistributive policies in order to equalize income levels within society and substantial numbers of citizens are committed to donating money and time to the needy and to participating in political protests in support of people deprived of their rights. Additionally, national studies highlighted also that citizens are not only committed to support people in need within their own country but to engage in acts of solidarity with those living in other European countries and beyond the European continent.

This book focuses on cross-national solidarity and allows for providing a richer account of solidarity in Europe than previous studies have done. Evidence presented in this book not only paints a vivid picture of social solidarity within European countries but also helps to ascertain and demarcate the role of European solidarity within this broader panorama. The findings of the previous chapters enable us to compare levels of solidarity between countries and to identify levels of support toward different target groups such as the disabled, the unemployed, and the refugees/migrants. Additionally, they also highlight the degree to which citizens are committed to support other fellow Europeans, when compared to the solidarity they exhibit with people living in their own country and outside of Europe.

The previous chapters have presented and discussed country-specific findings, thus highlighting the specificities of each national case. These insights require a comparative assessment and reflection on the project's findings. For this purpose, we will present the evidence gathered through our dataset by means of a direct comparison of country-specific levels of solidarity. In particular, we wish to highlight important manifestations of European solidarity by means of a series of tables describing the extent to which citizens in the eight countries under analysis are committed to practices of solidarity and redistributive policies at EU level. This evidence will be discussed in a concluding section, highlighting the main forces driving European solidarity and the implications of our findings for the future prospects of social cohesion in Europe.

European Solidarity: A Comparative Panorama

Our empirical analysis of European solidarity focuses on two manifestations. On the one hand, we deal with interpersonal forms of solidarity by comparing different levels of reported solidarity practices in eight European countries. On the other hand, we focus on the respondents' views on redistributional policies at the national and European level. In both respects, we wish to unveil the motivations and rationales guiding and patterning these forms of solidarity.

In the first step, we direct our attention to interpersonal, social solidarity. Our questionnaire had asked respondents to indicate the kind of activities they have been engaged in support of other people. They could report about a variety of conventional and unconventional activities (Grasso 2011, 2016), specifically the following six items: attended a march/protest/demonstration, donated money or time, bought or refused to buy products, engaged as a passive member or as an active member of an organization. For simplicity reasons, we examined whether citizens showed interpersonal solidarity by engaging in at least one activity.

Table 10.1 summarizes the findings by differentiating the answers of our respondents according to the six target groups of our study. The find-

Table 10.1 Personal support of other people

	People in your own country (%)	People in other countries within the EU (%)	People in countries outside the EU (%)	Disability rights (%)	The unemployed (%)	Refugees/ asylum seekers (%)	Total N
Denmark	47	23	35	44	27	30	2183
France	47	25	30	50	24	20	2098
Germany	51	31	40	52	27	34	2064
Greece	62	35	36	62	58	36	2061
Italy	47	32	33	49	36	28	2087
Poland	59	35	37	65	40	27	2119
UK	38	19	25	35	19	22	2221
Switzerland	59	34	45	67	33	33	2083
Total	51	29	35	53	33	29	16,916

'Have you ever done one of the following in order to support the rights of people/groups? Attend a protest, donate money or time, buy or boycott a product, passive or active membership in an organization'

Source: TransSOL (Horizon2020, GA, no. 649435)

ings show that a considerable number of European citizens report having been engaged in solidarity activities for other people, including donating money or time, protesting and engaging in voluntary associations. Concerning the spatial dimension, we see that practiced solidarity is strongest at the national level and that solidarity with fellow Europeans is lower than the support for people outside the EU. As we will see below, this seems to reflect the attachment of citizens to the various reference groups, because citizens feel most attached to their own country and to humankind, while fewer respondents feel European. At the same time, solidarity is more diffused in regard to disabilities, when compared to the jobless and refugees or migrants. Consequently, our data reflects what we would expect when taking previous studies into consideration (Burgoon 2014; Bauer et al. 2013; Oorschot 2000).

Differences in levels of solidarity emerge when disaggregating the findings according to our eight countries. However, it is interesting to note that these levels of solidarity are more similar than one would expect considering the findings of previous comparative studies (e.g., Bauer et al. 2013; Burgoon 2014). Particularly Greek and Polish citizens (and to a lesser extent also Italians) reported high levels of participation in activities of support toward people within and outside their country, and these rates are close to—or even higher than—the levels of solidarity in the other, supposedly more active countries. This could reflect the situation of crisis, uncertainty and transition experienced in these countries. Particularly in the case of Greece, we know that the economic and financial crisis since 2008—as well as the refugees crisis of 2015/2016—have unleashed a wave of social solidarity initiatives (Sotiropoulos and Bourikos 2014; Giugni and Grasso 2016; Grasso and Giugni 2016). But also in other countries, the support for refugees and asylum seekers is rather high, when remembering that previous studies see these target groups far behind other potential recipients (e.g., Oorschot 2000, 2006). This observation applies to Denmark, Germany, Greece and Switzerland. The dramatic hardship experienced by refugees on their way to and through Europe to their countries of destination incited a wave of 'welcoming' initiatives in these countries (Evangelinidis 2016). In this sense, our data reveals that European citizens tend to deliver in terms of voluntary engagement in time of crisis and emergency situations.

In the second step, we move to another manifestation of solidarity, namely, public support for policies of redistribution and burden sharing. Table 10.2 gives us a first impression by summarizing the findings

Table 10.2 Eliminating inequalities

	Not at all important (%)	Not very important (%)	Neither (%)	Fairly important (%)	Very important (%)	Total N
Denmark	5.4	12.7	33.1	32.8	16	2183
France	2.4	5.8	20.3	37.5	34	2098
Germany	2	6.2	22.8	39.3	29.7	2064
Greece	1.8	3.5	16.7	35.1	42.9	2061
Italy	1.4	3	14.9	40	40.7	2087
Poland	2.6	5.4	21.7	36.5	33.8	2119
UK	3.6	6.7	28.5	35.8	25.4	2083
Switzerland	3.2	7.9	22.3	38.9	27.7	2221
Total	2.8	6.5	22.6	37.0	31.1	16,916

'In order to be considered fair, what should a society provide? Eliminating big inequalities in income between citizens'

Source: TransSOL (Horizon2020, GA, no. 649435)

of a question measuring the general disposition of citizens to support a fair distribution of wealth. We see that every third respondent agrees that the goal of eliminating big inequalities is 'very important' and the proportion increases to more than two-thirds of the population when adding those who view this as 'fairly important'. Differences between the eight countries are very pronounced and reflect what we know from other studies about the support of redistributive policies within countries (Svallfors 1997; Blekesaune and Quadagno 2003; Burgoon 2014; Grasso et al. 2017). A complex set of factors plays a role, among them the level of prevailing inequalities, the standards of redistribution already in place, predominant political orientations and values.

For our own purposes, however, it is more telling to look at the differences in public support for redistribution at the global and European level. Table 10.3 presents the evidence in regard to the global scope of redistribution. Respondents were asked to indicate how important it should be for the EU to help people in developing countries. A strong majority of respondents supports the attempts of the EU to help countries outside of Europe in fighting poverty and promoting development, with 62% supporting and only 14% opposing these measures. Even though the biggest share thinks that this global commitment is only fairly important, every fifth respondent indicated that this engagement is very important.

Table 10.3 Development aid

	Not at all (%)	Not very (%)	Neither (%)	Fairly important (%)	Very important (%)	Total N
Denmark	4	8	26	43	19	2183
France	5	9	32	38	16	2098
Germany	3	6	18	46	28	2064
Greece	6	7	21	44	22	2061
Italy	4	7	18	46	26	2087
Poland	5	16	35	35	8	2119
United Kingdom	6	9	27	37	21	2083
Switzerland	3	8	20	44	25	2221
Total	5	9	25	42	20	16,916

'The European Union provides development aid to assist certain countries outside the EU in their fight against poverty and in their development. How important do you think it is to help people in developing countries?'

Source: TransSOL (Horizon2020, GA, no. 649435)

When we move to the European level, we see that public support for EU-internal help is much more limited, particularly if specific measures of redistribution and burden sharing are at stake. Our questionnaire listed two questions that aimed at measuring redistributional preferences. On the one hand, we asked respondents whether they support the EU in pooling funds to help EU countries having difficulties in paying their debts. On the other hand, we wanted to know whether respondents agree to grant the EU with more funds in order to help refugees. In regard to Switzerland, respondents answered in a more hypothetical manner, but their responses are not very different to those of EU citizens. For the other countries, the picture is rather mixed.

In regard to fiscal solidarity between member states, the supporters outweigh the opponents only slightly (41% vs. 30%), with 29% undecided respondents (see Table 10.4). The biggest group of supporters are located in Italy (66% against 16% opponents) and Greece (64% vs. 11%). Poland leans more toward the helping side (39% vs. 20%), but this is also due to the number of undecided respondents. In Denmark, Germany and the United Kingdom the share of opponents is bigger than the group of supporters, with 38% versus 28%, 41% versus 33% and 41% versus 34%. These findings show that countries on the giving and receiving side stress differently the idea of fiscal solidarity. While the population in countries that

Table 10.4 Fiscal solidarity: pay public debts

	Strongly disagree (%)	Disagree (%)	Neither (%)	Agree (%)	Strongly agree (%)	Total N
Denmark	14	24	34	23	5	1939
France	15	19	30	28	8	1903
Germany	15	26	25	27	6	1914
Greece	7	4	24	38	26	1975
Italy	5	11	18	47	19	1928
Poland	8	12	42	33	6	1938
United Kingdom	18	23	25	27	7	1861
Switzerland	14	22	31	28	5	1992
Total	12	18	29	31	10	15,455

'The EU is currently pooling funds to help EU countries having difficulties in paying their debts. To what extent do you agree or disagree with this measure?'
Source: TransSOL (Horizon2020, GA, no. 649435)

have mastered the financial and economic crisis are more skeptical toward measures of fiscal solidarity, the countries affected more strongly by these crises tend to stress more overtly the fact that EU member states should conform to one of their values, namely, interstate help and solidarity. This contrast is even more evident when considering that the share of respondents fully agreeing with measures of fiscal solidarity is very low everywhere, with an exception of Italy and Greece.

In regard to EU funds in support of refugees, we find very similar results. Table 10.5 shows that the group opposing more funds for EU measures slightly outweighs the supporters (39% vs. 35%), again with a considerable share of undecided respondents. Supporters of this measure are more numerous in Germany (47%), Denmark (41%) and Greece (39%), while least diffused in France, (26%), Italy (27%) and Poland (29%). Again, those countries faced with higher rates of forced migrants and thus more dependent on European solidarity are those calling for more financial help from all member states. Before this backdrop, it comes as no surprise that the Danish, the Germans and the British are among those 'strongly supporting' this redistribution.

These findings highlight that public support for at least some kinds of EU-internal solidarity measures is rather moderate. However, there are important reasons we should abstain from comparing this modest support directly with the more extended endorsement of humanitarian aid for

Table 10.5 Fiscal solidarity: help refugees

	Strongly oppose (%)	Somewhat oppose (%)	Neither (%)	Somewhat support (%)	Strongly support (%)	Total N
Denmark	16	17	25	27	14	2183
France	26	19	29	21	5	2098
Germany	12	17	24	35	12	2064
Greece	24	15	23	31	8	2061
Italy	21	25	28	23	4	2087
Poland	18	19	33	24	5	2119
United Kingdom	20	18	27	26	10	2221
Switzerland	21	25	20	28	6	2083
Total	20	19	26	27	8	16,916

'Would you support or oppose your country's government offering financial support to the European Union in order to help refugees?'

Source: TransSOL (Horizon2020, GA, no. 649435)

developing countries. Measures of fiscal solidarity within the EU imply a more far-reaching commitment of member states than humanitarian aid. In fact, the magnitude and the implications of EU-internal fiscal solidarity seem to provide reasons for why public support might be more modest and for why the share of citizens fully agreeing with EU-internal measures of solidarity is lower. Among other factors, we need to consider that many policy areas within the EU are patterned by the idea of subsidiarity, and this means that nation-states take the responsibility for problem solving. The moderate support for EU-internal solidarity in some respects is thus to be taken for what it is: citizens are less enthusiastic about authorizing their governments to help other EU member states' governments in solving the problems with their debt and refugees.

The moderate support for measures of fiscal solidarity raises the question of what motivates respondents to be more cautious. An answer is provided by a question included into our survey. It asked respondents to specify the potential reasons for granting or denying fiscal support to other EU countries. The results presented in Table 10.6 show that fiscal solidarity is conditional and seems to privilege reciprocity. In fact, our respondents are not ready to support other EU countries in trouble unconditionally. Only a minority of 19% testifies that fiscal solidarity is a matter of moral duty. The largest group subscribes to the idea of reciprocity, fairness, trustworthiness and deservingness (see Lengfeld et al. 2015;

Table 10.6 Fiscal solidarity: reasons

	Denmark	France	Germany	Greece	Italy	Poland	UK	CH	Total
Financial help has also beneficial effects for the own country	20	13	15	19	16	24	15	13	17
It is our moral duty to help other member states that are in need	18	16	21	27	20	20	17	15	19
Member states should help each other, as somewhere along the way every country may require help	33	37	45	59	52	49	31	42	44
Financial help should not be given to countries that have proven to handle money badly	40	37	40	22	26	38	42	38	35
Don't know	19	17	9	8	13	11	16	12	13
Total N	2183	2098	2064	2061	2087	2119	2083	2221	16,916

'There are many reasons to state for or against financial help for EU countries in trouble. Which one of the following best reflects how you feel?' Multiple answers possible (in %)

Source: TransSOL (Horizon2020, GA, no. 649435)

also Wheeless 1978; Thielemann 2003). Fiscal solidarity is a matter of giving and receiving for almost every second respondent, and one out of three citizens thinks that help should be given only to those countries that handle help responsibly. While countries diverge in the extent to which they subscribe to these statements, there is no doubt that both considerations are the most widely shared forms of reasoning everywhere. Accordingly, European solidarity suffers immediately, when citizens have the feeling that support measures are one-sided and potentially misused. Interestingly enough, citizens' judgments about fiscal solidarity within the EU do not seem to be very different to what we know about public norms guiding public support of redistribution within national welfare states (Bowles and Gintis 2000; Oorschot 2006; León 2012).

Solidarity with Non-EU Citizens: Attitudes Toward Migration and the Inclusion of Migrants

Migration policies have become a highly salient issue within the public sphere (Green-Pedersen and Otjes 2017). The growing inflows of forced migrants from the Middle East during the summer of 2015 have certainly contributed to this development. In particular, it has put the topic of European solidarity on the public agenda. In the previous section, we showed that almost every third respondent had been engaged in practices of support for migrants, especially in those countries that were on the migration routes of refugees and were confronted with a bigger need. But what can we say about policy preferences? Do citizens support immigration policies that welcome refugees within their country, and do they approve also of European policies of 'burden sharing'? These aspects are important for our analytic purposes. Citizens' attitudes toward immigration and immigration policies are an important indicator of the society's openness toward non-nationals and thus also for the inclusivity of solidarity. For this reason, we included a series of questions in our survey that were geared towards measuring public attitudes toward policies addressing groups migrating into one's country from the EU and from outside of it. A particular focus in this respect were Syrian refugees fleeing their war-torn country.

Table 10.7 looks first at respondent opinions in terms of the types of measures they think their government should pursue in terms of economic migrants from within the European Union. As we can see, across countries most people tend to accept economic migration in so far as 'there are jobs they can do'. Lower proportions are more liberal agreeing to 'allow all those who want to come'. In particular, Greeks and Poles tend to be the most welcoming followed by Italians and Germans and Danes, then the French with the Brits and the Swiss being the least welcoming with only 10% selecting this option. Indeed, the Brits and Swiss display the highest

Table 10.7 Immigration policies for EU citizens (in %)

	Allow in all those who want to come	Allow people to come as long as there are jobs they can do	Put strict limits on the number allowed to come	Prohibit people from these countries coming here	Don't know	Total
Denmark	14.6	52.1	18.9	3.8	10.7	100
France	13.0	42.2	25.1	8.1	11.6	100
Germany	16.3	46.2	26.1	4.8	6.7	100
Greece	22.0	44.7	23.0	4.2	6.1	100
Italy	16.7	48.5	20.7	5.7	8.3	100
Poland	20.0	44.2	19.1	5.3	11.5	100
Switzerland	7.2	46.4	36.8	4.2	5.4	100
United Kingdom	9.7	41.2	31.8	8.0	9.4	100
Total	14.9	45.7	25.2	5.5	8.7	100

'For each of the following groups, what measures do you think the government should pursue? People from European Union coming to ***COUNTRY*** to work?'

Source: TransSOL (Horizon2020, GA, no. 649435)

proportions of respondents agreeing that there should be 'strict limits on the number allowed to come'. Up to 8% of individuals in the UK would completely prohibit economic migration from the EU (8.1% also in France).

The same question was put to respondents in relation to non-EU citizens, too, in order to get a sense of what the impact of EU citizenship might be. Table 10.8 presents these results, which show that people are considerably less welcoming across countries compared to the results for EU migrants presented in Table 10.6. The most welcoming are Italians with about 8% suggesting all the people who want to come should come, followed by 7.8% of Greeks, 7% of Germans, 6.2% in France and Poland, 5.6% in Denmark, 5.3% in the UK and only 4.5% in Switzerland. In Denmark, Italy, Greece and Poland respondents are more likely to support economic migration provided there are jobs; whereas, in France, Germany, Switzerland and the UK respondents are more likely to prefer putting 'strict limits on the number allowed to come' from non-EU countries. Up to 14.5% of people in France want to completely prohibit non-EU people from coming to their country, followed by 12.3% of Germans and about 9–10% in the other nations adopting this very unforgiving position on migration.

Table 10.8 Immigration policies for non-EU citizens (in %)

	Allow in all those who want to come	Allow people to come as long as there are jobs they can do	Put strict limits on the number allowed to come	Prohibit people from these countries coming here	Don't know	Total
Denmark	5.6	40.3	31.8	10.7	11.6	100
France	6.2	32.8	34.3	14.5	12.2	100
Germany	7.0	32.1	40.3	12.3	8.3	100
Greece	7.8	38.0	37.2	11.1	5.9	100
Italy	8.0	46.6	27.4	9.3	8.8	100
Poland	6.2	34.8	33.7	11.9	13.4	100
Switzerland	4.5	35.3	45.1	9.2	5.8	100
UK	5.3	37.0	37.2	10.5	10.0	100
Total	6.3	37.1	35.9	11.2	9.5	100

'For each of the following groups, what measures do you think the government should pursue? People from non-EU countries coming to ***COUNTRY*** to work?'

Source: TransSOL (Horizon2020, GA, no. 649435)

These findings raise the question of how strong the support for immigration is in regard to Syrian refugees, given that forced migration due to war was very high during the years 2015 and 2016 and underlined much of the public debates about immigration policies. Table 10.9 summarizes the answers to the question of whether Syrian refugees should be treated differently than the two more general groups discussed previously. Here the UK, Denmark and Switzerland stand out as the countries more likely to say higher numbers should be admitted. In most countries however, the largest proportions of citizens prefer either keeping the current numbers or admitting even lower numbers (the latter is particularly true in Greece and Italy). In Poland 36.3% argued that none should be allowed to come at all, followed by France with 25% taking this harsh position, 22% in Italy, 20% in the UK, around 17% in Denmark and Greece and 12–13% in Germany and Switzerland. The latter results show that these citizens have more restrictive preferences when refugees from Syria are concerned, as compared to the other two groups, that is, non-EU citizens and EU citizens. However, the fact that the general population seems to be more cautious about admitting Syrian refugees should not lead us to believe that solidarity is merely ethnically patterned. In fact, our questions addressed the preferred numbers of admitted migrants. The fact that respondents are more restrictive toward Syrian refugees might

Table 10.9 Immigration policies for Syrian refugees (in %)

	Admit higher numbers	*Keep numbers coming about the same*	*Admit lower numbers*	*Should not let any come in*	*Don't know*
Denmark	17.1	29.0	27.0	16.8	10.1
France	10.0	21.1	29.8	25.0	14.1
Germany	9.3	35.8	37.0	12.7	5.3
Greece	8.6	18.9	49.5	16.9	6.1
Italy	8.7	23.4	34.8	22.0	11.1
Poland	9.2	24.5	15.8	36.3	14.2
Switzerland	15.6	38.0	27.3	12.2	7.0
UK	18.1	24.9	24.8	20.0	12.3
Total	12.1	27.0	30.6	20.2	10.0

'How do you think your country should handle refugees fleeing the war in Syria?'
Source: TransSOL (Horizon2020, GA, no. 649435)

be conditioned by the higher number of migrants coming from these areas in the year preceding our survey and thus by considerations about the capacity of the respondents' countries to integrate them. As we have seen from previous tables, the support for immigration policies is conditional on respondents' views of the capabilities of the situation of the labor market, that is, one could conceive, on the ability to give migrants available job opportunities within the country. These findings converge with previous research in showing that the economic context matters when immigration policies are concerned. The economic strain perceived by citizens has a direct effect on the preferences for how restrictive immigration policies should be but also for the perceptions of ethnic threat that could be seen to fuel calls for restrictive measures, too (Gang et al. 2013; Setten et al. 2017).

These observations illustrate that conditionality is also at stake when solidarity with non-EU citizens is concerned. Our questionnaire included one item that aimed to measure this conditionality by asking respondents about the conditions under which migrants should gain access to social benefits. Table 10.10 shows that only a minority of 12% is against granting migrants access to social benefits and services categorically. Access is generally conceived as being conditional on two things: they should have worked and paid taxes (42%), and they should become citizens of the country (30%). A minority of respondents (16%) is more generous, granting migrants access unconditionally or after a limited time of residence. In this sense, findings tend to indicate that for most citizens, solidarity is understood as rights-based and

Table 10.10 Migrants and social rights

	Immediately on arrival (%)	After living 1 year (worked or not) (%)	After worked and paid taxes 1 year (%)	After citizenship (%)	Never (%)	Total N
Denmark	7	9	37	36	11	2183
France	5	9	41	26	18	2098
Germany	9	13	46	24	7	2064
Greece	8	8	34	35	15	2061
Italy	8	7	38	36	12	2087
Poland	7	8	43	32	10	2119
UK	6	8	46	27	14	2083
Switzerland	6	9	52	23	10	2221
Total	7	9	42	30	12	16,916

'When should migrants obtain rights to social benefits and services as citizens do?'
Source: TransSOL (Horizon2020, GA, no. 649435)

thus tied to some notion of citizenship, that is, delimited by legal entitlements and mutual obligations (e.g., receiving social benefits and paying taxes or contributions). As such, this suggests that public policies furthering the active participation of migrants in the labor force and their naturalization could be beneficial to further support with respect to the norms of redistributional solidarity echoed in our data.

European Union Membership and Attachment: Correlates of Solidarity?

The findings discussed above have provided indications that Europe is a potential frame of reference impacting on the readiness of citizens to support others. Solidarity might thus be intricately tied to feelings of satisfaction and belongingness with regards to the EU. In conceptual terms, we assume that solidarity as a relation of (mutual) support is tied to (imagined) groups, which means that feelings of identity and belongingness should promote the individual's readiness to engage in solidarity with members of these groups (Hunt and Benford 2004; Stets and McCaffree 2014). At the same time, levels of satisfaction with the EU might condition the readiness to help other European and/or European governments, as well. A closer inspection of these factors is important, because they might help to explain the moderate rates of solidarity with other European people and countries unveiled at least with respect to certain indicators from our previous analyses. Indeed, the more moderate rates of European solidarity could be conditioned by lower rates of identification and satisfaction with the EU. In order to validate these assumptions, we need to take a closer look at these public attitudes and attachments toward the EU.

The satisfaction with the EU relates to more cognitive and instrumental considerations and motivations. Along these lines, we included a series of questions in our survey that encouraged respondents to evaluate the EU membership of their country, following the example of previous studies (Anderson and Reichert 1996; Hooghe and Marks 2007; Guerra and McLaren 2016). It is to be expected that EU-skeptic attitudes will go hand in hand with a lower disposition to act in solidarity with other European people. Citizens might be more cautious to support measures of European solidarity if they believe that the EU works badly. Hence, it is crucial to know how widely diffused is a negative assessment of the EU.

Table 10.11 presents results from respondents on whether they feel that on balance their country's membership of the EU was good, bad or neither a good nor a bad thing. In Switzerland, we asked about potentially joining the EU. Reflecting once more the patterns found previously, the Swiss think joining the EU would be bad, and the Greeks think that being members of the EU is a bad thing. All the others think it is on balance a good thing, but the gap is smaller in the UK, Italy and France than in Denmark and particularly Germany and Poland.

Table 10.11 EU membership good/bad (in %)

	A good thing	A bad thing	Neither good nor bad	Don't know	Total
Denmark	38.9	25.3	26.3	9.6	100
France	34.4	26.5	29.8	9.3	100
Germany	53.3	15.6	26.6	4.5	100
Greece	30.7	34.0	31.1	4.2	100
Italy	35.8	30.6	26.4	7.2	100
Poland	62.7	9.2	20.9	7.2	100
Switzerland[a]	8.0[a]	67.6[a]	18.1[a]	6.3[a]	100
UK	40.3	35.4	18.0	6.4	100
Total	37.8	30.8	24.6	6.9	100

'Generally speaking, do you think that your country's membership of the European Union is ...?'
Source: TransSOL (Horizon2020, GA, no. 649435)

[a] *In Switzerland we asked about joining the EU (joining the EU would be...)*

This evaluation could be tied to a more rational calculation about the advantages and disadvantages of EU membership. For this reason, we added a question asking respondents if they think their country has more directly benefited from being a member of the EU (in Switzerland we asked if they benefited from not being members). Table 10.12 presents the results. In Switzerland, over 70% think the country has benefited from not being part of the EU. In Greece, in Italy and—by a tiny margin—in France, higher proportions think the country has not benefited from membership. Even in the UK, a higher percentage felt they benefited from membership. In Denmark, Germany and Poland, again attitudes are very positive in terms of feeling that the countries benefited from being part of the EU.

Next to these more general evaluations of EU membership, we also asked respondents to assess the situation of the labor market, if the country were to be outside of the EU. As Table 10.13 shows, respondents had more difficulties here in giving clear indications. Overall, the proportion of respondents who believe that not being a member is detrimental for the labor market is higher when compared to those who say that the number of jobs would increase outside the EU. This is particularly true for Germany and Poland, in part also for Denmark and Italy. More Greek people believe that the labor market would perform better outside the EU. And the Swiss are convinced that a membership would have bad effects on the labor mar-

Table 10.12 Benefited from EU membership (in %)

	Benefited	Not benefited	Don't know	Total
Denmark	48.6	29.8	21.7	100
France	36.2	37.6	26.2	100
Germany	58.5	27.4	14.2	100
Greece	37.2	53.1	9.6	100
Italy	28.2	52.7	19.1	100
Poland	70.9	14.3	14.8	100
Switzerland[a]	70.3[a]	13.4[a]	16.3[a]	100
UK	43.7	37.0	19.3	100
Total	49.4	32.9	17.7	100

'Taking everything into account, would you say that your country has on balance benefited or not from being a member of the European Union?'

Source: TransSOL (Horizon2020, GA, no. 649435)

[a] *In Switzerland we asked if the country benefited or not from NOT being a member of the European Union*

Table 10.13 Effect on jobs and employment if country was *outside* the EU (in %)

	Would be good	Would be bad	Would make no difference	Don't know	Total
Denmark	16.2	37.8	21.7	24.3	100
France	23.8	27.6	27.8	20.8	100
Germany	14.4	43.7	26.5	15.4	100
Greece	38.4	31.2	16.5	14.0	100
Italy	25.9	35.4	21.9	16.8	100
Poland	10.6	52.1	18.1	19.2	100
Switzerland[a]	11.3[a]	49.6[a]	25.0[a]	14.1[a]	100
UK	26.5	33.0	24.3	16.1	100
Total	20.8	38.9	22.7	17.6	100

Source: TransSOL (Horizon2020, GA, no. 649435)

[a] In Switzerland we asked if the country was *in* the EU

ket, too. Across the countries, a sizeable proportion ranging from about 17% in Greece and almost 30% in France think it would make no difference, and between 14 and 24% of respondents are not sure.

Overall, we see considerable skepticism with reference to EU membership, which corroborates a general trend within the European citizenry identified by previous studies (McLaren 2007; Hooghe and Marks 2007; Leconte 2015). Against this backdrop, it is interesting to see how people in our eight countries would vote if there were a referendum on the EU membership of their country (in Switzerland we asked about joining). Results in Table 10.14 show once more that across countries, Switzerland prefers to stay outside and Greece would prefer to leave; there is a very slight preference for leaving in the UK much in line with the actual referendum from June 2016. Once more gaps are smaller in Italy and France than in Denmark, Germany and Poland, showing that the latter tend to be more Europhile, while citizens in the former countries lean more toward Euroskepticism.

This grouping is replicated when asking respondents if they believe that the UK should remain or leave the EU. Table 10.15 shows that a slightly higher proportion of UK respondents felt the UK should leave than those saying it should remain. The same applies to respondents from Switzerland, Greece, France and Italy, who corroborated once more Euroskeptic tendencies, whereas the Danes, Germans and Polish think the UK should stay. These citizens tend to defend the idea of the EU and the need to keep the countries within it.

270 C. LAHUSEN AND M. GRASSO

Table 10.14 Referendum on EU membership (in %)

	Remain[a]	Leave[a]	Would not vote	Don't know	Total
Denmark	47.6	32.1	4.2	16.1	100
France	42.7	30.3	7.6	19.4	100
Germany	61.3	23.5	6.0	9.3	100
Greece	37.7	46.3	7.9	8.1	100
Italy	43.1	36.1	6.4	14.5	100
Poland	64.0	14.8	7.8	13.4	100
Switzerland[a]	10.5[a]	74.3[a]	5.7[a]	9.5[a]	100
UK	44.3	45.2	3.7	6.8	100
Total	48.7	32.6	6.2	12.6	100

'If there was a referendum on your country's membership of the EU how would you vote?'

Source: TransSOL (Horizon2020, GA, no. 649435)

[a]*In Switzerland we asked about joining the EU*

Table 10.15 Should the UK remain a member or leave the EU? (in %)

	Remain	Leave	Don't know	Total
Denmark	45.1	34.5	20.4	100
France	30.3	46.6	23.1	100
Germany	51.7	35.7	12.6	100
Greece	32.2	51.7	16.1	100
Italy	39.8	43.2	17.0	100
Poland	59.0	19.5	21.5	100
Switzerland	26.3	55.1	18.7	100
United Kingdom	45.3	47.1	7.6	100
Total	41.1	41.7	17.2	100

Source: TransSOL (Horizon2020, GA, no. 649435)

In Table 10.16 we look at the relationship between membership of the EU and fiscal solidarity. The results show that there is a clear relationship between both: respondents more favorable to EU membership are also more likely to support fiscal solidarity.

Finally, we move to a question that tackles more directly the affective or emotional dimension of EU identification, because respondents were encouraged to assess their attachment to the European Union as well as to other entities including the world/humanity, one's country and region and one's city. Table 10.17 indicates that the EU scores the lowest levels

Table 10.16 Solidarity and support for EU membership (% a good thing)

Agreement with pooling funds to help countries in debt (see Table 10.4)	Supports EU membership
Strongly disagree	15.2
Disagree	28.0
Neither	35.1
Agree	55.5
Strongly agree	57.0
Don't know	24.0
Total	39.0

Source: TransSOL (Horizon2020, GA, no. 649435)

Table 10.17 Attachments (% fairly and very attached)

	European Union	The world/humanity	Country	Region	City
Denmark	33.4	64.1	90.8	62.2	80.3
France	47.1	72.7	88.6	80.5	79.0
Germany	53.3	69.0	83.7	79.1	82.1
Greece	32.3	73.8	90.5	85.0	85.0
Italy	49.1	73.4	78.1	80.2	82.3
Poland	65.8	79.9	89.8	87.8	87.6
Switzerland	28.1	74.6	89.1	84.0	81.1
United Kingdom	40.1	67.7	82.5	75.8	79.7
Total	43.5	71.9	86.7	79.3	82.1

'Please tell me how attached you feel to …?'
Source: TransSOL (Horizon2020, GA, no. 649435)

of attachment compared to the other spatial entities. The strongest attachment to the EU is clearly in Poland, followed by Germany, Italy and France, then the UK, Denmark, Greece and Switzerland. When we compare the attachment to the EU with the instrumental assessment of the EU membership (Table 10.8), we see that the proportions of people who feel attached to the EU match clearly the rates of those respondents considering EU membership to be a good thing. In France and Italy, almost every second respondent feels attached to the EU, but this does not prevent them from assessing their country's membership of the EU more critically. In Denmark, the relation is inversed, because the feelings of attachment are less diffused as the impression that EU membership is

Table 10.18 Solidarity and attachment to the EU (% fairly and very attached)

Agreement with pooling funds to help countries in debt (see Table 10.4)	Attached to the EU
Strongly disagree	18.2
Disagree	31.2
Neither	43.5
Agree	59.0
Strongly agree	58.7
Don't know	30.6
Total	43.5

Source: TransSOL (Horizon2020, GA, no. 649435)

good for their country. We thus see that people's feelings and instrumental reasonings converge, but not necessarily in all countries.

All these findings show that citizens identify with the European Union, even though these relations are nuanced. However, we should assume that citizens with a more developed European identity might be more supportive of the idea of European solidarity. In order to assess this assumption, it is necessary to measure the relationship between preferences for European solidarity and attachment to the European Union. For this purpose we use two questions introduced before: support for fiscal redistribution within the EU (see Table 10.4) and attachment to the EU (see Table 10.17). This allows us to have a look at the extent to which support for fiscal solidarity within the EU coincides with feelings of attachment to the EU. Table 10.18 shows that those who share the strongest feelings of attachment to the European Union are also those that are most likely to support the pooling of funds to help countries in debt.

Understanding Solidarity as a Social Force: Preliminary Conclusions

Solidarity is a pressing issue of our times. The various crises affecting the European Union since 2008 have increased the call for solidarity between the European people, especially when dealing with the consequences of the Great Recession and/or the welcoming of refugees fleeing from war, persecution and poverty. The evidence presented in this book paints a nuanced picture of solidarity within Europe. We found that a strong majority of respondents supports the attempts of the EU to help countries outside Europe in fighting poverty and promoting development; every second respondent reports having engaged in solidarity activities for people in their country, including donating money or time, protesting and engaging in voluntary associations; and European citizens strongly support solidarity-based (redistributive) public policies with almost three-quarters considering the reduction of big income inequalities as an important goal.

However, our data revealed at the same time that solidarity is not universally and unconditionally granted. The analysis of the motives of people to support fiscal solidarity within the EU, for instance, shows that the largest group subscribes to the idea of reciprocity and deservingness. In this sense, our findings subscribe largely to those insights provided by previous research. The group of people with a universalist or cosmopolitan sense of solidarity are largely in the minority. For most people, solidarity is more strongly tied to specific groups or entities (Markovsky and Lawler 1994; Hunt and Benford 2004; Stets and McCaffree 2014), and very often solidarity is closely tied to the notion of citizenship (Miller 2000; Keating 2009). This is particularly evident when solidarity touches social rights and obligations, as, for instance, with regard to policies of redistribution at the national or European level. As our own data has shown, respondents prefer to restrict the access to social benefits to fellow citizens, to those working or paying taxes. And in regards to fiscal solidarity within the EU, citizens most strongly believe that solidarity should conform to norms of reciprocity and trustworthiness (see also Lengfeld et al. 2015; also Wheeless 1978; Thielemann 2003). Additionally, our results showed that those who share feelings of attachment to the European Union are also those that are most likely to support the pooling of funds to help countries in debt. These citizens seem to acknowledge that European citizenship is in place and that members of this community are thus expected to support each other.

In sum, citizens' views about fiscal solidarity within the EU tend to follow a rationale that is very similar to the one underlying public support of national welfare policies (Bowles and Gintis 2000; Oorschot 2006; León 2012). Additionally, these attitudes are not very distant from motives guiding civic and social solidarity within interpersonal relations and informal networks, because these solidarity relations are also governed by ideas of reciprocity, fairness, trustworthiness and deservingness (Markovsky and Lawler 1994; Oorschot 2000; Komter 2005; Molm et al. 2009). Solidarity seems to be patterned similarly across various reference groups, be that peers or neighbors, fellow citizens, Europeans or people outside Europe.

The findings of this book do not only provide important lessons about the rationale guiding solidarity at various levels of organization—the national, the European and the global. They have also given indications about the social and political factors inhibiting or limiting solidarity and thus about those groups within the population that are closer or more distant from practices and attitudes of solidarity. In this way, a number of lessons can be drawn from the national studies.

In the first instance, solidarity seems to follow a cumulative logic. Citizens actively supporting other people in their country are more probably engaged also in solidarity with people within the EU and beyond, while people who are more passive in regard to one reference group will be also probably be more inactive with respect also to the others (see Kiess et al. in this book). Hence, the difference between activity and inactivity seems to be more important than the target group to which solidarity is directed. However, this cumulative logic is certainly not universally applicable, particularly with respect to exclusive or antagonistic groups that mobilize their constituencies for their own sake and against others. Additionally, we have seen that solidarity across borders is less common within the European populations than solidarity practices within borders. However, our data indicate that solidarities are not necessarily exclusive and antagonistic. We might even hypothesize that most active people are engaged in multiple ways, even if these solidarities are patterned—in their proportions—along concentric circles of proximity and distance.

The analyses assembled in this book also give indications about those social and political factors that impact on solidarity disposition and practices. Among the main factors to be highlighted are the following. First, interpersonal trust seems to be an important precondition and resource explaining the commitment of citizens to supporting others. The importance of this factor has been highlighted in all chapters of this book. Solidarity is more probable when citizens consider the recipient of their help as trustworthy, thus testifying that norms of deservingness and reciprocity are at stake here, too (see also Wheeless 1978; Oorschot 2000; Brown and Ferries 2007). Second, religiosity influences solidarity as well, even though not all chapters testify to the importance of this factor for their countries. Religious people are more active in support of others than non-religious respondents, independent of the target group this support is directed at. As argued by others, religion plays a role not only because of the ethical claims it makes but also since we examine institutionalized forms of religiosity that imply collective forms of help and care (Abela 2004; Lichterman 2015).

Third, solidarity has a strong political component, not least because the idea of solidarity is part of the oratory of many social movements and their mobilization attempts (Giugni and Passy 2001; Hunt and Benford 2004; Scholz 2008). Additionally, we have been argued in this book that solidarity has a political dimension *per se*, since it is more often than not implicitly or explicitly linked to rights and obligations stipulated within a specific group. This assumption is corroborated by the national studies also in regard to forms of interpersonal solidarity. In fact, solidarity practices can be differentiated along the distinction between civic and political orientations (see Fernandez in this book). Additionally, respondents testifying that they have been engaged in practices of solidarity are more often interested in politics (see Maggini or Cinalli and Sanhueza in this book), are more involved in unconventional forms of participation (see Kalogeraki in this book) and/or are more active as newspaper readers (see Montgomery et al. in this book). Their practiced solidarity seems to be motivated also by a dissatisfaction with government policies toward the respective target group (see Kiess et al. in this book). Poland is an interesting exception, because analyses identify it as disaplying commitment to transnational solidarity that is not politically motivated (see Kurowska and Theiss in this book).

Fourth, in most countries, contacts with and attachments to the specific target groups (people with disabilities, the jobless, refugees) and identification with spatial entities (the nation, Europe) make a difference with respect to promoting solidarity practices. The British case illustrates that solidarity practices may be also unevenly distributed within the territory, with higher rates of support for various target groups in Scotland and Northern Ireland (see Montgomery et al. in this book).

Finally, we see that socio-demographic traits and social structural resources play a less consistent and important role, when compared to the previously discussed factors. While previous research has highlighted the importance of some of these factors, among them gender (Neill and Gidengil 2006), age and biographical availability (Beyerlein and Bergstrand 2013; Grasso 2014), education (Bauer et al. 2013; Grasso 2013) or occupational and class status (Wilson 2000), our own analyses do not draw a consistent picture. Age and gender do not play a consistent role across countries, although biographical availability seems to be relevant for volunteering in Greece. Socio-economic status plays a role in various countries, but the relevant factors change from country to country. It is either higher education (Denmark, Germany and Poland), income and occupational status (Denmark and Poland) or the respondents identifying with the middle classes (Italy) that matter in explaining solidarity practices.

These inconclusive findings are probably linked to the design of our analyses, since a more focused study on specific forms of solidarity practices (e.g., donating money or attending protest events for specific target groups) might have identified more specific social profiles of engaged people. However, the aim of our analyses was to measure more general dispositions and practices of solidarity. In this regard, the lesser relevance of socio-demographic and social structural traits is telling in itself. Solidarity practices are not restricted to specific strata of the population but tied to different groups within society (Giugni and Grasso 2015).

What do we learn from these findings for making sense of the prospects of European solidarity? On the one hand, we have to expect that solidarity across borders is unlikely to be prioritized by European citizens. And this seems to be particularly true for European solidarity. This has to do with the fact that the feelings of attachment and identification with Europe and the European Union are less developed than those to one's own country, region or town. Europeans tend to be more engaged with respect to fellow citizens and people in their proximity, and this also means that practices of solidarity targeting other EU countries are secondary. To this, we have to add that the discontent with the European Union seems to translate into a weaker disposition to support redistribution between states, and possibly also between citizens. The rise of Euroskeptical sentiments in the population (McLaren 2007; Hooghe and Marks 2007; Leconte 2015) and the growing importance of populist parties rallying for nationalist and xenophobic agendas (Taggart 2004; Krouwel and Abts 2007; Kriesi and Pappas 2015) have the potential to diminish the prospects of European solidarity within the citizenry.

However, against these negative views we argue that on balance there is more hope and that there is room for a further development of European solidarity (see also Börner 2014; Gerhards et al. 2016). The lessons drawn from our analyses seem to boil down to one major proposition. If European citizens privilege solidarity with fellow citizens, and if their solidarity is conditional on the active involvement of the targeted recipients in a relation of trust and reciprocity, then the idea of social citizenship becomes a turntable for the development of European solidarity. So far, European citizens claiming their social rights are referred back to their country of residence, since, within the EU, social citizenship is tied back to the nation-state. Truly European measures of redistribution are needed to bolster the idea of a European social citizenship, such as redistributive programs to which all European citizens contribute and from which they receive support in times of trouble. The reservation which citizens voice against redistributive measures among European member states may just reflect a general feeling that there is not yet a fair system of rules in place that balances the mutual rights and obligations of the European people within the EU. The European Union is not yet an accomplished political community establishing and guaranteeing common social rights and obligations. The development of social rights and social citizenship, as widely discussed in the public sphere (Eder and Giessen 2001; Schmitter and Bauer 2001; Ferrera 2004; Keating 2009; Ross and Borgmann-Prebil 2010), could be an important instrument to increasingly develop and promote the readiness of citizens to support other European citizens—through either interpersonal help or public policies of redistribution moving forward into the future.

REFERENCES

Abela, A. M. (2004). Solidarity and Religion in the European Union: A Comparative Sociological Perspective. In P. Xuereb (Ed.), *The Value(s) of a Constitution for Europe* (pp. 71–101). Malta: European Documentation and Research Centre.

Anderson, C. J., & Reichert, M. S. (1996). Economic Benefits and Support for Membership in the EU: A Cross-National Analysis. *Journal of Public Policy, 15*(3), 231–249.

Anheier, H. K., & Salamon, L. M. (1999). Volunteering in Cross-National Perspective: Initial Comparisons. *Law and Contemporary Problems, 62,* 43–66.

Bauer, T. K., Bredtmann, J., & Schmidt, C. M. (2013). Time vs. Money – The Supply of Voluntary Labor and Charitable Donations Across Europe. *European Journal of Political Economy, 32,* 80–94.

Beyerlein, K., & Bergstrand, K. (2013). Biographical Availability. In D. A. Snow, D. D. Porta, B. Klandermans, & D. McAdam (Eds.), *The Wiley-Blackwell Encyclopedia of Social and Political Movements* (pp. 137–138). New York: Wiley-Blackwell.

Blekesaune, M., & Quadagno, J. (2003). Public Attitudes Toward Welfare State Policies: A Comparative Analysis of 24 Countries. *European Sociological Review, 19*(5), 415–427.

Börner, S. (2014). From National to European Solidarity? The Negotiation of Redistributive Spaces. In S. Börner & M. Eigmüller (Eds.), *European*

Integration, Processes of Change and the National Experience (pp. 166–188). Basingstoke: Palgrave Macmillan.
Bowles, S., & Gintis, H. (2000). Reciprocity, Self-Interest, and the Welfare State. *Nordic Journal of Political Economy, 26,* 33–53.
Brown, E., & Ferries, J. M. (2007). Social Capital and Philanthropy: An Analysis of the Impact of Social Capital on Individual Giving and Volunteering. *Nonprofit and Voluntary Sector Quarterly, 36*(1), 85–99.
Burgoon, B. (2014). Immigration, Integration, and Support for Redistribution in Europe. *World Politics, 66*(3), 365–405.
Eder, K., & Giessen, B. (2001). Conclusions: Citizenship and the Making of a European Society – From the Political to the Social Integration of Europe. In K. Eder & B. Giessen (Eds.), *European Citizenship Between National Legacies and Postnational Projects* (pp. 245–269). Oxford: Oxford University Press.
Evangelinidis, A. (2016). The Greek State's Response to the Refugee Crisis and the Solidarity Movement. *Contemporary Southeastern Europe, 3*(1), 32–36.
Ferrera, M. (2004). Social Citizenship in the European Union. Toward a Spatial Reconfiguration? In C. K. Ansell & G. di Palma (Eds.), *Restructuring Territoriality. Europe and the United States Compared* (pp. 90–121). Cambridge: Cambridge University Press.
Gang, I. N., Rivera-Batiz, F. L., & Yun, M.-S. (2013). Economic Strain, Education and Attitudes Towards Foreigners in the European Union. *Review of International Economics, 21*(2), 177–190.
Gerhards, J., Lengfeld, H., & Häuberer, J. (2016). Do European Citizens Support the Idea of a European Welfare State? Evidence from a Comparative Survey Conducted in Three EU Member States. *International Sociology, 31*(6), 677–700.
Giugni, M., & Grasso, M. T. (2015). Environmental Movements in Advanced Industrial Democracies: Heterogeneity, Transformation, and Institutionalization. *Annual Review of Environment and Resources, 40,* 337–361.
Giugni, M., & Grasso, M. T. (2016). How Civil Society Actors Responded to the Economic Crisis: The Interaction of Material Deprivation and Perceptions of Political Opportunity Structures. *Politics & Policy, 44*(3), 447–472.
Giugni, M., & Passy, F. (Eds.). (2001). *Political Altruism? Solidarity Movements in International Perspective.* Lanham, MD: Rowman & Littlefield.
Grasso, M. T. (2011). *Political Participation in Western Europe.* D.Phil. Thesis, Nuffield College, University of Oxford.
Grasso, M. T. (2013). The Differential Impact of Education on Young People's Political Activism: Comparing Italy and the United Kingdom. *Comparative Sociology, 12*(1), 1–30.
Grasso, M. T. (2014). Age-Period-Cohort Analysis in a Comparative Context: Political Generations and Political Participation Repertoires. *Electoral Studies, 33,* 63–76.

Grasso, M. T. (2016). *Generations, Political Participation and Social Change in Western Europe*. London: Routledge.

Grasso, M. T., & Giugni, M. (2016). Protest Participation and Economic Crisis: The Conditioning Role of Political Opportunities. *European Journal of Political Research*, 55(4), 663–680.

Grasso, M. T., Farrall, S., Gray, E., Hay, C., & Jennings, W. (2017). Thatcher's Children, Blair's Babies, Political Socialisation and Trickle-down Value-change: An Age, Period and Cohort Analysis. *British Journal of Political Science*. https://doi.org/10.1017/S0007123416000375.

Green-Pedersen, C., & Otjes, S. (2017). A Hot Topic? Immigration on the Agenda in Western Europe. *Party Politics*. Online first, Published August 31, 2017. https://doi.org/10.1177/1354068817728211.

Guerra, S., & McLaren, L. M. (2016). Public Opinion and the European Union. In M. Cini & N. P.-S. Borragán (Eds.), *European Union Politics* (5th ed., pp. 352–364). Oxford: Oxford University Press.

Hafner Fink, M. (2012). Political Participation, Democratisation and Citizens' Values in Europe. *Teorija in Praksa*, 49(3), 544–565.

Hooghe, L., & Marks, G. (2007). Sources of Euroscepticism. *Acta Politica*, 42(2), 119–127.

Hunt, S. A., & Benford, R. D. (2004). Collective Identity, Solidarity, and Commitment. In D. A. Snow, S. A. Soule, & H. Kriesi (Eds.), *The Blackwell Companion to Social Movements* (pp. 433–457). Oxford: Blackwell.

Keating, M. (2009). Social Citizenship, Solidarity and Welfare in Regionalized and Plurinational States. *Citizenship Studies*, 13(5), 501–513.

Komter, A. E. (2005). *Social Solidarity and the Gift*. Cambridge: Cambridge University Press.

Kriesi, H., & Pappas, T. S. (Eds.). (2015). *European Populism in the Shadow of the Great Recession*. Colchester: ECPR Press.

Krouwel, A., & Abts, K. (2007). Varieties of Euroscepticism and Populist Mobilization: Transforming Attitudes from Mild Euroscepticism to Harsh Eurocynicism. *Acta Politica*, 42(2), 252–270.

Leconte, C. (2015). From Pathology to Mainstream Phenomenon: Reviewing the Euroscepticism Debate in Research and Theory. *International Political Science Review*, 36(3), 250–263.

Lengfeld, H., Schmidt, S., & Häuberer, J. (2015, April 1). *Is There a European Solidarity? Attitudes Towards Fiscal Assistance for Debt-Ridden European Union Member States*. Report No. 67, University of Leipzig.

León, F. J. (2012). Reciprocity and Public Support for the Redistributive Role of the State. *Journal of European Social Policy*, 22(2), 198–215.

Lichterman, P. (2015). Religion and Social Solidarity. A Pragmatist Approach. In L. Hustinx, J. von Essen, J. Haers, & S. Mels (Eds.), *Religion and Volunteering*.

Complex, Contested and Ambiguous Relationships (pp. 241–261). Cham: Springer.

Markovsky, B., & Lawler, E. J. (1994). A New Theory of Group Solidarity. In B. Markovsky, K. Heimer, & J. O'Brien (Eds.), *Advances in Group Processes* (pp. 113–137). Greenwich, CT: JAI Press.

McLaren, L. (2007). Explaining Mass-level Euroscepticism: Identity, Interests, and Institutional Distrust. *Acta Politica, 42*(2), 233–251.

Miller, D. (2000). *Citizenship and National Identity*. Cambridge: Polity Press.

Molm, L. D., Collett, J. L., & Schaefer, D. R. (2009). Building Solidarity Through Generalized Exchange: A Theory of Reciprocity. *American Journal of Sociology, 113*(1), 205–242.

Neill, B., & Gidengil, E. (Eds.). (2006). *Gender and Social Capital*. New York: Routledge.

van Oorschot, W. (2000). Who Should Get What, and Why? On Deservingness Criteria and the Conditionality of Solidarity Among the Public. *Policy & Politics, 28*(1), 33–48.

van Oorschot, W. (2006). Making the Difference in Social Europe: Deservingness Perceptions Among Citizens of European Welfare States. *Journal of European Social Policy, 16*(1), 23–42.

van Oorschot, W., Arts, W., & Gelissen, J. (2006). Social Capital in Europe. Measurement and Social and Regional Distribution of a Multifaceted Phenomenon. *Acta Sociologica, XLIX*, 149–167.

Ross, M., & Borgmann-Prebil, Y. (Eds.). (2010). *Promoting Solidarity in the European Union*. Oxford: Oxford University Press.

Schmitter, P. C., & Bauer, M. W. (2001). A (Modest) Proposal for Expanding Social Citizenship in the European Union. *Journal of European Social Policy, 11*(1), 55–65.

Scholz, S. J. (2008). *Political Solidarity*. University Park, PA: Penn State University Press.

van Setten, M., Scheepers, P., & Lubbers, M. (2017). Support for Restrictive Immigration Policies in the European Union 2002–2013: The Impact of Economic Strain and Ethnic Threat for Vulnerable Economic Groups. *European Societies, 19*(4), 440–465.

Sotiropoulos, D. A., & Bourikos, D. (2014). Economic Crisis, Social Solidarity and the Voluntary Sector in Greece. *Journal of Power, Politics & Governance, 2*(2), 33–53.

Stets, J. E., & McCaffree, K. (2014). Linking Morality, Altruism, and Social Solidarity Using Identity Theory. In V. Jeffries (Ed.), *The Palgrave Handbook of Altruism, Morality, and Social Solidarity* (pp. 333–351). New York: Palgrave Macmillan.

Svallfors, S. (1997). Worlds of Welfare and Attitudes to Redistribution: A Comparison of Eight Western Nations. *European Journal of Sociology, 13*(3), 283–304.

Taggart, P. (2004). Populism and Representative Politics in Contemporary Europe. *Journal of Political Ideologies, 9*(3), 269–288.

Thielemann, E. R. (2003). Between Interests and Norms: Explaining Burden-Sharing in the European Union. *Journal of Refugee Studies, 16*(3), 253–273.

Wheeless, L. R. (1978). A Follow-up Study of the Relationship Among Trust, Disclosure, and Interpersonal Solidarity. *Human Communication Research, 4*(2), 143–157.

Wilson, J. (2000). Volunteering. *Annual Review of Sociology, 26,* 215–240.

Open Access This chapter is licensed under the terms of the Creative Commons Attribution 4.0 International License (http://creativecommons.org/licenses/by/4.0/), which permits use, sharing, adaptation, distribution and reproduction in any medium or format, as long as you give appropriate credit to the original author(s) and the source, provide a link to the Creative Commons license and indicate if changes were made.

The images or other third party material in this chapter are included in the chapter's Creative Commons license, unless indicated otherwise in a credit line to the material. If material is not included in the chapter's Creative Commons license and your intended use is not permitted by statutory regulation or exceeds the permitted use, you will need to obtain permission directly from the copyright holder.

Index

A
Activism
  political forms of solidarity, 198, 199, 201, 216
Activities, 8, 28
Age, 10
Altruism
  social dispositions, 195, 196, 199–201
Associational involvement, 10
Asylum, 2
Asylum policy, 2
Asylum seekers, 169–186
Attachment, 47–49, 58, 60, 61, 63, 256
Attachment to groups, 11
Attitudes, 2
Austerity, 1

B
Balibar, 1
Belongingness, 3
Biographical availability, 130

Bonding social capital, 108
Border control, 23
Boycott, 253
Bridging social capital, 104
Burden sharing, 262

C
Charitable, 5
Charitable dimension of solidarity, 130
Charitable donations, 10
Citizens, 3
Citizenship, 228, 232, 236, 238–245, 247
Civic engagement, 131
Civic groups and organizations, 9
Civic solidarity practices, 198, 204, 209, 210, 212, 215
Civil society organizations, 5
Claims-making, 10
Cognitive involvement in politics, 140
Cognitive political involvement, 140, 158

Collective, 10
Collective identities, 11
Communal life, 24
Communities, 11
Community, 3
Community-regarding
  motivational orientations, 201, 202, 212–213, 216
Comparative, 3
Comparative dataset, 8
Conditional, 27
Conditionality, 25, 75, 131
Contentious, 61
Contentious politics, 159
Cooperation, 2
Cosmopolitan identities, 3
Cosmopolitanism
  social dispositions, 200
Cosmopolitan philanthropy, 4
Crisis/crises, 1, 2
Cross-national, 3
Cross-national solidarity, 254
Cultural capital, 172, 173, 175, 178, 179, 184, 186

D
Denmark, 2, 3
Deprivation, 10, 45, 53, 58, 60, 61, 63
Deregulation, 21
Deservingness, 7, 26, 56, 131, 158
Deviants, 24
Devolved, 77
Disabilities, 256
Disabled, 8
Disabled people, 81
Dispositions, 8
Donated time or money, 253
Donating money, 4
Duties, 24

E
East, 23
Economic and financial crisis, 1
Economic growth, 24
Educational attainment, 136
Egalitarian, 19
Elderly, 254
Empathy, 63
EU citizenship, 23
EU membership, 268
European Financial Stability Facility, 1
European Paths to Transnational Solidarity in Times of Crisis, 3
European solidarity, 1, 10
European Stability Mechanism, 1
European Union, 1, 2, 6, 8
Eurosceptic, 2

F
Factors fostering solidarity practices in Italy, 133
Fair, 47
Fight against human trafficking, 2
Fiscal solidarity, 258
Five Star Movement, 142
Flexicurity, 20
France, 2, 3
Free movement, 23
Frequency of social connections, 130
Frontier controls, 2

G
Gender, 10, 89
Germany, 3
Global, 25
Greece, 3, 169–186
Grievances, 2
Group-boundedness, 5

H
Habermas, 1
Help, 8
Horizon 2020, 3
Human capital, 174, 176, 177, 179, 181, 183, 185, 186
Humanitarian, 5
Humankind, 256

I
Identity, 45, 91
Ideological orientations, 11, 131
Immigrants, 254
Immigration, 2, 8
Inclusiveness, 20
Income, 10
Income inequality, 9
Income level, 137
Individual contributions, 27
Individualistic welfare arrangement, 25
Informal networks, 9
Institutions, 2
Integration, 2
Interest in politics, 131
International solidarity, 1
Interpersonal help, 9
Interpersonal trust, 10, 130
Italy, 2, 3

J
Jobless, 254, 256

L
Labour market, 268
Left-right dimension, 142
Left-right ideology, 159
Left-right scale, 9
Libertarian vs. authoritarian values, 133
Libertarian values, 159
Life satisfaction, 90
Local, 26

M
Membership, 5
Member states, 3
Migrants, 10
Mobility, 23
Mobilization, 54
Moralizing solidarity, 24
Moral responsibility, 58
Motivations, 255
Mutual rights and obligations associated to group membership, 5

N
National community, 27
Neediness, 7
New cultural issues, 159
Newspaper readers, 89
Non-deserving, 24
Nondiscrimination, 23
Non-profit organizations, 253
Norms, 10
Northern Ireland, 77
Northern League, 142

O
Operationalization, 4
Opinion polls, 3
Other-regarding motivational orientations, 197, 198, 201, 202, 209, 210, 212–214, 216

P
Particularistic, 61
Party attachment, 131
Pensions, 8
People with disabilities, 133
Petitions, 253
Philanthropic particularism, 47
Poland, 3
Policies, 2
Policy measures, 1
Political activism, 29
Political allegiances, 8
Political behavior, 9
Political beliefs, 44, 45, 61
Political community, 20, 232, 246, 247
Political dimensions of solidarity, 9, 130
Political factors, 131
Political organizations, 10
Political orientations, 257
Political participation, 11
Political preferences, 131
Political preferences and orientation, 9
Political protests, 10
Political solidarity, 104, 106
Political solidarity practices, 197, 202, 203, 205, 207–215
Populism, 58, 61
Populist, 46
Populist parties, 2
Populist-right, 24
Post-materialist values, 9
Poverty, 8
Practices, 2
Pro-beneficiaries, 231, 232
Protest participation, 9
Proximity, 47, 49, 62, 63
'Public' activities, 10
Public policies of redistribution, 256

R
Race, 10
Rational calculations, 8
Recession, 2
Reciprocity, 5, 56, 131, 260
Redistribution, 45, 56, 257
Redistributive policies, 5, 157, 257
Redistributive preferences, 8
Refugee crisis, 58, 170, 171, 184, 185
Refugees, 2, 43, 82, 169–186
Refugees/asylum seekers, 8
Refugees or migrants, 256
Religion/religiosity, 8, 45, 53, 56, 58, 60, 63, 131, 158
Religious beliefs, 8
Republicanism, 230, 232, 243, 247
Resources, 10, 45, 48, 52, 54, 63
Rights and obligations, 5
Right-wing populist parties, 132

S
Scotland, 77
Security net, 22
Self-placement on the left-right dimension, 133
Self-regarding
   motivational orientations, 197, 201, 202, 209
Sick, 254
Skills, 10
Social and political dimensions of solidarity in Italy, 127
Social benefit, 265–266
Social capital, 8, 9, 46, 106, 130, 158, 173–175, 177–179, 183–186
Social capital measures, 132
Social class, 8, 10, 45, 53
Social cohesion, 2, 9
Social embeddedness, 88, 158
Social exclusion, 10

Social identification
  social dispositions, 196, 199, 214–216
Social inequalities, 9
Social movements, 5, 45
Social policies, 8
Social policy fields, 8
Social proximity, 7
Social relations, 10, 130
Social rights, 277
Social solidarity, 7, 106
Social status, 10
Social traits, 130
Socio-demographic characteristics, 10
Socio-demographic factors, 130
Socio-demographic traits, 8
Solidarity, 1, 74, 256
Solidarity disposition, 10
Solidarity in Italy, 129
Solidarity practices
  solidarity-based behaviour, 195, 215
Solidarity practices towards refugees, 133
South-East and South of Europe, 23
Spain, 2
Spatial, 48
Spatial dimension, 256
Stability and Growth Pact, 1
Subjective social class, 137
Support of voluntary associations, 5
Survey-based research, 7
Switzerland, 3

T
Targeted recipients, 7
Target groups, 8
Taxation/taxes, 4, 21, 266
Traditional, 26
Transnational solidarity, 27, 105
Transnational trust, 3
TransSOL, 3
Triggers of interpersonal solidarity, 156

Triggers of solidarity practices in the Italian context, 127
Trust, 24, 45, 46, 53, 56, 58, 60, 63

U
Unconventional protest, 253
Unemployed, 8, 83, 133
Unemployment, 2
United Kingdom, 2, 3
Universalism, 19
Universalist, 4, 63
Universalistic and unconditioned notion of solidarity, 132
Universalistic conceptions of solidarity, 156
Universal welfare, 27
Universal welfare states, 21

V
Vertical solidarity, 135
Voluntary engagement, 9, 10
Volunteer, 169–186
Volunteer Function Inventory (VFI)
  psychological perspective on prosocial behaviour, 197, 198, 200
Volunteering, 5
  volunteerism, 196
Voting behaviour, 142
Voting intentions, 140
Vulnerability, 8
Vulnerable groups, 19

W
Wealth redistribution, 8
Welcoming culture, 43
Welfare state, 5
Welfare state institutions, 9

X
Xenophobia/xenophobic, 58, 61

The manufacturer's authorised representative in the EU is Springer Nature Customer Service Centre GmbH, Europaplatz 3, 69115 Heidelberg, Germany. If you have any concerns regarding our products, please contact ProductSafety@springernature.com

Printed and bound by CPI Group (UK) Ltd, Croydon, CR0 4YY
23/03/2026
02076735-0012